T5-DHU-865

Japanese Business Management

In recent years the nature of the Japanese economy and expectations of it have changed quite dramatically. The bubble economy is no longer, and low growth and globalization are vital issues with which Japanese business management is getting to grips.

In this innovative new study, the views of Japan's leading experts on the globalization of Japanese business, management and industrial relations explain how traditional Japanese-style management is responding to the changes. The areas covered include the changes in management itself inside Japan and also how it is adapting itself when transferred overseas. There are also chapters on the formation of regional markets, technology transfer, the subcontracting system, ownership, work practices and industrial relations.

Japanese Business Management demonstrates how management is moving towards a 'hybrid-type' in overseas operations and towards a 'Western style' in Japan, where contractual principles are now being given much more weight. It will be invaluable reading for those wishing to obtain a more accurate picture of Japanese management in the 1990s.

Hasegawa Harukiyo is Lecturer in Japanese Studies at the University of Sheffield and is author of *The Steel Industry in Japan*. **Glenn D. Hook** is Professor of Japanese Studies at the University of Sheffield and is author of *Militarization and Demilitarization in Contemporary Japan*.

Sheffield Centre for Japanese Studies/Routledge Series
Series editor: Glenn D. Hook
Professor of Japanese Studies, University of Sheffield

This series, published by Routledge in association with the Centre for Japanese Studies at the University of Sheffield, will make available both original research on a wide range of subjects dealing with Japan and will provide introductory overviews of key topics in Japanese studies.

The Internationalization of Japan
Edited by Glenn D. Hook and Michael Weiner

Race and Migration in Imperial Japan
Michael Weiner

Japan and the Pacific Free Trade Area
Pekka Korhonen

Greater China and Japan
Prospects for an economic partnership?
Robert Taylor

The Steel Industry in Japan
A comparison with the UK
Hasegawa Harukiyo

Race, Resistance and the Ainu of Japan
Richard Siddle

Japan's Minorities
The illusion of homogeneity
Edited by Michael Weiner

Japanese Business Management
Restructuring for low growth and globalization
Edited by Hasegawa Harukiyo and Glenn D. Hook

Japanese Business Management

Restructuring for low growth and globalization

Edited by Hasegawa Harukiyo and Glenn D. Hook

London and New York

First published 1998
by Routledge
11 New Fetter Lane, London EC4P 4EE

Reprinted 1999, 2000

Simultaneously published in the USA and Canada
by Routledge
29 West 35th Street, New York, NY 10001

Routledge is an imprint of the Taylor & Francis Group

Typeset in Times by
J&L Composition Ltd, Filey, North Yorkshire

Printed and bound in Great Britain by
T.J.I. Digital, Padstow, Cornwall

British Library Cataloguing in Publication Data
A catalogue record for this book is available from the British Library

Library of Congress Cataloguing in Publication Data
A catalogue record for this book has been requested

ISBN 0–415–17256–X

Contents

Figures

Tables

Contributors

Abō Tetsuo (Chapter 4) is professor at the Institute of Social Science, University of Tokyo. Currently he is conducting research on the Japanese production system in Europe in comparison with the USA and Asia. He is the author of *Senkanki Amerika no Taigai Tōshi – Kinyū, Sangyō no Kokusaika Katei* (US foreign direct investment in the inter-war period – internationalization process of finance and industry), Tokyo: University of Tokyo Press, 1984, and the editor of *Hybrid Factory: The Japanese Production System in the United States*, New York: Oxford University Press, 1994. He has also published numerous articles on Japanese production systems in both English and Japanese.

Hasegawa Harukiyo (Chapter 2) is Lecturer in Japanese studies and the Director of the Centre for Japanese Studies at the University of Sheffield. Prior to moving to Sheffield in 1990 he was Professor of Economics at Kyoto Seika University. His recent publications include *Kigyō to Kanri no Kokusai Hikaku* (An international comparison of business and management), Tokyo: Chūō Keizaisha, 1993 (co-author), and *Steel Industry in Japan: A Comparison with Britain*, London: Routledge, 1996.

Glenn D. Hook (Chapter 1) is professor of Japanese Studies and director of the Graduate School of East Asian Studies at the University of Sheffield. He has published extensively on Japanese politics, international relations and East Asian regionalism in both Japanese and English. His recent books include *The Internationalization of Japan*, London: Routledge, 1992 (co-editor) and *Militarization and Demilitarization in Contemporary Japan*, London: Routledge, 1996.

Ikeda Masayoshi (Chapter 5) is professor of the Faculty of Economics, Chuo University. He has written extensively on small and medium enterprises in Japan with a focus on the automobile industry. He is the co-author of *Jidōsha Sangyō no Kokusaika to Seisan Shisutemu* (The internationalization of the automobile industry and production systems), Tokyo: Chuo University Press, 1990, and co-author, of *Kōzō Tenkan-ka no Furansu*

Jidōsha Sangyō (The French automobile industry under structural change), Tokyo: Chuo University Press, 1994.

Munakata Masayuki (Chapter 9) is professor of the School of Business Administration, Kobe University and currently serving as a board member of the Japan Society of Business Administration. His major research interests are in technology theory and its relation to management and the development of German management theories. He has written *Gijutsu no Ronri: Gendai Kōgyō Keiei Mondai e no Gijutsuronteki Sekkin* (The logic of technology: a technological approach to managerial issues in contemporary industries), Tokyo: Dōbunkan Shuppan, 1989, and *Doitsu Keieigaku no Shinten* (Development in the theories of German management), Tokyo: Chikura Shobo, 1992 (co-author).

Nakata Masaki (Chapter 6) is professor of comparative management in the School of Business Administration, Ritsumeikan University (Kyoto) and currently serving as an auditor of the Japan Society of Business Administration. His major publications include *Gendai America Kanrironshi* (History of management theories in contemporary America), Kyoto: Mineruva Shobo, 1985, and *Kigyō to Kanri no Kokusai Hikaku* (An international comparison of business and management), Tokyo: Chūō Keizaisha, 1993 (co-author). He is also a translator of *Capitalist Property and Financial Power* (John Scott, 1986).

Nishinarita Yutaka (Chapter 10) is professor of economic history at Hitotsubashi University and a member of the Japan Society of Social and Economic History. His publications include *Kindai Nippon Rōshi Kankeishi no Kenkyū* (A study on the history of industrial relations in the modern era), Tokyo: University of Tokyo Press, 1988, and *Gendai Nippon Keizaishi* (Economic history of modern Japan), Tokyo: Yūhikaku, 1992 (co-author). He recently published *Zainichi Chōsenjin no 'Sekai' to Teikoku 'Kokka'* (The *Gemeinschaft* of Korean workers in imperial Japan), Tokyo: University of Tokyo Press, 1997.

Ōhki Kazunori (Chapter 11) is professor of labour history at Japan Social Welfare University, Nagoya. He has written extensively on industrial relations and the labour movement in Japan and currently serves as the head of the Aichi Labour Research Institute. He is a board member of the Japan Research Institute of Labour Movement. His major works include *Rōdō Kumiai Undō no Konpon Mondai* (Fundamental issues in the labour union movement), Tokyo: Ōhtsuki Shoten, 1984, and *Henbō suru Sekai Kigyō Toyota* (Toyota, transformation of a world enterprise), Tokyo: Shin Nippon Shuppan, 1994. He recently published *Sangyō Kūdōka ni Dō o Tachimukau ka* (How to cope with industrial hollowing out), Tokyo: Shin Nippon Shuppan, 1996.

Okubayashi Kōji (Chapter 7) is professor of management in the School of Business Administration, Kobe University and currently a board member of the Japan Society of Business Administration. He has written numerous articles and books on management and organization of Japanese business. He is editor of *Henkakuki no Jinteki Shigen Kanri* (Human resource management in a period of transition), Tokyo: Chūō Keizaisha, 1995, and co-author of *Jūkōzō Soshiki Paradaimu Josetsu* (A new paradigm of soft-structured organization), Tokyo: Bunshindō, 1994.

Watanabe Takashi (Chapter 8) is professor of personnel management in the School of Business Administration, Ritsumeikan University in Kyoto. He is currently a board member of the Japan Society of Business Administration. He has written numerous books among which are *Gendai Ginkō Kigyō no Rōdō to Kanri* (Labour and management in modern banking institutions), Tokyo: Chikura Shobo, 1984; *Kōsubestu Kanri to Josei Rōdō* (Employment management by course selection and female labour), Tokyo: Chūō Keizaisha, 1995; and *Kigyō Soshiki no Rōdō to Kanri* (Labour and management of business organization), Tokyo: Chūō Keizaisha, 1995.

Yamashita Shōichi (Chapter 3) is professor and Dean of the Graduate School for International Development and Cooperation, Hiroshima University. He writes in both English and Japanese and his recent English publications include *Transfer of Japanese Technology and Management to ASEAN Countries*, Tokyo: Tokyo University Press, 1991 (editor); and 'Japan's role as a regional technological integrator and the black box phenomena in the process of technology transfer', in D. F. Simon (ed.) *The Emerging Technological Trajectory of the Pacific Rim*, New York: M. E. Sharpe, 1995. His recent research concerns the transfer of environment protection technology to China.

Preface

In the 'post-bubble' 1990s, Japanese political economy and business management are restructuring for low growth and globalization. Inevitably, a debate has arisen in both Japanese and British academic circles on the significance of these two forces, and their impact on the prevailing perceptions of Japanese management styles. Has Japanese management been spurred into transformation, or merely adjustment?

With this debate in mind, the Centre for Japanese Studies at the University of Sheffield decided to convene a seminar for British and Japanese academics and business specialists in order to discuss the implications of recent economic changes brought about by low growth and globalization. The result was the Inaugural Anglo-Japanese Business Seminar, held in The University of Sheffield on 16–18 March 1995, with the support of the Japan Foundation, the Chubu Electric Power Company, Sumitomo Life International, and Japan & Europe Motors (JEMCA).

Most of the chapters making up this volume are revised versions of the seminar papers. The three sections of the seminar are reflected in the division of this book: Part I Japanese business in globalization processes; Part II Restructuring in management; Part III Restructuring in labour. The primary concern of the organizers was to investigate and consider the most recent aspects of change taking place in Japanese business management as part of the Japanese political economy. The papers show the quality of work being performed on this theme on both sides of the world.

The editors wish to thank Mike Rigby (Sony), Itō Satoshi (DAKS Simpson) and Komori Osamu (Toyota) for their informative presentations on their respective management experiences in the UK. The contributors benefited enormously from the seminar participants and wish to thank, in particular, Raymond Loveridge (Aston), Geoffrey A. Broad (Salford), Lola Okazaki-Ward (Cranfield), John Scott (Exeter), Nick Oliver (Cambridge), John L. Halstead (Sheffield), Royden Harrison (Warwick), and Andrew Tylecote (Sheffield). They not only made invaluable remarks at the seminar, but later kindly provided us with detailed reports which helped the authors to improve the papers edited in this volume. We also wish to thank Hamada Ryūichi and Akeda Yasunobu (Chubu Electric), Tominaga Kenji

(Tekkō Rōren), Motani Tomomi (Sankei Shinbun), Hama Tetsurō (JEMCA), Kojima Atsushi (Yomiuri Shinbun), and Miyamoto Yōsuke (Embassy of Japan) for their participation and support in making the event successful. Watanabe Mitsuko, Ise Naoko, James Malcolm, Hugo Dobson and Paul Sweeny (Sheffield postgraduates) helped in the preparations for the seminar and provided administrative assistance. Ian Gow, Chairman of the School of East Asian Studies, kindly offered departmental support for the seminar and facilitated the publication of this book. Jenny Leech provided sterling service in making fair copies of the papers, which John Billingsley helped to edit. Without all of their support and encouragement neither the seminar nor the publication of this book would have been possible.

We are especially grateful to Christopher W. Hughes (now of Hiroshima University) for translating a number of the key papers and for taking overall responsibility for the satisfactory translation of all other papers in time for the seminar. Hasegawa Harutomo and Sven C. Scholven have provided unstintingly of their computing skills in reproducing all the tables and figures. We thank them for their many hours of work. We are also grateful to Routledge's anonymous referees for their valuable comments, and to Victoria Smith for her keen interest in the seminar and enthusiastic support for this publication.

Finally, following Japanese convention, the names in the text and notes are given with the family name followed by the given name. In writings in English, however, the personal name is followed by the family name. Except for place names commonly encountered in the West and names of institutions translated into English, all long vowels are indicated by a macron.

HH
GDH

Abbreviations

ABS	Anti-locking Brake System
AFTA	ASEAN Free Trade Area
APEC	Asia–Pacific Economic Cooperation
ASEAN	Association of South East Asian Nations
ASEAN 4	Association of South East Asian Nations (Thailand, Malaysia, Indonesia and the Philippines)
ASIC	Application Specific Integrated Circuit
BBC	Brand-to-brand Complementation
BMW	Bayerische Motor Werke
CD	Compact Disk
CIM	Computer Integrated Manufacturing
CKD	Complete Knock Down
CSIC	Custom Specific Integrated Circuits
DKB	Daiichi Kangyō Bank Ltd
DNC	Direct Numerical Control
DRAM	Dynamic Random Access Memory
DSP	Digital Signal Process
EC	European Community
EP-ROM	Electrically Programmable-Read Only Memory
EU	European Union
FDI	Foreign Direct Investment
FMS	Flexible Manufacturing System
FOB	Free on Board
GM	General Motors
IAT/IGM/IAO/HBS	Institut für Arbeit und Technik/IG Metall/ Fraunhofer-Institut für Arbeitswirtschaft und Organisation/Hans-Bocker-Stiftung
IMF, JC	International Metal-workers Federation, Japan Council
IR	Industrial Robot
IT	Information Technology
JETRO	Japan External Trade Organization

JIT	Just in time
JMNESG	Japanese Multinational Enterprise Study Group
JPN	Japanese
JVC	Victor Company of Japan Ltd
KD	Knock Down
ME	Micro-electronics
MIT	Massachusetts Institute of Technology
MITI	Ministry of International Trade and Industry
MPU	Micro Processor Unit
NAFTA	North America Free Trade Agreement
NEC	Nippon Electric Co. Ltd
NIEs	Newly Industrializing Economies
OECD	Organization for Economic Co-operation and Development
OJT	On-the-Job Training
OMAs	Orderly Market Agreements
PIA	Parts, Price, Improvement of Action
PM	Production and Maintenance
QC	Quality Control
QCD	Quality Control Development
R&D	Research and Development
RISC	Reduction Instruction Set Computer
SII	Structural Impediments Initiative
SOMPS	Study of Mazda's Production System
SPV	Supervisor
SRAM	Static Random Access Memory
TQC	Total Quality Control
UAW	United Automobile Workers
UK	United Kingdom
US	United States
USA	United States of America
VA	Value Analysis
VCRs	Video Cassette Recorders
VE	Value Engineering
VERs	Voluntary Export Restraints
VIP	Vehicle Innovation Programme

Glossary

Asahi Shinbun	Asahi newspaper
Dekasegi	Migrant wage labour
Dōmei	Japanese Confederation of Labour
Ekonomisuto	Economist (weekly magazine published in Japan)
Heisei Recession	Heisei Era began in 1989, while the recession began in May 1991
Honkō Kumiai	Union of Permanent Employees
Ie	House
Jichirō	All Japan Prefectural and Municipal Workers' Union
Jishu Kisei	Voluntary Export Restraints
Jōmukai	Committee of Executive Directors
Kaizen	Continuous improvement
Kanban	Notices signalling the need for new components
Kantō Keieisha Kyōkai	Kanto (geographical region centring on Tokyo) Employers' Association
Karōshi	Death from overwork
Keiretsu	Horizontal and/or vertical inter-company relations
Keizai Dōyūkai	Japan Committee for Economic Development
Kigyō Shūdan	Enterprise groups
Kokurō	National Railway Workers' Union
Korōkyō	Public Enterprise Union Confederation
Kōsei Torihiki Iinkai	Fair Trade Commission
Madogiwa Zoku	Middle-aged and older employees who have been demoted
Mura	Village
Nikkeiren (Nihon Keieisha Dantai Renmei)	Japan Federation of Employers Associations

Nihon Keizai Shinbun Hen	Nihon Keizai Newspaper
Nihon Rōdō Kenkyūkikō	Japan Institute of Labour
Nihon Seisansei Honbu	Japan Productivity Centre
Nikkei Sangyō Shinbun	Nikkei Sangyo Newspaper
Nikkyōso	Japan Teachers' Union
Nōryokushugi Kanri	Personnel management based upon individual ability
Ōen	Assistance
Ōkurashō	Ministry of Finance
Rengō	Japanese Trade Union Confederation
Rōdō Rōsei Kyoku	Bureau of Labour and Labour Issues
Rōdōshō	Ministry of Labour
Rōso Kaigi	Labour Union Conference
Sanbetsu	Congress of Industrial Unions
Sanji	Councillor
Sanshu no Jingi	Three Sacred Treasures
Shokugyō Anteihō	Employment Security Act
Shukkō	Dispatch
Shuntō	Spring Labour Offensive
Sōdōmei	Japan Federation of Labour
Sōhyō	General Council of Trade Unions of Japan
Sōrifu (Tōkei Kyoku)	Prime Minister's Office (Statistics Bureau)
Tan i Sanpō	Unit Industrial Report Organization
Tekkō Renmei	Japan Iron and Steel Federation
Tekkō Rōren	Japanese Federation of Iron and Steel Workers' Unions
Tenseki	Change of company
Tōkei Geppō	Monthly statistics
Tsūsanshō	Ministry of International Trade and Industry (MITI)
Tsūshō Hakusho	MITI Whitepaper
Yokusan	Imperial Rule Assistance (Association)
Zaibatsu	Financial groups (combines) existing in pre-war Japan
Zenmin Rōkyō	All Private Enterprise Union Confederation
Zenrōren	National Confederation of Trade Unions or National Liaison Council of Labour Unions

Introduction

The authors of this book are for the most part leading Japanese intellectuals known for their outstanding work in political economy, management, and labour relations.[1] In publishing their work in English, we aim to provide the reader with an up-to-date understanding of Japanese perspectives on a range of important issues currently affecting Japan's role in the global and regional political economies, management in manufacturing industries,[2] and labour relations in contemporary and historical contexts. How, in the 'post-bubble' 1990s, is Japanese business management restructuring for low growth and globalization? This is the central question addressed in this work.

Individually and collectively, the chapters form a coherent whole, permitting a comprehensive understanding of the major trends and conditions affecting Japanese business and management in the 1990s. In the range of approaches presented here we can identify the influence of the end of the Cold War, which has eroded any intellectual confidence in socialism, and the impact of globalization processes, which has called into question a purely domestic approach to Japanese business management.[3] The common thread tying the book together is what we call a 'structural' analysis, which is rooted in a view of 'pro-active' globalization. It is structural in the sense that we seek to identify and examine three areas of business studies as relevant to capital accumulation: Part I Japanese business in globalization processes; Part II Restructuring in management; Part III Restructuring in labour. It is pro-active in the sense that globalization, insofar as Japan is concerned, is taking the form of a positive expansion of capital, technology and managerial techniques to overseas locations, which sets in motion reciprocal dynamics on Japan's domestic business management and labour.

The influence of Japanese management methods in Asia, the Americas and Europe has been an important topic of concern among Western academics, and much research has been carried out in North America and the UK on a wide range of issues, from 'the secrets' of Japanese management to the threats arising from inward investments. Their congeners in Japan, in contrast, have sought to shed light on how the end of high economic growth in the mid-1970s and increasing globalization in the 1980s and 1990s have transformed domestic management, being drawn naturally to examine their effects on what has been termed 'Japanese-style management'.[4] Thus, academics in different parts of the world have come to focus on two broad areas, although to date little attempt has been made to bring these two together in a general assessment of Japanese management nor, indeed, has any analysis in English yet been carried out from the Japanese perspective. It is this lacuna that our book seeks to fill.

Two major areas require attention. The first concerns the scope and degree of change in Japanese-style management itself. What happens to the 'original' under the impact of low economic growth and globalization? The second concerns the nature of transplant management. What happens to Japanese-style management when it is transferred overseas? We thus provide an analysis and assessment of Japanese business management, both at home and abroad, following the bursting of the bubble and the growing influence of globalization.

Although each chapter deals with specific issues related to political economy, management and labour, altogether the contributors present the hypothesis that the end of high growth and subsequent globalization have created pro-active Japanese influence abroad (the other side of the same coin is known as 'Japanization' in Britain), while at home the same process has brought about a large-scale restructuring of business management and labour practices. Investigation into transplant management, on the one hand, and recent change in domestic management, on the other, brings to light the following points for discussion:

1 Japanese transplant management implies a dual transformation, that is, transformation of Japanese management, and transformation of local management. More precisely, transplant management is 'hybrid' management and manifests strength precisely because it is 'hybrid' in a variety of ways.
2 Domestic management in Japan has been affected to such an extent by low economic growth and globalization that the adjustments carried out at home must be considered in quite stark terms: Do they represent a fundamental departure from so-called Japanese-style management?
3 The change in domestic management will induce changes in labour; that is, in industrial relations and labour movements. How, then, will labour change and what are the implications for employees and working conditions in general? This will have profound implications for social relations in Japan.

The areas in which the above issues arise exist as a coherent whole in the 'pro-active' globalization of Japanese business. And it is precisely as a consequence of the uneven nature of capitalist development that Japanese business exerts a global influence. This is in three crucial respects:

1 the relative rise of Japanese capitalism to the point where Japan now stands as a major exporter of capital;
2 the relative rise of East Asian capitalism to the point where Japanese capital is welcomed as a means for promoting industrialization;
3 the relative decline of Anglo-American capitalism to the point where capital and technological transfers from Japan are useful to regenerate their manufacturing industries.

Thus, the global influence of Japanese management occurs via transplant management as part of a new political economy, which is emerging out of the dynamics of world capitalism. This influence will continue so long as the current dynamics of contemporary capitalism provide favourable conditions for Japan's global giants, while their capital investments continue to serve the objectives of the host economies.

Japanese influence differs depending upon where capital is invested as seen in East Asia, Europe, and North America. In East Asia, for example, Japanese-style management can be transferred more directly, whereas in Europe and North America it is constrained more by local factors arising out of pre-existing employment practices and labour relations. In the UK, Japanese transplant management is taken as the benchmark of 'Japanization' in UK management, whereas in Japan transplant management is viewed as a transformation of Japanese-style management.

The major elements of Japanese-style management – lifetime employment, seniority promotion, enterprise unions, *keiretsu* and subcontracting relations – arose primarily as a consequence of the rapid and high economic growth achieved through post-war industrialization, rather than as a universal formula for economic success or as a consequence of a unique cultural tradition. Change had already started to emerge as early as the mid-1970s, as seen in the introduction of *Nōryokushugi Kanri* (personnel management based upon individual ability) in a number of Japanese companies. Globalization has forced management to pursue drastic restructuring of management organization and employment practices, causing a large-scale departure from established management norms. The degree and direction of such change, along with its theoretical implications, are addressed in many of the chapters in this book. The approach taken is frequently different from that found in Anglo-American studies of Japanese management.

ANGLO-AMERICAN PERSPECTIVES

The perspective adopted in studying Japanese business is not rooted exclusively in national academic culture, as globalization processes affect the nature of the academic as well as the business enterprise. Still, as is clear from wartime studies of the Japanese, which in the cooler light of the post-war years now appear as grotesque simplifications of a complex land and people, the political and economic as well as academic environments do exert a telling influence on a researcher's choice of topic and approach. The 'value-free' social scientist exists more in the mind of the positivist than in the common room. It is not surprising, therefore, to find studies of Japanese business influenced by the changes in the producer nation as well as in Japan. The latter's spectacular rise to economic superpower status created a whole industry devoted to discovering the secrets of the Japanese 'miracle'. By driving a nail into the coffin of complacency about the international competitiveness of Anglo-American capitalism, Japanese business has been thrust to the centre of attention for many social scientists, whether at home or abroad. Japanese management has been at the heart of their concern.

In terms of their focus and attention, the main Anglo-American perspectives can be grouped into four types:

- the 'production system' perspective;
- the 'Japanization' perspective;
- the 'labour process' perspective;
- the political economy perspective.

'Production system' perspective

The 'production system' perspective is based upon the analysis of production technology and work organization, as represented by American authors Womack *et al.* (1990), or Kenney and Florida (1993). These writers examine the ways in which a particular production system may be more advanced than another, and how far it may differ from the older, Fordist model, with the value premise being rooted in discovering the source of Japanese competitiveness.[5] The former take the view that the Japanese production system is no longer a variant of Fordism, but rather should be characterized by a new concept, such as 'lean production'. In the same vein, Kenney and Florida offer another new concept to characterize the Japanese production system, namely the 'innovation-mediated production' system. Whether in terms, of 'lean production' or 'innovation-mediated production system', both agree that Japan has constructed a new model (concept) embodying elements of 'efficiency', 'rationality', and resulting competitiveness from which others can learn. Their aim is to ask whether the Japanese or Fordist model is more 'competitive' (i.e. the competitiveness debate) and how the Japanese model can be distinguished from Fordism.

From a slightly practical perspective, but still with the same aim of identifying the source of competitiveness, is the investigation by Liker *et al.* (1995) of technology management practices in the major Japanese companies. Further development of this objective in a more academic approach can be found in Aoki and Dore (1994), who focus upon institutional arrangements and their interconnectedness as a system. It is here where the contributors to Aoki and Dore seek to identify sources of competitiveness.

Thus this perspective in which a number of ramifications are included reflect a view of reactive globalization, as they are looking for ways to revitalize the declining manufacturing industry in the Anglo-American world by learning from Japanese competitiveness. The answer offered is to renew the old Fordist system and to create flexibility in the rigid and outdated institutional arrangements.

'Japanization' perspective

The 'Japanization' perspective, as represented by Oliver and Wilkinson (1992), is advocated by those who have directly experienced Japanese inward investment and its influence upon British industry, in management as well as in labour. In this sense, the 'Japanization' approach reflects the unique and mature conditions of the British political economy, as subject to a reactive process of globalization. 'Japanization' embraces two aspects – one concerning Japanese transplant management and industrial relations, and the other its influence upon local British management and industrial relations. The discussion ranges from a concrete investigation of the influence exerted by transplants, at one level, to a normative assessment of their importance for British management, labour and the economy in general, at another.

The 'Japanization' perspective thus can be said to reflect the thinking of British academics concerned with the need to revitalize British manufacturing, yet nervous about the end result of Japanese influence upon the economy and industrial relations. In this latter regard, 'Japanization' appears as a way to shift the balance in management–labour relations, leading to further loss of union power which began with the Thatcher government in the 1980s. It seems, therefore, that interest is in both production systems and social relations, reflecting the current condition of the British economy and the declining strength of trade unions.[6]

'Labour process' perspective

The 'Labour process' perspective emphasizes the nature of social relations in the labour process evolving within Japanese management (Elger and Smith 1994). Along with authors such as Turnbull (1988) and Garrahan and Stewart (1992), this perspective is rooted in a critical view of the 'Japanization' process and indeed 'Japanization' itself. The core of the argument is that the Japanese production system has not replaced the existing concept of capitalist production, with all the exploitative features and worker control intact. Garrahan and Stewart, for example, take the 'Nissan Way' as a 'new regime of subordination' which rests upon 'control through quality, exploitation via flexibility, and surveillance via teamworking' (Garrahan and Stewart 1992: 139). By extension, their bedfellows are Dohse *et al.* (1985), who argue that Japanese management is a more sophisticated system of exploitation under conditions in which management prerogatives are much stronger due to the decline of union power.

This 'labour process' perspective can be seen as another manifestation of Western academics taking a critical approach to capitalist production systems – not for them a view of Japanese management or production systems as a new concept, model or paradigm. Rather, Japanese management is seen as an enhanced system of control and exploitation under capitalist social relations, with the issue of revitalizing the British manufacturing industry being of secondary importance to a critique of 'Japanese-style capitalism'.

Political economy perspective

The political economy perspective focuses upon Japanese foreign direct investment, an inevitable consequence of the country's growth into an economic superpower and integration with the rest of the world (Strange 1993). This perspective, as in Morris (1991), and Campbell and Burton (1994), is rooted firmly in the British political economy. In other words, Japan's global integration is seen in terms of the potential benefits for Britain, with 'Japanization' being regarded as positive (Strange 1993). This reflects an attitude towards accommodating pro-active Japanese globalization within the reactive process of the British political economy.

Although these mainly Anglo-American perspectives thus reflect the conditions extant in each national economy, they also reflect perceptions of reactive globalization, largely triggered by the pro-active globalization of Japan. This is in sharp contrast to Japanese academics, who now find themselves in the midst of pro-active globalization.

JAPANESE PERSPECTIVES

Two general stages of development can be identified in Japan's post-war industrialization: first, the rapid growth following industrial recovery; and second, the globalization processes of recent years. Academic interest in Japan has also shifted in response to these altered conditions.

The trend in the earlier period (1955–73) was for academics to study American business practices and theories, which provided a theoretical basis for the introduction of American practices into Japanese management. This was necessarily pragmatic, as massive imports of advanced technologies and mass production methods, mainly from the USA, occurred during this period. The dominant perspective then was thus a Japanese version of American business management. During the rapid economic growth period, the imported production and management systems were modified and processed within the Japanese social and cultural context.

When runaway growth terminated with the oil shock of 1973, Japan entered a period of much lower economic growth, and Japanese business was forced to move into the international arena, seeking world markets and new investment opportunities. As a result, Japanese management and production systems came under increasing scrutiny overseas, and this attention focused Japanese academic enquiries on identifying within the domestic management and production systems specifically 'Japanese' elements. The conference theme for a 1977 meeting of the Japan Society of Business Administration, for instance, was 'Japanese-style management', which followed the trend to attempt to identify 'unique' characteristics of Japanese business management (for representative work, see e.g. Hazama 1971; Tsuda 1977; Iwata 1984). This perspective, which aimed to shed light upon specific elements of Japanese management, tended to ascribe the success of Japanese business to unique traditional factors, in particular Japanese 'culture' as manifest within managerial structures.

Almost a decade later, the same Society in 1989 addressed the issues of transfer and localization of Japanese management. The main aim in this conference was to highlight the universal or rational factors inherent in Japanese management. On this occasion, 'universal' rather than 'unique' factors were prominent explanations for successful transplant management (for representative work, see e.g. Okubayashi 1988; Shimada 1988; Abō 1994). This view maintains that within Japanese management a substantial degree of 'universal', rational management practices exist, and that these can be recreated elsewhere, even in the local management of overseas transplants. In this we can see how the dominant Japanese academic perspective has shifted from one emphasizing culture-specific factors to one emphasizing the global applicability of Japanese management. In the 1990s, as globalization has proceeded further, the 'universalists' have taken over from the 'particularists', a shift which reflects the formation of a pro-active perspective on Japanese globalization.

In 1996, when the feedback effects of low economic growth and globalization upon domestic management have been felt keenly by business academics, the topic chosen for the Society's conference was 'Themes of Contemporary Management Studies', with three sub-themes: 'Reconstruction of Business Management', 'Business Activities and Civic Life' and 'Business Activity and its Regulation'. The 1996 conference thus focused upon the domestic dimension of management and its impact upon civic life, suggesting a completely different set of theoretical concerns to those of the high-growth period and those of globalization in low economic growth. Our contributors also reflect such a shift in perception about Japanese business activities: one group reflects the concerns of globalization, another that of domestic management, and a third that of labour and industrial relations.

Although each author applies his own approach in addressing a specific area of business activity and management, the book as a whole should provide an overall picture of Japan's global presence and Japanese management. Current thinking may be characterized as a perspective rooted in 'pro-active', as opposed to 'reactive', globalization, where the globalization of capital, labour and business organization is manifest in a new dimension of Japanese business and needs an overall understanding. The contributors can be divided into three groups. In the first we can place Hook, Hasegawa, Yamashita and Abo, who seek to investigate the process and consequence of Japanese globalization as well as its implications. This group tends to adopt a pro-active perspective on Japanese globalization in the three core regions of the global political economy. In general, the current globalization of Japan has been seen, at least until now, as a positive and inevitable phenomenon emerging rapidly after the end of the Cold War, although the authors are concerned about potential conflicts and the negative consequences of Japanese globalization. The second group, embracing Ikeda, Nakata, Okubayashi and Watanabe, examines the restructuring of Japanese management, which is seen as demanding constant rethinking in the context of the corporate environment. These authors see such a restructuring as the response of business strategy, but in terms of academic perception, such a restructuring can be taken as a process of Japan converging with a Western logic of capital accumulation at a time when, ironically, Western academics and practitioners tend to see Japan's traditional specificity as elements of competitive strength. The third group consists of Munakata, Nishinarita and Ōhki. Each seeks to investigate the self-reactive processes inherent in the production systems and social relations as manifest in industrial relations and the labour movement. Whereas Japanese industrial relations have been viewed by most Western academics studying Japanese business as an institutional element which functions effectively in promoting competitiveness, these authors take a more critical view. Their chapters look at business both from the perspective of productive forces as well as from that of social relations.

Overall, then, this volume investigates capital accumulation as manifest in pro-active Japanese globalization, with a focus on the overseas operations of Japanese business, organizational and institutional changes, and industrial relations and labour movement.

STRUCTURE OF THE BOOK

The three groups of authors outlined above provide the structure for the book. In Part I the contributors are concerned to examine the complex dynamics of Japan's role in the three core regions of the global political economy, focusing both on the general level of the Japanese presence in the three cores as well as the specific level of transplant activities.

Hook, in 'Japanese Business in Triadic Regionalization', sets out a general perspective on the globalization of Japanese business by focusing on the Japanese penetration of the three core regions of the global economy – North America, Europe and East Asia. The chapter investigates the trade and investment patterns of Japan in the triadic cores; the nature of these investments in terms of the specific manufacturing and other sectors targeted; and any problems that the emerging trade and investment patterns have given rise to, such as trade friction with the USA and Europe. The focus is on the 1980s and 1990s, especially after the bursting of the economic bubble.

The issue of localization as an integral part of Japanese globalization is explored by Hasegawa in 'Japanese Global Strategies in Europe and the Formation of Regional Markets'. He notes that this process is followed by the subsequent formation of regional markets for both products and part supplies. Hasegawa's analysis, based upon the most recent Japan External Trade Organization (JETRO) surveys, indicates that an increase in localization in management is an inevitable part of globalization and has far-reaching implications for Japanese-style management – namely, that localization of Japanese management in Europe implies a process of transformation of Japanese management itself, while it is also a process of influencing local management.

Yamashita's chapter on 'Japanese Investment Strategy and Technology Transfer in East Asia' examines the process of Japanese foreign direct investment (FDI) in East Asia including the recent increase in China. He focuses on the electrical machinery and automobile industries, examining the pattern of investment, technology transfer, and education and training in Japanese transplants. He identifies forces of both competition and co-operation between Japan and East Asia, but as an overall perception he sees that both Japan and other East Asian economies benefit from the dynamics of globalization, especially if an ideal circular structure of economic development, such as an 'Asian Economic Co-operation Zone', can be established.

In 'Changes in Japanese Automobile and Electronic Plants in the USA: Evaluating Japanese-style Management and Production Systems', Abo compares the results of his research in 1989–93 with that carried out in 1986–89. He identifies some significant changes between the two periods and points to implications in the change from the direct import of managerial resources to the application of managerial 'logic' in local social and historical context. He thus argues that 'hybrid' approach is useful in explaining the situation of Japanese transplant management.

Part I thus investigates the manifestation of Japanese pro-active globalization in the three core regions, which is promoted by the export of capital, technology and managerial techniques. It can be seen as a new stage of Japanese capitalism catching up with the West in the area of capital exports. The impact of this pro-active globalization can be seen in the transformation of so-called Japanese-style management.

In Part II the contributors focus on the transformation in management, examining the impact of globalization on the operations of Japanese business as well as a number of the important changes in the structure of companies in the wake of the longest recession in the post-war period.

Ikeda's contribution, 'Globalization's Impact upon the Subcontracting System', investigates the increase in competition under globalization, focusing upon the domestic subcontracting system in the automobile industry. Ikeda's detailed analysis sheds light on domestic de-industrialization under Japanese globalization as well as on the organizational strength of Japanese business. The expansion of overseas production into East Asia and especially into China has made auto-manufacturers downgrade the importance of the second and third levels of the *keiretsu* and, as a result, subcontracting firms are left to compete on their own merits in the market. Some of the subcontracting firms may merge, reorganize, or even close down. Indeed, Ikeda points out that globalization and the subsequent increase in competition are enforcing a restructuring of the domestic subcontracting industrial structure to an extent never seen before. This drastic remodelling of subcontracting will transform the structure itself into a much sharper and slimmer hierarchy, while accommodating the cheap labour of East Asia and China into an international subcontracting system.

Nakata's 'Ownership and Control of Large Corporations in Contemporary Japan' examines Japanese corporate ownership and its relationship to corporate control and rule. In the early 1990s, enterprise groups increased their cohesiveness, as expressed in average and aggregate shareholding within groups. This is in marked contrast to the general trend in the latter half of the 1980s, in which period inter-corporate relations in each enterprise group declined. Nakata's comment on the increased percentage of shareholding by life insurance companies, fire and marine insurance companies and pension funds implies that financial institutions as a whole are becoming more influential than manufacturing companies in each enterprise group, and thus may exert influence upon the nature of corporate control and rule. He suggests that this can be taken as a sign of a move towards a system much of the Anglo-American model. Although top management expanded during the high economic growth period, with the lowering in the rate of economic growth, power is now increasingly concentrated in a smaller and higher placed group in the top management hierarchy, as in the West.

In 'Small Headquarters and the Reorganization of Management' Okubayashi discusses the theoretical implications of the recent change in corporate organization based upon his 1985 and 1993 surveys. He establishes two major factors for the restructuring of corporate organization, one economic and the other technological. The economic factor is the continued recession in the 1990s, while the technological one is the spread of micro-electronics and information technology. Based on a classification of organizations into management organization and workplace organization, he shows how management organization has been changing to a flat organization, with the delegation of administrative decision-making functions towards lower levels of management, namely to section heads. On the other hand, workplace organization has changed from a rigid type to a more flexible type, which he calls an organic organization. The single-product, mass-production system which requires rigid management organization is now being replaced by a multi-product, medium-size production system, which requires flat organic organization, namely a change to what he calls a 'loosely structured organization'.

Watanabe's 'The Rise of Flexible and Individual Ability-oriented Management' investigates the nature of the 'career course' system, a new method of employment recently introduced into Japanese companies in response to the changing corporate environment. He shows that the new system has an ambivalent nature: on the one hand, it creates further division among employees through increased competition and undermines the power of labour unions. This system has created core and periphery workforces in both men and women employees and resulted in reduced workforces, wage costs, and longer working hours. Yet, on the other hand, it can also be seen as a reasonable response by management to the diversified perceptions and attitudes of workers. Workers themselves have now changed their values and perceptions of work itself. Flexibility in recruitment, career, education and training, and working hours has been a hallmark of Japanese companies in recent years. Although the 'career course' system provides only a limited degree of choice in employment conditions, it is a move away from traditional management based upon collective concepts, towards a more flexible system with relatively higher emphasis on individual employees. Watanabe foresees the arrival of large-scale 'co-operative' social relations which foster the creation of independent and autonomous human beings, who may each transform themselves from a 'company person' to an 'independent individual', who can appreciate both social and family life.

Chapters 5 to 8 in Part II thus examine the inward impacts of the proactive globalization of Japan and that of continued low economic growth, shedding light on the process and implications of such change and seeking new concepts which can explain the departure from the existing management concepts formulated during the high economic growth period. In Part III the contributors examine with a critical eye the contemporary and historical nature of production systems, industrial relations and the labour movement in Japan, taking into account work practices and the role of unions.

'The End of the "Mass-production" System and Changes in Work Practices', by Munakata, focuses upon the discussion of 'massproduction' and 'flexibility' in the light of the persistent debate over the Japanese production system, which is often referred to as 'Japanese manufacturing techniques', 'Japanese-style production system', the 'Japan model', 'lean production' or 'Toyotism'. After defining the system as an advanced stage of mass production and rejecting the view that it represents a 'paradigm shift' from Fordism, Munakata shows how the strength of the system derives from an integration of mechanical and organic principles. The Japanese production system is able to resolve the friction between productivity, quality and flexibility by improving the trade-off between the requirement of ensuring order in the system (mechanical principle), and the full utilization of worker potential (organic principle), made possible through a stable nation state and the closed nature of Japanese society, which itself has been changing in recent years.

In 'Japanese-style Industrial Relations in Historical Perspective' Nishinarita analyses 'Japanese-style' industrial relations from a historical perspective and critically comments on the popular cultural approach and the universalist approach. He maintains that the structure of industrial relations is unique to each period in history and should be investigated as such, rather than seeing them as a reflection of the historical development of some single prototype. 'Seniority based wages' and 'lifetime employment' are consequences of particular historical conditions, and they can be explained either by the 'livelihood guarantee' hypothesis or 'specific skill' hypothesis, or by both. Indeed, industrial relations were not originally 'co-operative' but shifted from 'conflictual' to 'co-operative' through 'recovery', 'high growth' and 'stable growth' periods. Nishinarita offers a unique interpretation of the QC circle movement, which increased dramatically in the 1970 to 1980s as a supplement to labour integration, which cannot be created by formal 'co-operative' industrial relations alone. 'Co-operative' enterprise unions and QC circles remain as the organizational structure of Japanese-style industrial relations, while seniority based wage/salary promotion will be replaced further by an individual ability-oriented promotion system – a move towards modified Japanese-style industrial relations.

Ōhki's 'New Trends in Enterprise Unions and the Labour Movement' reviews how industrial relations have changed, as reflected in the formation, development and transformation of enterprise unions. He explains the way in which enterprise unions in large corporations, one of the most important mainstays of the rapid economic growth of post-war Japan, are now in the throes of transformation and what consequences are emerging for workers and small and medium enterprises. In the latter half of the 1970s, enterprise unions developed into 'company unions'; during this time, the Japanese production system created what is now known as 'lean' production systems. This situation now faces the need for further change towards a more international division of labour which encompasses Asia in its production system. In the 1990s negative criticism of company unions and their federation, Japanese Trade Union Confederation (*Rengō*), has increased, as employees of small and medium enterprises and casual workers have been driven into further difficulties and worsened economic conditions under continued low growth and globalization. This opposition has gathered around another national organization, National Confederation of Trade Unions (*Zenrōren*), which has succeeded to the tradition and experience of class-conscious industrial unions and the labour movement. Ōhki thus examines how such difficulties have emerged out of the policies and strategies of company unions as well as *Rengō* and how the rival organization, which is autonomous and horizontal, is gaining strength by accommodating workers who are not organized by the *Rengō* unions.

No digest of Japanese academic perspectives under the economic conditions of low growth and pro-active globalization has yet appeared in English, despite the increasing importance of the research underway. Business and management issues under these conditions need to be examined in terms of the forces of capital accumulation, which is manifest in domestic as well as overseas operations, and industrial relations and labour movement which evolve within them. Although each chapter does not refer to this overall theme directly, readers should be able to gain a deeper understanding of the major business issues which have emerged as part of Japanese business management's restructuring for low growth and globalization.

Hasegawa Harukiyo
Glenn D. Hook

NOTES

1 The book is based upon the papers presented by Japanese academics who attended the Inaugural Anglo-Japanese Seminar on Japanese Business organized by the Centre for Japanese Studies at the University of Sheffield on 16–18 March 1995.
2 We regard manufacturing industry as still relatively important for academic studies, although the actual volume of foreign direct investment in the service sector accounts for more than that of manufacturing. There are at least four reasons for this focus: (1) production systems and relevant management and organization remain an important area of business studies; (2) manufacturing industry plays an important role for the expansion of the service industry; (3) international competitiveness is determined to a large extent by how manufacturing industry is organized and managed; (4) manufacturing is a crucial determinant of labour relations, often bringing into clear focus the question of unionization.
3 Among business studies academics in Japan there were traditionally two schools of thought: one which has been influenced by American management theories and the other by critical thought based upon Marxism. With the demise of the major socialist states and their economic failures plain to see, confidence in critical thought it has been largely lost among the latter academics. Hence they are now searching to find grounds on which to remain critical. Readers will find in this volume authors expressing critical thought as well as those expressing more confidence, reflecting a positive evaluation of pro-active globalization in the 1990s.
4 Of course, there is no clear-cut model of Japanese-style management per se; it is rather an abstraction and generalization from individual realities for the purpose of our discussion. We distinguish between 'Japanese-style management' and

'Japanese management' in this book. The former is Japanese management as summarized by reference to life-time employment, seniority promotion, and enterprise unions in addition to representative features of production methods such as JIT, teamworking and TQC, etc. When we use Japanese management, in contrast, we are referring to management as practised in Japan.

5 Womack *et al.* use the term 'lean production' and stress that 'the fundamental ideas of lean production are universal – applicable anywhere by anyone' (Womack *et al.* 1990: 9), while Kenney and Florida conceptualize it as 'innovation-mediated production' and argue that such features are now 'visible across the landscape of global capitalism' (Kenney and Florida 1993: 14). Thus they argue for the creation of a new universal concept of production system and organization.

6 As an extension of this discussion, Fruin (1992) and Shiomi and Wada (1995) adopt a more objective and historical approach to the influence of one type of management on the rest of the world. These authors investigate historically how and to what extent one typical type of production and institutional arrangement can be transferred and diffused, and examine the varying ways differences in social and cultural elements are accommodated.

REFERENCES

Abō, T. (ed.) (1994) *Hybrid Factory: The Japanese Production System in the United States*, Oxford: Oxford University Press.

Aoki, M. and Dore, R. (eds) (1994) *The Japanese Firm: Sources of Competitive Strength*, Oxford: Oxford University Press.

Campbell, N. and Burton, F. (eds) (1994) *Japanese Multinationals: Strategies and Management in the Global Kaisha*, London: Routledge.

Dohse, K., Jürgens, U. and Malsch, T. (1985) 'From "Fordism" to "Toyotism"? The social organisation of the labour process in the Japanese automobile industry', *Politics and Society*, 14, 2: 115–146.

Elger, T. and Smith. C. (eds) (1994) *Global Japanization?: The Transnational Restructuring of the Labour Process*, London: Routledge.

Fruin, W. M. (1992) *The Japanese Enterprise System: Competitive Strategies and Cooperative Structures*, Oxford: Oxford University Press.

Garrahan, P. and Stewart, P. (1992) *The Nissan Enigma: Flexibility at Work in a Local Economy*, London: Mansell Publishing Ltd.

Hazama, H. (1971) *Nihonteki Keiei* (Japanese-style management), Tokyo: Nihon Keizai Shinbun.

Iwata, R. (1984) *Nihonteki Keiei Ronsō* (Discussions on Japanese-style management), Tokyo: Nihon Keizai Shinbunsha.

Kenney, M. and Florida, R. (1993) *Beyond Mass Production: The Japanese System and Its Transfer to the US*, Oxford: Oxford University Press.

Liker, J. K., Ettlie, J. E. and Campbell, J. C. (eds) (1995) *Engineered in Japan: Japanese Technology Management Practices*, Oxford: Oxford University Press.

Morris, J. (ed.) (1991) *Japan and the Global Economy: Issues and Trends in the 1990s*, London: Routledge.

Okubayashi, K. (ed.) (1988) *ME Gijutsu Kakushin kano Nihonteki Keiei* (Japanese style management under evolution of micro-electronic technology), Tokyo: Chūō Keizaisha.

Oliver, N. and Wilkinson, B. (1992) *The Japanization of British Industry*: Oxford: Blackwell.

Shimada, H. (1988) *Hūman uea no Keizaigaku* (The economics of Humanware), Tokyo: Iwanami Shoten.

Shiomi, H. and Wada, K. (eds) (1995) *Fordism Transformed: The Development of Production Methods in the Automobile Industry*, Oxford: Oxford University Press.

Strange, R. (1993) *Japanese Manufacturing Investment in Europe: Its Impact on the UK Economy*, London: Routledge.

Tsuda, M. (1977) *Nihonteki Keiei no Ronri* (Logic of Japanese management) Tokyo: Chūō Keizaisha.

Turnbull, P. J. (1988) 'The limits to "Japanization" – just-in-time, labour relations and the UK automotive industry', *New Technology, Work and Employment*, 3, 1 Spring 1988: 7–20.

Womack, J. P., Jones, D. T. and Roos, D. (1990) *The Machine that Changed the World*, New York: Rawson Associates.

Part I

Japanese business in globalization processes

1 Japanese business in triadic regionalization

Glenn D. Hook

This chapter seeks to provide an overview of Japanese business in the triadic regions of the global economy, North America, Europe, and East Asia. The three chapters to follow in Part I deal separately with issues of Japanese business management in these three core regions, whereas my aim here is to focus more generally upon how Japanese business is embracing triadic regionalization, especially in the 'post-bubble economy'[1] of the 1990s. The chapter has four main purposes: first, to show that, despite predictions of the global economy dividing into three blocs, Japan has embraced interregionalization, not just East Asian regionalization. In other words, the Japanese economy is embedded in a complex web of economic interconnectedness in the three core regions of the globe, suggesting that interregionalization as well as regionalization are integral to Japanese trade strategies. Second, to outline how, in responding to the pressures of globalization and regionalization, Japanese business has developed a triadic investment strategy. This is manifested clearly in the patterns of investment pursued by key Japanese manufacturers in North America, Europe, and East Asia. Third, to indicate that, in pursuing a strategy of exporting manufactures and boosting foreign investment, Japanese companies have set in motion a dual transformation, at home as well as abroad. Specifically, changes in the domestic political economy are linked intricately to the movement of Japanese manufacturers abroad, not least in cost-cutting and other changes within companies and the 'hollowing out' of industries. These points will be dealt with in greater detail in some of the later chapters of the book. Finally, to highlight how, with the bursting of the Japanese economic bubble, trade, investment and production patterns now differ considerably from the 1980s, when the Plaza Accord[2] pushed Japanese companies to invest in the advanced economies. The focus now is increasingly on East Asia.

In essence, then, the two predominant trends in the world political economy, globalization and regionalization, are reshaping profoundly the political economy of Japan. The quantitative increases in economic interconnectedness, as manifested in the complex patterns of cross-border trade, finance, and production, highlight the salient features of economic globalization. This growth in quantity implies a qualitative change in the degree of cross-regional economic links at the heart of globalization. In this sense, interregionalization is a part of globalization, too. At the same time as globalization is transforming the Japanese political economy, however, a concomitant trend towards regionalization is boosting intraregional interconnectedness, as with the deepening and widening of the European Union (EU), and the emergence of new regional institutional frameworks in the form of the North American Free Trade Agreement (NAFTA), Asia–Pacific Economic Cooperation (APEC), Association of South East Asian Nations (ASEAN) Free Trade Area (AFTA), and others. As a result, economic interconnectedness at the regional level is similarly shaping the political economy of Japan. In some quarters, the triadic regionalism at the heart of regionalization in Europe, the Americas and East Asia is painted in the alarmist pictures of a world dividing into competing regional blocs, but the complex interweaving of the dual trends towards both globalization and regionalization draws our attention to how, in the emerging world order, the links between as well as within the three core regions of the global economy need to be taken into account (Gamble and Payne 1996). For these reasons, the role of Japanese business in both globalization and regionalization will be examined below, with the emphasis being placed on the issues of trade and investment in the 1980s and 1990s. The historical developments shaping the Japanese response to globalization and regionalization, although important, have been addressed elsewhere (see Hook 1996).

TRIADIC TRADE RELATIONS

The globalization and regionalization of Japanese business can be understood by reference to trade, foreign direct investment (FDI) and the ratio of production and other economic activities carried out beyond the shores of Japan. To start with trade, Japan has established itself as the paramount mercantilist state through maximizing the export of manufactured products, especially consumer durables, while minimizing the import of foreign manufactures. The three core regions of the global economy account for the overwhelming proportion of both Japanese exports and imports, with East Asia[3] accounting for an increasing ratio in the 1990s. As a share of total dollar-based exports in 1995, the USA accounted for 27.3 per cent, EU 15.9 per cent, and East Asia 42.2 per cent, made up of NIEs (Hong Kong, Singapore, South Korea, Taiwan) 25.1 per cent, ASEAN 4 (Indonesia, Malaysia, Philippines, Thailand) 12.1 per cent, and China 5.0 per cent. As a share of total dollar-based imports in 1995, the USA accounted for 22.4 per cent, EU 14.5 per cent, and East Asia 34.4 per cent, made up of NIEs 12.3 per cent, ASEAN 4 11.4 per cent, and China 10.7 per cent. In this way, the triadic political economy in 1995 accounted for just over 85 per cent of Japanese exports and just over 70 per cent of imports on a dollar-based value, suggesting the degree to which Japan is embedded triadically in the global economy. The strengthening of this trend from the mid-1980s onwards can be seen from Figures 1.1 and 1.2.

The Japanese trade relationship with the USA is central to our understanding of the globalization and regionalization of the Japanese political economy. The trade surpluses with the USA, which frequently have led to

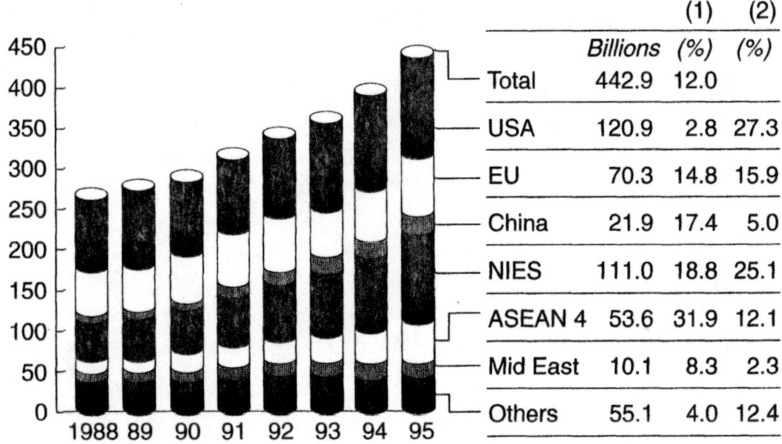

	Billions	(1) (%)	(2) (%)
Total	442.9	12.0	
USA	120.9	2.8	27.3
EU	70.3	14.8	15.9
China	21.9	17.4	5.0
NIES	111.0	18.8	25.1
ASEAN 4	53.6	31.9	12.1
Mid East	10.1	8.3	2.3
Others	55.1	4.0	12.4

Figure 1.1 Trends in Japanese exports (US$ billion)
Source: Figures from Ministry of Finance, reproduced from *Imidasu 97*: 101

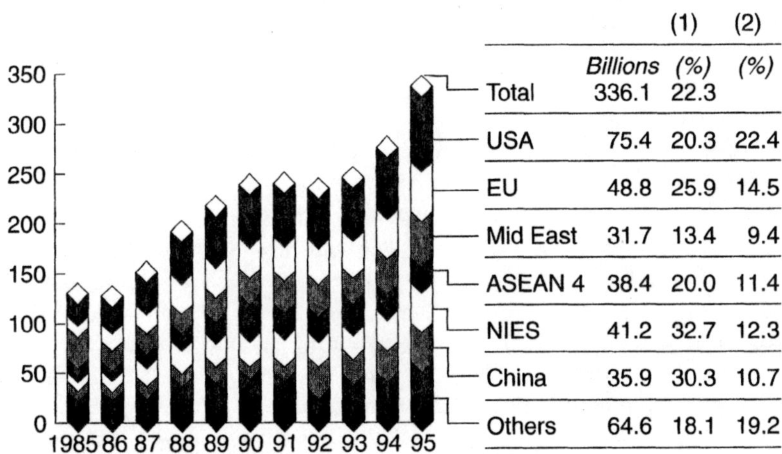

	Billions	(1) (%)	(2) (%)
Total	336.1	22.3	
USA	75.4	20.3	22.4
EU	48.8	25.9	14.5
Mid East	31.7	13.4	9.4
ASEAN 4	38.4	20.0	11.4
NIES	41.2	32.7	12.3
China	35.9	30.3	10.7
Others	64.6	18.1	19.2

Figure 1.2 Trends in Japanese imports (US$ billion)
Source: Figures from Ministry of Finance, reproduced from *Imidasu 97*: 101

the politicization of bilateral economic issues, have spurred Japanese government and industry to introduce a variety of measures in response. After a decline in the late 1980s, the surplus rose again between 1991–4, but then registered a decline in 1995 to $45.5 billion, reflecting the changing nature of the bilateral trade relationship. In 1995 imports from the USA, led by semiconductors and automobiles, registered a 20.3 per cent increase over 1994. In the case of Japanese exports to the USA, however, the increase was only 2.8 per cent, with capital goods registering a 2.3 per cent increase over 1994 (figures from MITI 1996: 18). Despite this, with the rise in the value of the dollar against the yen in 1996, Japanese exports to the USA of automobiles and other manufactures can be expected to rise again, boosting the surplus. The 1995 figures point to the success achieved by the USA in penetrating the Japanese market, as in the case of semiconductors, albeit in the context of the politicization of economic issues and the setting of numerical targets.[4]

Indeed, Japanese exports to the United States of especially automobiles, electronics and other consumer durables have given rise to numerous bilateral trade conflicts. Thus, in the face of US political pressure, manifest in a range of so-called *jishu kisei* (voluntary export restraints, VERs) and result-oriented agreements, Japanese exports have been restricted and imports from the USA boosted. The economic conflicts between the two have become more complex as time has passed, but have been basically of four different types (Kusano 1996: 73–6). The first major source of conflict has been Japanese exports to the USA. Whether colour televisions and steel in the 1970s, automobiles and machine tools in the 1980s, or semiconductors and auto-parts in the 1990s, the politicization of trade issues has led to export restraints being imposed on Japan. In response, Japanese business has moved production facilities offshore, both to North America and to East Asia, where 'launch platforms' for export to the North American market have been created. A second major conflict has been over the closed nature of the Japanese market, ranging from resistance to opening up the agricultural sector, as in the cases of citrus fruits and rice; the service sector, as with finance and insurance; and the industrial sector, as illustrated by semiconductors and pharmaceutical products. The third type of conflict has arisen as a result of investments in the USA. These conflicts became especially salient in the late 1980s, when Japanese investors bought US real estate and companies, including such high-profile acquisitions as Sony's purchase of Columbia. Finally, in the late 1980s conflict arose over structural features of Japanese society and political economy, with the distribution system, corporate cross-shareholding, the balance between savings and investment, and so on, being subject to attack. This culminated in the 1989 Structural Impediments Initiative,[5] through which the USA sought to penetrate the Japanese market. In this way, the politicization of economic issues and activities, and the processes set in motion by the Japanese response to US pressures, brought about fundamental changes in both the domestic political economy and the global and regional roles of Japanese business.

Similarly, trade surpluses with the European Union (European Community) have led to the politicization of Euro-Japanese economic relations, with Japan being subject to a whole range of pressures by both the members and the Commission. The surplus enjoyed by Japan in the 1980s registered a fall at the end of the decade, but rose again in 1991 and 1992. It has been thenceforth in decline, however, with the surplus in 1995 dropping to $21.5 billion, again reflecting the changing nature of the trade relationship. In 1995 imports from the EU12 were led by machinery, especially automobiles, which registered a 36.9 per cent increase over 1994. In the case of Japanese exports to the EU, general machinery exports increased, but a marked decrease occurred in the export of automobiles, which dropped to 12.4 per cent in 1995, compared with 18.2 per cent in 1988 (MITI 1996: 23–4). The 1995 figures are testimony to the increasing success of European automakers, especially the German BMW, in gaining access to the Japanese market as well as a reflection of autogiants like Nissan and Toyota moving autoproduction to Europe.

As with the USA, a number of economic conflicts have arisen between Japan and the EU, with the bilateral relationship between the two being dominated by trade issues in the 1970s and 1980s. The conflicts over automobiles, colour televisions, video recorders, pharmaceuticals, and so on, were typical. However, without the US–Japan Security Treaty,[6] which has served as a lever for the USA in exerting pressure on Japan in trade negotiations, along with difficulties arising out of differences among EU members as well as between members and the Commission, Europe often has been in a weaker negotiating position than the USA.[7] Despite this, national governments and the Commission have followed the American lead in attempting to deal with made-in-Japans through VERs and anti-dumping legislation. In the case of automobiles, for instance, the threat of protectionist measures by the British government in 1978 led the Japanese auto-makers to restrict exports to below 10 per cent of the market. Similar restrictions on auto-exports also were agreed with other European countries. By 1986 VERs had been instituted on a European Community-wide basis, with manufacturers holding growth to around 10 per cent, with further restrictions, which remain in force until 1999, being imposed in 1991. Similar types of VERs have been placed on the export of electronics products. One of the most notorious cases is the French attempt in the early 1980s to restrict Japanese exports of video-cassette recorders (VCRs) by the use of a variety of tactics, such as requiring documentation related to the exports to be prepared in the French language and using a small number of customs officers in the provinces to deal with custom clearance. In the end, as in the case of automobiles, VCRs became subject to an EC-wide VER agreement in 1983 (for details, see Hosoya 1989).

Nevertheless, these bilateral negotiations at the national and Commission levels have not prevented the Japanese government from appealing to international mechanisms in order to try to resolve bilateral issues. This is the case with the government's 1988 decision to take the EC to the General Agreement on Trade and Tariffs over so-called 'screwdriver plants'. Indeed, in 1990 Japan won the case it had brought against the 1987 EC Council decision to regulate these plants, which imposed a limit of 60 per cent as the ratio of components originating from Japan in assembly plants in the EC. Even now, however, local content is influenced by the European Community Rules on Origin. In this way, trade conflicts between Japan and Europe have been dealt with through both multilateral and bilateral measures, although the movement of production facilities to Europe has been one of the major ways for Japan to deal with the conflicts.

In the case of trade links with East Asia, the pressure brought to bear on Japan as a result of the trade surplus with the USA and the EU cannot be matched by the East Asian governments, despite the nation's larger surpluses, as their economies are enmeshed in a subordinate web of economic relationships in comparison with the economies of the other two legs of the triad. The trade links between Japan and East Asia point to a growing interconnectedness, with a major increase in the 1995 dollar-based imports from the NIEs of 32.7 per cent over the previous year, led by a 128.8 per cent boost in imports of computers and other office equipment, a 87.8 per cent upswing in semiconductors and other electronic components, together with a 50.0 per cent growth in mineral fuel. Similarly, an 18.8 per cent increase was registered in exports, led by a 53.3 per cent growth in organic compound, a 46.6 per cent expansion in metal processing machinery, and a 37.9 per cent rise in semiconductors and electronic components. In the case of ASEAN, in 1994 a 20.0 per cent increase in imports occurred over the previous year, led by a 110.5 per cent expansion in computers and other office equipment, a 51.5 per cent rise in audio-visual equipment, and a 45.3 per cent growth in semiconductors and other electronic components. A 31.9 per cent increase occurred also in exports, with a 74.3 per cent expansion in metal processing machinery, a 58.3 per cent growth in organic compound, and a 49.4 per cent increase in semiconductors and other electronic components, and a 49.5 per cent upswing in automobiles. Finally, imports from China increased by 30.3 per cent over the previous years, with steel rising by 158.9 per cent, semiconductors by 90.2 per cent, computers and other office equipment by 80.8 per cent, and audio-visual equipment by 58.2 per cent. Exports increased by 17.4 per cent, led by computers and other office equipment 80.8 per cent, metal processing machinery 78.8 per cent, and semiconductors and other electronic components 30.3 per cent (MITI 1996: 33–7). The significant role of Japan not only as an exporter but also as an importer of a whole range of manufactured goods from East Asia is clearly illustrated by these figures, and by the fact that 'by the first half of 1995, 89 per cent of the calculators, 62 per cent of the colour televisions, 55 per cent of the hair dryers, 30 per cent of the copying machines and 28 per cent of the video-cassette recorders bought in Japan were imported, mostly from east Asia' (*Financial Times* 1996, 11 June).

The picture of economic interconnectedness drawn by the above figures on imports and exports shows the extent to which triadic trade relations link Japan intricately to the three core regions of the global political economy. The success of Japanese business in pursuing a strategy of exporting manufactures set in motion a process of transformation in both the nations with which Japan trades as well as within the country itself. The surplus enjoyed with North America and Europe politicized trade issues, leading Japanese newspapers to run 'trade war' headlines. Faced with eroding international competitiveness, the advanced economies resorted to political pressure on the Japanese government in order to restrict the flow of made-in-Japans outwards and boost the flow of made-in-Americas (or made-in-Europes) inwards. The mutually reinforcing dynamics between imports and exports have meant that, among the three core regions, East Asia has now grown in importance as the source of imports and as a market for exports. In other words, precisely as a result of the success of Japan in pursuing a mercantilist policy of maximizing exports and minimizing imports, pressures to open the market to foreign manufactures have been exerted by the advanced regional cores of North America and Europe, with Japanese business responding by developing a triadic investment strategy with an increasing focus on East Asia.

TRIADIC INVESTMENT STRATEGY

Thus, in the wake of the economic conflicts between Japan and the USA and Europe in the 1980s, the growth of East Asia as a market as well as a production platform, and the general rise in the value of the yen during the past decade, which has made investments in neighbouring countries especially attractive, many Japanese businesses have forged ahead with strategic investments in the three core regions of the global economy. The major boost in Japanese FDI following the Plaza Accord of 1985 reached a peak in 1989, at the height of the Japanese bubble economy, and then fell back in the early 1990s after the bursting of the bubble. The upturn came in 1993, with a 5.5 per cent increase over the previous year. The 1994 figures also show a rise of 14 per cent over the previous year, bringing the total FDI up to 60.8 per cent of the 1989 high. As a share of total FDI in 1995, Table 1.1 shows that North America accounted for 45.2 per cent; Europe accounted for 16.7 per cent; whereas Asia[8] now accounted for 24.0 per cent. Table 1.1 also points to the shift of Japanese investment to East Asia in the 1990s, which has been especially at the expense of Europe, as illustrated by the change in the overall share of the three core regions 1990–5. In 1990, North America accounted for 47.8 per cent (a drop of 2.6 per cent to 1995), Europe accounted for 25.1 per cent (a drop of 8.4 per cent), and Asia

Table 1.1 Japanese FDI (percentage, dollar base)

	North America	*Europe*	*Asia*
Total 1951–94	43.7	19.4	16.4
1990	47.8	25.1	12.4
1991	45.3	22.5	14.3
1992	42.7	20.7	18.8
1993	42.4	22.0	18.4
1994	43.4	15.2	23.6
1995	45.2	16.7	24.0

Sources: JETRO 1996: 31, 509 and JETRO 1997: 25

accounted for 12.4 per cent (a rise of 11.6 per cent nearly doubling the percentage). In this way, investments in the 1980s, which reflected the emergence of a triadic strategy on the part of Japanese multinationals, are being transformed in the 1990s by the march into Asia of small and medium-sized enterprises as well as the giants.

Investments in the advanced economies of North America and Europe, especially the USA and the UK, have been made in the manufacturing and non-manufacturing sectors, reflecting the need to maintain market access as well as the rise of Japan as an important player in non-manufacturing industries. In the 1970s and 1980s investments were used in order to set up production facilities in the three core regions of the global economy as well as to make inroads into commerce, finance, real estate, and so on. In the case of the USA, Japanese FDI has been concentrated in machinery in the manufacturing sector; and commerce, financial institutions and services in the non-manufacturing sector. In the case of the UK, FDI has focused overwhelmingly on machinery in the manufacturing sector and finance in the non-manufacturing sector. In the wake of the growth of a regional production network in the 1990s (Bernard and Ravenhill 1995), however, these two core regions now are being eclipsed by investments focusing on East Asia, especially China, as discussed below.

The consumer electronics and auto industries have been at the heart of the Japanese manufacturing presence in these two economies, especially in the 1970s and 1980s. As far as electronics is concerned, Sony and Matsushita built plants in the USA in the early 1970s. Other electronic giants like Mitsubishi, Toshiba and Sharp followed later in the decade. Hitachi and JVC entered in 1982; NEC in 1985, with the latter deciding to close operations in 1990. Behind this move was the growing competition in the 1980s from the newly rising East Asian economies, especially South Korea. This East Asian challenge led Japanese television manufacturers to move the labour-intensive parts of production across the border to Mexico. In the case of Hitachi, moreover, television production in the USA has recently been abandoned altogether in favour of production in

Mexico. In Toshiba's case, television components are supplied by the NIEs, Japan and from elsewhere within the USA to Toshiba's Tennessee factory (Ōno and Okamoto 1995: ch. 4). In this way, Japanese electronics manufacturers are creating an international division of labour in the production of consumer electronics, with Toshiba's strategy highlighting the degree to which production networks are interregional, not just regional.

In the case of Europe, Japanese companies have sought to maintain a presence in the EU market by moving production facilities to different parts of the Community, especially to the UK. Of the 728 Japanese manufacturers operating in Europe at the end of January 1994, for instance, the largest number, 206, was located in the UK, with 183 being makers of electrical/electronic goods and parts (JETRO 1994: ch. 1). Sony built a television factory in Wales in 1974, with Matsushita and Toshiba setting up their own production facilities at the end of the decade. Other electronic giants, such as NEC, JVC, and Mitsubishi, also have established UK plants. These companies produce and market colour televisions, VCRs, CD players, electronic components, and so on, for the UK market as well as for other markets in Europe. In this way, the UK has become a major production platform for Japanese electronic and electrical companies seeking to exploit the European market.

As far as East Asian FDI is concerned, one of the striking features of the 1990s is the relative decline of the Asian NIEs and the growing importance of ASEAN as a destination for Japanese manufacturing investments. In 1986, for instance, of the 21.1 per cent of global FDI destined for Asia, the NIEs took 15.1 per cent and ASEAN 5.1 per cent. In 1990, of the 19.8 per cent of global FDI destined for Asia, the NIEs took 5.2 per cent and ASEAN 13.1 per cent. By 1993 the Asian percentage of global investment had reached 32.9 per cent, with the NIEs taking 6.6 per cent and ASEAN 13.2 per cent. (*Ekonomisuto* 1994, 5 July: 32). As can be seen from Table 1.2, however, the striking feature of Asian FDI in the 1990s is the phenomenal increase in investments in China: an increase from 4.8 per cent of Asian FDI in 1990 to 36.4 per cent in 1995. While the implementation of the AFTA and liberalization measures will continue to ensure the attrac-

Table 1.2 Japanese FDI in China (unit: million dollars)

	Amount	*Per cent of total FDI*	*Per cent of Asian FDI*
1990	349	0.6	4.8
1991	579	1.4	9.8
1992	1,070	3.1	16.5
1993	1,691	4.7	25.5
1994	2,565	6.2	27.0
1995	4,473	8.8	36.4

Sources: JETRO 1996: 31 and JETRO 1997: 25

tiveness of ASEAN to Japanese business, China has become the focus of investment activity in the 1990s as it offers both production and marketing opportunities for the small and medium-sized as well as the large companies. In other words, Japanese companies can take advantage of low production costs in China, especially in labour-intensive industries, making investment attractive from the perspective of production, but the size of the Chinese market offers opportunities for market-led investment, too.

The growth in FDI is reflected by the more than doubling in number of Japanese companies registered overseas during the last decade, with the number reaching 17,015 in October 1995. The setting up of these companies has been concentrated overwhelmingly in the three core regions of North America, Europe and East Asia. Although an upswing occurred in manufacturing companies moving into North America and Europe in 1994, after a fall between 1990 and 1993, the main increase was in East Asia. Thus, although the global number of Japanese companies registered overseas increased in 1995 by only 6 per cent over the previous year, the expansion in Asia was 15 per cent, the highest rise since 1987. The manufacturing focus of these investments is clear: an increase in 1994 of 30 per cent over the previous year, whereas a drop occurred in the non-manufacturing sector (*Tōyō Keizai Tōkei Geppō*, May 1996: 19). This growth in the number of Japanese companies in East Asia, especially China, demonstrates how small and medium-sized as well as large companies are moving into Asia in the wake of the transformation of the Japanese economy, where smaller companies need to follow the giants into East Asia in order to survive.

The changing pattern of investments in the post-bubble 1990s is at the same time influenced by the increase in reinvestment made by overseas Japanese companies. Surveys by the Ministry of International Trade and Industry (MITI), for instance, show that between 1989 and 1993 the amount of reinvestment almost doubled. Indeed, in 1993 this amounted to more than the total of FDI from Japan, giving a grand total of 24 billion dollars. This is particularly the case in Asia, where in 1993 the amount reinvested was the largest to date, and higher than reinvestments in both North America and Europe. These investments reflect the establishment of regional headquarters in the three core regions of the global economy, with Japanese business in especially the USA and Asia making investments in third countries. This is in contrast to the pattern in the 1980s, when most investments were made from headquarters in Japan.

Thus, many of Japan's business giants have implemented a triadic headquarters strategy, setting up headquarters in North America, Europe, and Asia outside Japan. According to a 1990 survey conducted by the *Keizai Dōyūkai* (Japan Committee for Economic Development), of the 304 companies to respond to the survey, 48 per cent already had established headquarters in the USA, with another 5.6 per cent planning to set one up within a year, and 25.9 per cent planning or thinking about setting one up in a few years. In the case of Europe, 27.6 per cent already had established headquarters, with 72.2 per cent planning to set one up within a year, and 34.3 per cent planning or thinking about setting one up in a few years. In East Asia (excluding Japan headquarters), 17.1 per cent already had established headquarters, with 22.2 per cent planning to set one up within one year, and 36.1 per cent planning or thinking about setting one up in several years (*Keizai Dōyūkai* 1991: 92). This trend can be seen in the case of the electronic giants Sony, Toshiba, and Hitachi, which already have established regional headquarters in Japan, Singapore, the USA and Europe (for details, see Ishii 1992). This highlights how, in responding to globalization and regionalization, Japanese companies are employing a strategy of maintaining activities in all three core regions of the global economy.

INVESTMENT MOTIVATIONS

It was not really until the late 1980s, after the 1985 Plaza Accord, that Japanese companies became serious triadic investors. In looking back on the last decade, the surge in FDI can be seen to have been a response to a number of pressures on Japanese business (Iwaki 1993). In the first place, as indicated by our earlier reference to the Plaza Accord, a major motivation for investing overseas has been the rise in the value of the yen. The increased value of the yen following the Plaza Accord provided an added spur to the globalization and regionalization of Japanese business. The sharp rise in value – from 260 yen to the dollar in February 1985 to 237 yen to the dollar in September 1985 to 160 yen to the dollar in July 1986 – eroded the international competitiveness of Japanese exporters. This led Japanese business to boost FDI in the three core regions of the global economy, particularly the USA and Europe. These investments went ahead in order to maintain markets, despite the lack or low level of profitability in the advanced economies of North America and Europe, in contrast to East Asia (on profitability, see Hashimoto 1995: 585–8). The steep rise in the value of the yen in 1993–5 proved another major impetus for Japanese business to invest abroad. With the yen breaking through the 100 yen-to-the-dollar barrier and trading in the 90s in June 1994, and even trading under 80 yen to the dollar for a brief spell in April 1995, the ability of small and medium-sized as well as large enterprises to maintain international competitiveness by domestic measures like cost-cutting appeared no longer viable. The pressure from the high yen thus led Japanese business in the mid-1990s to focus on East Asia, especially ASEAN and China (with new interest in Vietnam), as the place for further investments.

Indeed, the ability of Japanese companies to pass on part of the costs associated with the yen's rise had been curtailed severely by the mid-1990s. On the one hand, further rationalization and cost-cutting within the company or among component suppliers had reached new limits; on the other, the renewed international competitiveness of US companies had made it difficult to raise prices. This meant that, in contrast to the rise in the yen after the 1985 Plaza Accord, when Japanese auto-makers were within six months able to recoup around 60 per cent of the loss arising from the yen's rise, in the mid-1990s the auto-giants could only pass on around 30 per cent (Furuta 1995: 45). This suggests that, in order to respond to pressures generated by hikes in the value of the yen, which can occur in an instant in the globalized currency markets, business cannot rely on time-consuming restructuring and rationalization in order to maintain international competitiveness, even if new limits can be found to cost cutting. Moving production overseas provides an answer. The electronics and electrical industry is illustrative: Sony, Matsushita and Hitachi respectively decided to increase the overall ratios of overseas production to 45 per cent by the end of 1994; 50 per cent by the end of the same year; and 70 per cent by 1996 (Furuta 1995: 47). It is thus not surprising that, in a survey carried out in February 1994 by MITI, we find 71 per cent of the 63 companies which replied to the survey planning to expand the ratio of overseas production during the year, with 56 per cent doing so in order to 'respond effectively to local demand', 49 per cent in order to 'respond to worsening profits on exports', and 36 per cent 'for reverse imports' (cited in Furuta 1995: 46).

A second reason for the increase in overseas investments by Japanese business is as a reaction to regionalism, especially in Europe. Indeed, in the late 1980s and the beginning of the 1990s the fear of 'fortress Europe' led many of Japan's leading companies to set up offices or plants in Europe in the lead-up to the creation of the single market. In particular, Japanese manufacturers sought to ensure their products would still gain access to the European market after the 'single market' came into force. The FDI made in the UK by Japanese consumer electronics and electrical makers, auto-makers and other manufacturers was thus not only a means to ensure access to the UK market, but also to the continental European market. Similarly, the coming into force of NAFTA in January 1994 acted to stimulate – albeit less so – Japanese companies to further invest in North America and Mexico. As with their US competitors, Japanese auto-manufacturers already had developed a strategy to carry out production across the border in Mexico as well as in the United States. Similarly, electrical and electronic machinery manufacturers operate 'twin plants' in the US–Mexican border region, with Mexican cheap labour being used for components assembly. Unlike the case of the EU, therefore, the creation of NAFTA did not exert a major impact on Japanese companies, many of which had already developed a production strategy to take advantage of Mexican proximity to the USA (Fukushima 1994: 34). Finally, as far as regionalism in Asia is concerned, Japan has been at the centre of 'contested regionalism' (Hook 1996a), with a key role for the nation being envisioned in both the exclusionary East Asian Economic Caucus, as proposed by Prime Minister Mahathir of Malaysia, and APEC, as now pushed forward by the USA.

The Japanese commitment to APEC is a commitment to 'open regionalism', which 'contains no element of exclusionary discrimination against outsiders' (Garnaut and Drysdale 1994: 2). In this sense, investments in the members of APEC, mostly the East Asian economies and the USA, have been carried out largely as part of the triadic strategy of Japanese business, with a focus on Europe as well as East Asia and the USA, rather than as an explicit response to NAFTA as new regionalism.

Third, overseas investments have been carried out in order to ameliorate trade conflicts, especially USA–Japan trade conflicts, and as a precaution against the use of some of the heavier weapons in the US arsenal, such as the Super 301 provision of the 1988 Omnibus Trade and Competitiveness Act. As we have seen earlier, Europe and the USA have imposed restraints on Japanese exports, which have been carried out under the euphemism of voluntary export restraints (VERs) as well as orderly market agreements (OMAs). These have been used by the USA against Japanese exports of colour televisions, steel, automobiles, machine tools, semiconductors, auto-parts, and so on. Thus, overseas investments often have been made in order to respond to the political pressure brought to bear to restrict exports from Japan as a result of trade conflicts and protectionist impulses. The importance of trade conflicts as a motivation for investing in the USA can be seen from the major surge in FDI by Japan's auto-giants following the highly politicized automobile trade conflict of the early 1980s and the introduction of VERs on Japanese cars. The continuing importance of the export of automobiles and auto-related products to the USA is clear from the fact that, of the US trade deficit with Japan, approximately two-thirds is considered to be auto-related (*Nihon Keizai Shinbun Hen* 1995: 2). This no doubt helps to explains reports in October 1995 that the Central Intelligence Agency had tapped the phone of MITI Minister Hashimoto Ryūtaro in a bid to discover Japan's negotiating position in the recent auto negotiations (*Nihon Keizai Shinbun Hen* 1995: 1). In East Asia, such investments have been carried out with a view to establishing production platforms in order to launch products into the North American and European markets as well as to penetrate the East Asian markets themselves. In the case of East Asian investments, therefore, Japanese business is producing for markets outside the region as well as for national and regional markets. In the case of Matsushita, for instance, air conditioners produced in Malaysia are exported to the US markets as well as back to Japan and are increasingly sold to the burgeoning middle classes of East Asia itself. In this way, investments carried out in response to the politicization of economic issues between Japan and the advanced economies have helped to transform the global, regional and domestic political economies of the three core regions of the global economy.

Fourth, overseas investments by the large Japanese manufacturing companies have exerted a 'pull effect' on the small and medium-sized subcontractors and other related *keiretsu* companies to invest overseas, too. In purchasing components and other necessities in the manufacturing process, large manufacturers often prefer to rely on the same subcontractors and other companies used in Japan, due to confidence in the quality of the products, delivery deadlines, and so on. At the same time, the movement overseas of Japanese manufacturers is gradually leading to a 'hollowing-out'[9] of manufacturing industries, leaving the small and medium-sized enterprises struggling to find orders in Japan. This movement of small and medium-sized enterprises, along with the giants, thus serves to help reproduce the 'dual structure' of the Japanese production system in East Asia. In order to maintain their own competitiveness, increasing numbers of small and medium-sized enterprises have little choice but to move overseas. As in the auto-industry, these companies are taking advantage not only of business opportunities created by the location of the big Japanese auto-makers, but of national auto-makers in East Asia, too. In this way, some small and medium-sized companies also are developing their own global and regional strategies (Yamada 1995: 15).

Finally, Japanese business often makes overseas investments as part of global or regional strategies. Such strategies can be pursued in a variety of ways, but of particular importance is the Japanese role in 'strategic alliances' with other global players from the USA and Europe, in particular; and as part of a new division of labour, especially in the context of the development of a regional production system in East Asia. Japan's global players seek to gain technical and other expertise by linking with key US and European industries in research and development, as in the micro-chip and computer industries, in order to stay at the forefront of technological innovation. Such strategic alliances can also serve to spread the costs of development among the big global players. The 1990 alliance between the Mitsubishi and Bentz groups is illustrative of the increasingly important role Japanese companies are now playing globally.

At the same time, one of the striking features of the 1990s is the gradual emergence of a regional production system centring on Japan (for details, see Bernard and Ravenhill 1995). This relocation of production facilities to other parts of East Asia is part of a restructuring of the regional political economy. Still, the newly emerging division of labour does not fit a simplistic view of Japanese investments in developing East Asia in labour-intensive industries, thereby enabling Japanese companies to escape the high costs of labour within Japan and take advantage of the relatively cheaper costs of labour in developing East Asia, although this is one aspect of the movement overseas. Rather, the emerging regional production system reflects an international division of labour within Japanese companies, as investments in the NIEs, ASEAN and China are creating a network of Japanese subsidiaries and other companies as part of a regional system of intra-industry development, production and trade, where even the research and development element of the production system is carried out in East Asia. Indeed, the vast majority of Japanese manufacturers recognize the importance of conducting research and development overseas (JETRO 1994: ch. 5). This is illustrated by Matsushita's decision to establish research and development facilities for air conditioners in Malaysia.

In comparison with North America and Europe, the globalization of Japanese business continues to lag behind, reflecting Japan's later start as a major foreign direct investor. In 1985, for instance, the percentage of total production (measured in terms of sales) carried out overseas was only 3 per cent for Japan, whereas it was around 17 per cent for the USA and Germany. By 1992 the Japanese rate had more than doubled to 6.2 per cent, with the US rate rising to 26 per cent and the German rate to 18.2 per cent. In particular, the percentage of overseas production is high in the case of both Japanese electrical and electronic machinery (12.6 per cent in 1993) and transport machinery (17.3 per cent in 1993) (JETRO 1996: 42). In terms of intra-firm trade, a significant number of Japanese companies in East Asia and the USA exports back to Japan, as a 1995 survey carried out by JETRO shows: 46.4 per cent of the surveyed companies in the USA exported components or semi-finished products back to the company in Japan, with 53.9 per cent exporting finished goods. In the case of Asia, the figures were 50.3 per cent and 72.2 per cent. The lowest percentage was for those companies in the EU, respectively 22.5 per cent and 27.4 per cent, reflecting the large proportion of companies which source from other companies in the EU (JETRO 1996: 45).

Furthermore, many companies reinvest locally or in other economies in East Asia in order to respond to local or regional demands as well as to export back to Japan from the third country in which investments have been made. The growing importance of such reinvestment in East Asia is confirmed by a 1995 JETRO study in Hong Kong, Thailand, Malaysia and Singapore, which showed that, of the 573 companies to respond to the survey, 18.7 per cent had invested already in a third country and a further 35.3 per cent of companies was considering making such investments. This trend was especially strong in Hong Kong and Singapore, indicating the growing importance of offshore Japanese companies for understanding the transformation of the regional economy. As can be seen from Figures 1.3 and 1.4, the largest number of investments by companies in Hong Kong is in China (Figure 1.3), whereas companies in Singapore focus more on Malaysia (Figure 1.4, JETRO 1996: 35–6)

CONCLUSION

In this way, the trade, investment and production patterns outlined above point to differences between Japanese investments in Europe and the USA, especially in the wake of the Plaza Accord, and investments in East Asia in the post-bubble 1990s. In the former case, the investments made in the manufacturing industries, such as automobiles or consumer electronics, established production facilities aimed at exploiting the national and regio-

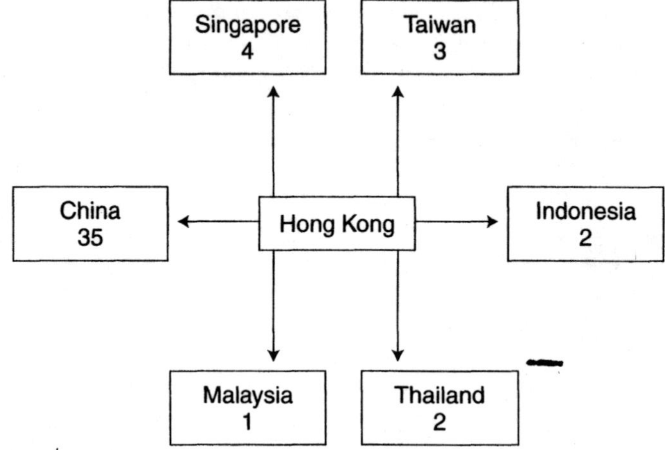

Figure 1.3 FDI by Japanese companies based in Hong Kong
Source: JETRO 1996: 36

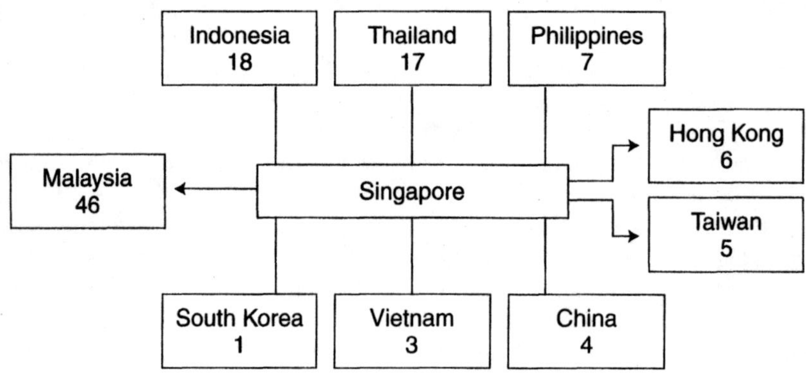

Figure 1.4 FDI by Japanese companies based in Singapore
Source: JETRO 1996: 36

nal markets in the 1980s. The Japanese transplants in the USA produced mainly for the North American market, as in the UK they produced mainly for the European market. As we have seen, however, in the 1990s Japanese manufacturers in the USA are exporting back to Japan, too, reflecting the further globalization of Japanese business. In East Asia, Japanese investments have moved gradually from the NIEs to ASEAN and increasingly to China, reflecting attempts to take advantage of cheaper production costs as well as to exploit market opportunities in East Asia. Surveys show that a marked increase occurred between 1992 and 1994 in those companies which gave as their reasons for investing in China developing new markets, and exporting back to Japan, and not simply as a way to secure cheap sources of labour (*Rōdō Undō* 1995: 17). In this way, the Japanese, Chinese and other East Asian economies are being tied together in a complex regional production system linking Japanese companies and their subsidiaries and *keiretsu*-related and other companies overseas.

Nevertheless, the trade, investment and production patterns we have outlined above suggest that interregionalization, not just regionalization, is a powerful force in shaping the strategy of Japanese business. True, the attraction of East Asia has increased during the 1990s, and the regional production system can be expected to become more entrenched as we move towards the twenty-first century. As seen in the global strategies of the Japanese electronic giants, however, all three regions of the global political economy are important to Japanese business. So, despite the increase in trade and investment in the East Asia region, Japan still is linked closely through trade, investment and production with the other two core regions of the global economy. In the case of the USA, investments over the years mean that, not only does North America remain centrally as an absorber of made-in-Japans, but is increasingly functioning for Japanese manufacturers as a launch platform to export finished and semi-finished products back to Japan. In Europe, despite the fall in investment, the EU continues as an important absorber of manufactured products, with the UK remaining as an important launch platform for penetrating the continental European markets.

In the future, the Japanese political economy will continue to respond to global, interregional and regional pressures. On the one hand, this will mean a continuing Japanese presence in the three core regions of the global political economy, and a growing presence in East Asia. On the other, the Japanese response to external pressures will continue to reshape the domestic political economy. This should mean that, in the same way that Japan penetrated the region and the globe in especially the last two decades, the region and the globe will further penetrate Japan in the first two decades of the next. The continuing flow of imports and investments into Japan, and the accompanying flow of people, will bring about a profound change in the nature of Japanese society. In this can be seen another important consequence of the globalization and regionalization of the Japanese political economy.

ACKNOWLEDGEMENT

I would like to thank Meiji University for support of this research.

NOTES

1 The 'bubble economy' is a metaphor used to refer to the hyperinflation of Japanese assets (e.g. stocks and shares, land and property) starting in the mid-1980s and the collapse of asset prices in the 1990s. Prices expanded in the

mid-1980s, as in a bubble forming, and collapsed in the 1990s, as in a bubble being pricked.

2 The Plaza Accord is the name given to the 1985 agreement made at the Plaza Hotel, New York by the Group of Five Countries (G5: USA, Great Britain, France, West Germany, Japan) with a key aim being to co-ordinate macroeconomic policies and realign exchange rates. As a result of this agreement the value of the Japanese yen rose sharply in value against the dollar.

3 'East Asia' is used here to refer to the Association of South East Asian Nations four of Indonesia, Malaysia, the Philippines, and Thailand; the Asian Newly Industrializing Economies of Hong Kong, Singapore, South Korea, Taiwan; and China.

4 The USA and Japan made an agreement in 1986, renewed 1991–6, which sought to increase the US share of the Japanese semiconductor market. The USA has now captured more than 20 per cent of the market. For details on the friction between the Japanese and US semiconductor industries, see Tsuchiya (1995).

5 Under the Structural Impediments Initiative (SII) the US government called on Japan to address structural problems, such as over-saving and the lack of investment opportunity; differences between domestic and foreign prices; distribution; high cost of land; *keiretsu* and other restrictive trading practices; and the financial *keiretsu*.

6 On the treaty's role in US–Japan relations, see Hook (1996b: ch. 3).

7 This weakness in comparison with the USA is recognized by the Commission. See, for instance, Commission of the European Communities (1995).

8 In the JETRO figures 'Asia' includes the following countries and territories: Indonesia, Hong Kong, Singapore, Thailand, Malaysia, South Korea, China, Taiwan, the Philippines, India, Vietnam, Pakistan, Bangladesh, Sri Lanka, Brunei, and others.

9 On 'hollowing out', see Harrison and Bluestone (1988).

REFERENCES

Bernard, M. and Ravenhill, J. (1995) 'Beyond product cycles and flying geese. Regionalization, hierarchy, and the industrialization of East Asia', *World Politics*, 47: 171–209.

Commission of the European Communities (1995) 'Europe and Japan: the next steps', *Com* (95) 73, Final.

Ekonomisuto (1994) 5 July.

Financial Times (1996) 11 June.

Fukushima, E. (1994) *NAFTA to Nihon e no Eikyō* (NAFTA and its influence on Japan), Tokyo: JETRO.

Furuta, A. (1995) 'Dai ni ji endaka shokku to Nihon kigyō no gurobalizēshon' (Shock of the second yen rise and the globalization of Japanese companies), *Chūkyō Keizai Kenkyū*, 4, 2: 43–66.

Gamble, A. and Payne, A. (eds) (1996) *Regionalism and World Order*, London: Macmillan.

Garnaut, R. and Drysdale, P. (1994) 'Asia Pacific regionalism: the issues', in R. Garnaut and P. Drysdale (eds) *Asia Pacific Regionalism. Readings in International Political Economy*, London: HarperCollins, 1–7.

Harrison, B. and Bluestone, B. (1988) *The Great U-turn in Corporate Restructuring and the Polarizing of America*, New York: Basic Books.

Hashimoto, T. (1995) 'Nihon kigyō no Ōbei genchi seisan ni kansuru ichi kōsatsu' (A view of the present conditions of Japanese transplants in the USA and Europe), *Keizai Gaku*, 57, 4: 47–57.

Hook, G. (1996) 'Japan and the construction of Asia Pacific', in A. Gamble and A. Payne (eds) *Regionalism and World Order*, London: Macmillan,169–206.

Hook, G. (1996a) 'Japan and contested regionalism', in I. Cook, M. Doel, and R. Li (eds) *Fragmented Asia: Regional Integration and National Disintegration in Pacific Asia*, Aldershot: Avebury, 12–28.

Hook, G. (1996b) *Militarization and Demilitarization in Contemporary Japan*, London: Routledge.

Hosoya, C. (1989) *Nichibeiō no Keizai Masatsu o Meguru Seiji Katei* (The political process relating to economic conflict between Japan, the United States and Europe), Tokyo: Sōgō Kenkyū Kaihatsu Kikō.

Imidasu 97, Tokyo: Shūeisha.

Ishī, S. (1992) *Nihon Kigyō no Kaigai Jigyō Tenkai: Gurobaru Locarizeshon no Jittai* (The development of Japanese enterprises' overseas business: the state of global localization), Tokyo: Chūō Keizaisha.

Iwaki, A. (1993) 'Kokusai keizai blokkuka to takokuseki kigyō' (The creation of an international bloc economy and multinational corporations), *Oberlin Ekonomikkusu*, 23: 15–36.

JETRO (1994) *Zaiō Nikkei Seizōgyō Keiei no Jittai* (1994 *ban*) (Management conditions amongst Japanese manufacturers in Europe), Tokyo: Nihon Bōeki Shinkōkai.

JETRO (1996) *JETRO Hakusho* (JETRO White Paper), Tokyo: Nihon Bōeki Shinkōkai.

JETRO (1997) *JETRO Hakusho* (JETRO White Paper), Tokyo: Nihon Bōeki Shinkōkai.

Keizai Dōyūkai (1991) *Heisei Ni nen Ban. Kigyō Hakusho* (1990 Business White Paper), Tokyo: Keizai Dōyūkai.

Kusano, A. (1996) 'Nichibei keizai masatsu: renzokusei to tayōsei' (US–Japan economic friction: continuity and diversity), *Kokusai Mondai*, 431: 72–86.

MITI (Ministry of International Trade and Industry) (ed.) (1996) *Tsūshō Hakusho* (MITI White Paper),Tokyo: Ōkurashō Insatsukyoku.

Nihon Keizai Shinbun Hen (1995) *Dokumento Nichibei Jidōsha Kyōgi. 'Shōri naki Tatakai' no Jisshō* (Documentary of the US–Japan automobile negotiations. Evidence of a fight without victory), Tokyo: Nihon Keizai Shinbunsha.

Ōno, K. and Okamoto, Y. (1995), *EC, NAFTA, Higashi Ajia to Gaikoku Chokusetsu Tōshi. Hatten Tojōkoku e no Eikyō* (The EC, NAFTA, East Asia and foreign direct investments and the influence on developing countries), Tokyo: Ajia Keizai Kenkyūjo.

Rōdō Undō. Rinji Zōkan (1995) December.

Tōyō Keizai Tōkei Geppō (1996) May.

Tsuchiya M. (1995) 'Nichibei handōtai masatsu no bunseki' (An analysis of the friction between the Japanese and American semiconductor industries), *Hōgaku Seijigaku Ronkyū*, 25: 343–73.

Yamada, M. (1995) 'Jidosha buhin meka no 21 seiki e no tenbō' (Prospects towards the 21st century for auto-component makers), *Chūshō Kigyō Kihō*, 3: 10–20.

2 Japanese global strategies in Europe and the formation of regional markets

Hasegawa Harukiyo

This chapter seeks to examine, mainly through an analysis of Japan External Trade Organization (JETRO) surveys, localization of Japanese foreign direct investment (FDI) in Europe as part of the growing globalization of trade and industry, taking account of the dynamic linkage between 'localization' and 'globalization'. It is in the context of this dynamic that 'regional markets' occur.[1]

The first part of this chapter thus takes a broad look at recent Japanese investment in Europe, concentrating on trends in manufacturing industries, with the second section going on to assess the range and depth of localization. Localization is a manifestation of globalization impinging on the local level. So we are lead to ask how, given the continuing trends in global business activity, new regional markets come into being.

The globalization of Japanese enterprises is, on the one hand, the product of a relative surplus of corporate capital resulting from the end of high economic growth and the appreciation of the yen. In this situation, the natural business logic for Japanese companies is to invest overseas and become multinational, thus showing pro-active globalization.[2] At the same time, this is also induced by the logic of the receiving side as typical in the case of the UK, which is manifest as reactive globalization.[3] Such dynamics of globalization necessitate localization and in turn create regional markets wherein the integration of major trade and investments occur.[4]

JAPANESE GLOBALIZATION IN EUROPE[5]

This section examines a number of recent trends in Japanese investment in Europe in order to clarify the salient features of globalization processes. The first area to be considered is the motivation for and nature of investment by country and industry. The formation of a large capital surplus in Japan occurred after the high domestic growth period ended in the mid-1970s. This has provided the principal stimulus for Japan's overseas advance as capital requires an outlet, and the degree of stimulus depends on the relationship of existing capital to economic growth in any given national economy. Should domestic growth slacken, a surplus capital arises which will seek an outlet for recycling its accumulation elsewhere. This in turn affects corporate strategies, not only in seeking new ground for growth and profitability, but also to cope with the extra competition through mergers and acquisitions, and diversification of business activities.

In Japan such a change in the corporate environment emerged following the so-called 'oil shocks' of the early 1970s, which signalled a shift from high to low growth in the Japanese economy; worldwide recession in 1985–6 simultaneously set limits on Japanese exports, resulting in an increased relative surplus of capital. Nevertheless, the existence of surplus capital is not in itself sufficient to promote overseas capital investment. More immediate causes for this move, such as aggravated trade friction with the USA, appreciation of the yen and relative 'strength' of production systems in Japan (Hasegawa 1996: 6–14)[6] can be identified.

The resolution of trade conflicts was first attempted by *jishu kisei* (voluntary export restraints, VERs) and then externally by the application of the protective clause known as Super 301 by the US government.[7] This forced Japanese corporations to consider 'export-substitute' investments. Yen appreciation as a result of the G5 Plaza Accord in 1985 created serious difficulties for Japan in terms of exports, but facilitated rapid overseas direct investment. The relative strength of Japanese production systems moreover could maintain confidence in cost and quality even in overseas operations as seen in the automobile and electro-electrical manufacturing industries (Sakamoto 1992). These major factors, together with more specific local ones which will be explained later, induced Japanese corporations to shift investment abroad.[8] Figure 2.1 shows the increasing trend of Japanese foreign investment in the world and in Europe, although in relative importance its position in Europe is still much smaller than that of the USA and intra-European investments (Sachwald 1995).[9]

Japanese FDI began to increase in the 1970s, escalating greatly in the 1980s.[10] As Figure 2.1 shows, the growth was particularly high in the latter half of the 1980s, largely due to worsening trade friction and the yen's appreciation after 1985. The FDI in Europe also increased dramatically in the latter half of the 1980s, peaking in 1989.[11] The decrease since 1990 to 1992 can be explained by the recession in both Japan and the rest of the world, the completion of major investment projects and a shortage of human resources for overseas operations (Tejima 1993). But this has changed to an increase again from 1993 and reached a level of 52.7 billion US dollars in 1995, while that of Europe was 8.8 billion US dollars. In East Asia, however, the relative importance of manufacturing investments has increased dramatically in the 1990s shifting the trend of investment towards East Asia and in particular to China, as discussed in Chapter 1. The direct investment in China ranks second largest (8.7 per cent) next to

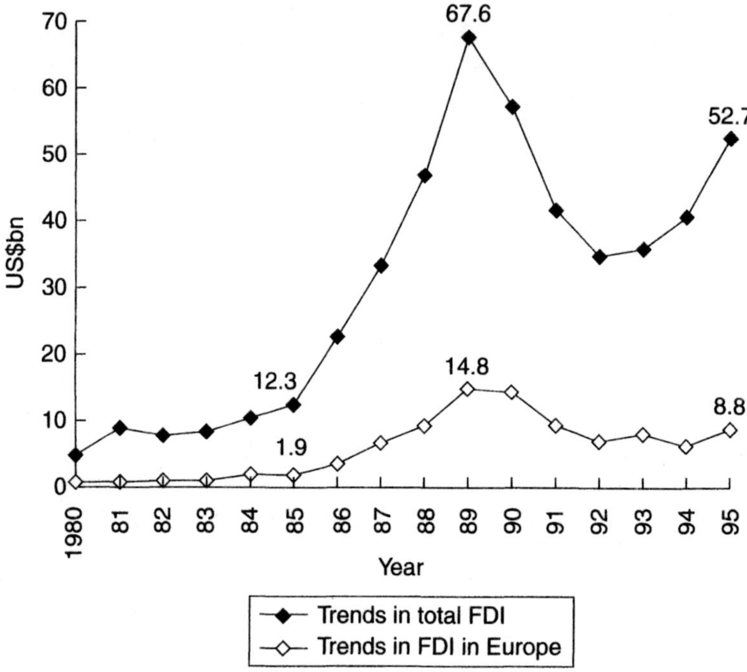

Figure 2.1 Recent trends of Japanese FDI in total and in Europe (US$ billion)
Source: Ōkurashō 1996

the US (44.1 per cent) in 1995, then followed by the UK (7.7 per cent) and Australia (5.2 per cent) (Ōkurashō 1996).

This chapter mainly addresses investment in manufacturing industries, as this is more directly relevant to issues of localization such as employment, management and regional markets (Aoyama 1988). However, the volume of investment in manufacturing has been relatively small. In the 1970s non-manufacturing investment accounted for 62 per cent, of which commerce took up 65.5 per cent. In the 1980s this rose slightly to 64.1 per cent, 41.6 per cent of which was commerce.[12] In the early 1990s (1991–2) it increased again, to 70.9 per cent (Tsūsanshō 1993: 210). Thus the relative importance of manufacturing remained at only around 30–40 per cent of all Japanese FDI through the 1980s and into the 1990s (Sachwald 1995).[13]

The primary investment motivation differs between regions. Trade friction, yen appreciation and de-industrialization were the activating factors for US investment, while low labour costs and the potential as an offshore production platform for exports to the rest of the world attracted Japanese money to Asia. Interest in Europe was as much if not more to ensure a foothold there after unification as to play a role in necessary regeneration. The UK emerged as the most suitable target zone for Japanese FDI by reason of the regeneration factor, which, to counteract de-industrialization, required capital investment suitable for attracting advanced production technology.[14] In addition, the UK has offered Japanese corporations far more favourable conditions than other nations, such as France and Germany. Some of the major political, economic and social factors favouring Japanese investment in the UK are as follows:

- UK government policies;[15]
- infrastructure, i.e. financial institutions, telecommunications, transport and supporting industries;
- productive labour force at relatively low cost;
- relatively low corporate tax;[16]
- enthusiasm of local governments to attract Japanese investment, especially incentives such as government subsidies for investment in depressed areas with high unemployment and traditional work culture;
- English language (the world business language, the chief foreign language taught in Japan).

The effect of Japanese current investment upon British industry and economy can be seen in general as 'positive' at least until now, in particular in terms of its contribution to trade and in the creation of employment.[17] At a more micro-corporate level this investment stimulates innovation and ameliorates conflictual industrial relations, making them more 'harmonious' – a topical issue among those who study the Japanese influence upon Britain. For Japanese companies as a whole Britain is seen as and functions as a production platform within 'Fortress Europe'.

Just how much the UK is preferred by Japanese corporations is illustrated in Figure 2.2, which shows cumulative investment in Europe by country. Holland's strength as a centre for commerce, distribution, finance and banking in Europe is clear, too. Germany and France are about the same in the volume of investment as well as the spread of investment among industrial sectors.

In Figure 2.3 we see the rapid increase in the number of Japanese manufacturing companies operating in Europe since 1985. It conforms with the general trend of Japanese investment in Europe overall shown in Figure 2.1. The difference is that the number of companies is still increasing, while the total amount of investment, including the non-manufacturing sector, peaked in 1989. Thus a slightly different phenomenon can be identified if non-manufacturing and manufacturing sectors are examined in detail. The line in Figure 2.3 indicates the number of UK-based Japanese companies. The UK's increasing importance for Japan in Europe, as well as the success of the British government in securing Japanese investment, is shown by the large increase in the UK's share over the period 1985–95. The number of new companies in 1995 was thirty six, exceeding that of previous years for the first time in six years. Britain

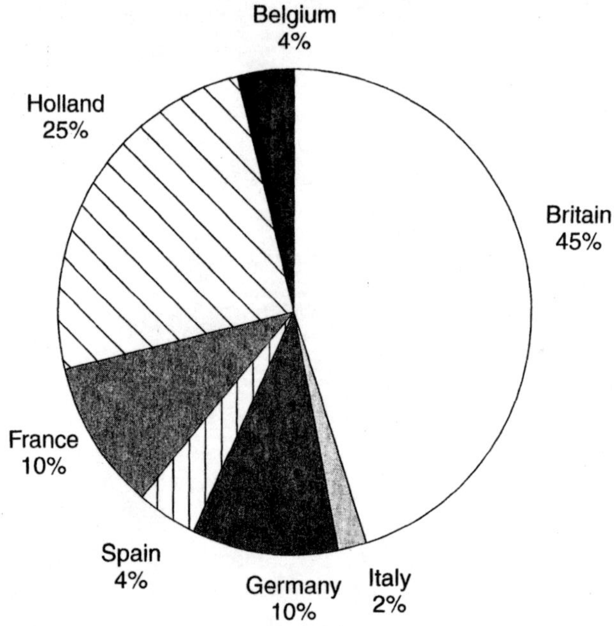

Figure 2.2 Japan's foreign direct investment in major European countries (cumulative total from 1951–95)
Source: JETRO 1997
Note: The total investment was US$83,263 million as of 31 March 1995.

has increased its importance still as the most suitable investment country with eleven new companies followed by France and Holland with six and five new companies respectively (JETRO 1996).

In contrast to the investment ratios shown in Figure 2.2, Figure 2.4 shows a relatively greater volume of Japanese activity in France and Germany, when manufacturing companies are considered, although the UK is still the favourite location.

Japanese investment in Europe by industry is rational, reflecting the industrial conditions of each country. The three major industries in the UK where Japanese investment is concentrated are respectively electronics and electric machinery, chemical products, and electronic components. General machinery has the greatest proportion in Germany, followed by electronics and electric machinery and electronic parts, while France is host to electronics and electric machinery, chemical products, and foodstuffs. Spain is involved with transport equipment, chemical products, and transport equipment parts, whereas in Italy it is clothing and textile products, chemical products and general machinery.

There are thus slight differences from country to country in terms of the industries where Japanese investment occurs. Three main investment areas can be identified. One is where Japanese companies have relative strength

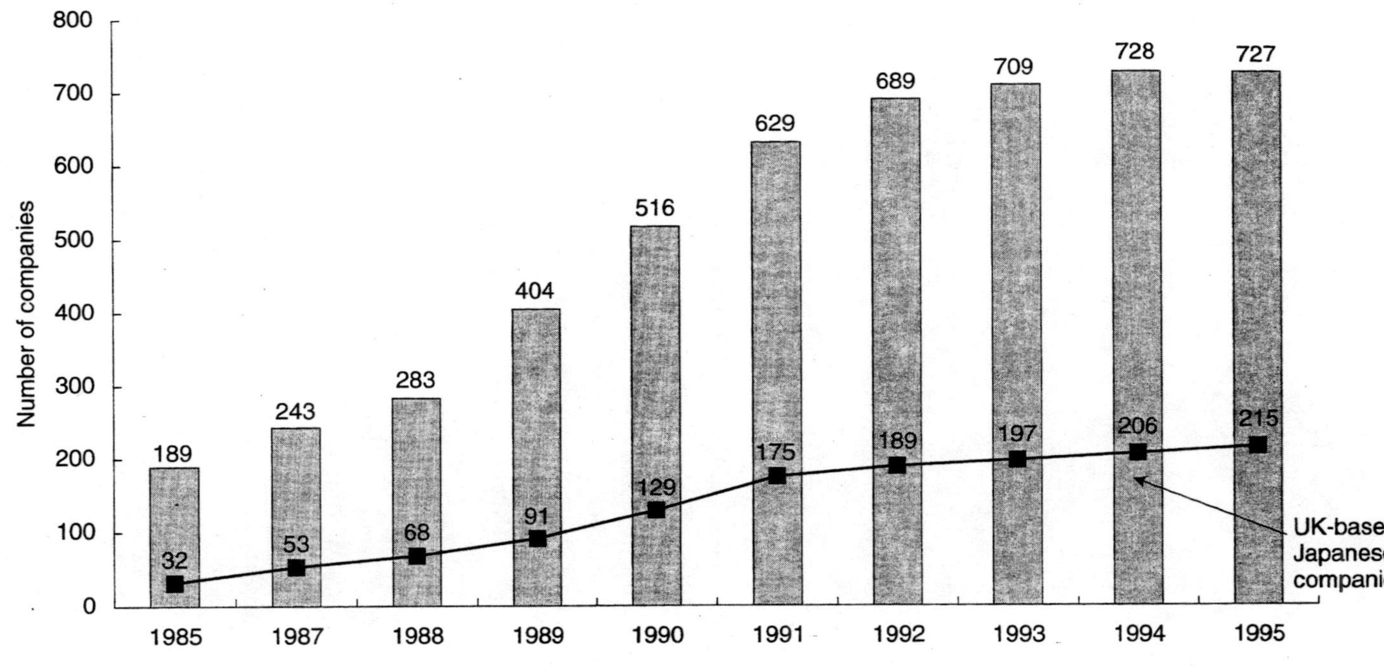

Figure 2.3 Number of Japanese manufacturing companies in Continental Europe and the UK (1985–95)
Source: JETRO (1996)
Note: a. The number of companies is the number at the end of December each year.
b. The line represents companies based in the UK.

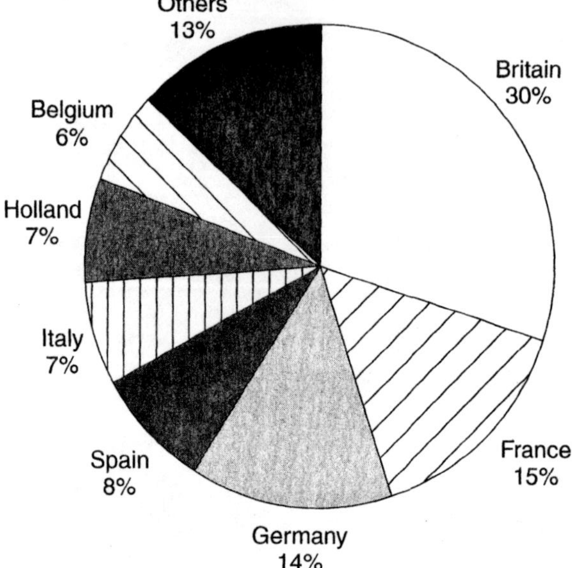

Figure 2.4 Japanese manufacturing companies in major European countries (as of December 1995)
Source: JETRO 1996
Note: The total number of companies operating in Europe in December 1995 is 727 in 18 countries.

(electronics and electric machinery); the second is where they can operate to mutual benefit with local enterprises (general machinery); and the third is where Japanese companies have relative weakness or can expect a particular benefit (chemical products, foodstuffs, clothing and textile products).

Table 2.1 shows the difference in profitability by world region. The most profitable region is in the home economy, followed by Asia. Europe is third and the USA is the lowest in profitability. If the prime business objective of Japanese companies is short-term profit, then the best corporate strategy would seem to be to stay in Japan and export from there. The second choice is to invest in Asia, exporting to other parts of the world from there.

Table 2.1 Profitability in different regions, 1985–90

	Ration of ordinary profit to net sales
USA	−0.03
Europe	2.1
Asia	3.7
Parent company in Japan	4.8

Source: Tsūsanshō 1993: 214

However, corporate strategy takes into account various factors when going global. Overall, a long-term perspective demands that companies spread investment over different regions, seeking overall synergetic effects to optimize total corporate performance. The investment in regions with lower profitability, such as Europe and North America, however, increases the challenge to maximize market share, thus intensifying competition in those regions.

The differing profitabilities, however, may influence corporate strategies in planning for future investment. If profitability in the USA remains generally negative, then large investment there is unlikely until its market expands through greater economic growth. The current percentage share of Japanese passenger cars (including both those exported and those made in the USA) in the total US automobile market is close to 30 per cent, and it is commonly felt that this is the maximum level that Japan can expect (Tejima 1993). The situation in Europe is also not so bright due to the continuing recession and the relatively strong resistance of car manufacturing companies in France and Italy. Such conditions will discourage future investment by Japanese car manufacturers unless the economy improves.[18] If further investment in Europe occurs it may well be in peripheral zones such as Eastern and Southern Europe. The profitability in Asia is attractive not only in terms of profitability per se, but also because the lack of any pre-existing local auto-industry has ensured freedom from constraint or conflict. Asia has thus become and will continue to develop as a production base for markets in Japan and the rest of Asia.

The economic recession of the 1990s is reflected in the reduction of investment and rationalization in business operations. Although progress in EU integration provided an expansion of business opportunities, a JETRO survey showed that 82 per cent of the companies approached had suffered from recent recessions; in response, 38.7 per cent had carried out redundancy measures, 36.6 per cent had reduced production, and 31.8 per cent had held back on investment. Of companies 51.2 per cent recorded a deficit in 1992 (JETRO 1994a).

Japanese companies have generally positive expectations of the ongoing integration of the European market. A JETRO questionnaire in 1994 (JETRO 1994a) showed the most common anticipated outcomes to be further simplication of customs procedure (62.6 per cent), expansion of the market (52.4 per cent), reduction of distribution costs (46.2 per cent), increased competition with European companies and the consequent unfavourable conditions for Japanese companies (40.5 per cent), and increased competition among Japanese companies (26.7 per cent).

In spite of some constraining factors for expansion, as mentioned, the general trend is towards further globalization, which will promote localization in various areas of business management and operation.

LOCALIZATION AS A PROCESS OF GLOBALIZATION

Localization is a process of globalization and aims to create compatible production systems appropriate to local and regional conditions under a global corporate strategy. This phenomenon is often described by Japanese business people as 'production where demand exists' or 'act locally, think globally'.[19]

There are two kinds of localization, internal and external. Internal localization is relevant to managerial function in enterprise, and implies delegation of managerial function to local people by translating Japanese managerial concepts into local practices, regulations, customs and values. External localization, on the other hand, involves relations elsewhere in areas such as parts supply, R&D and community activities. External localization is more visible and sometimes creates friction and tension with existing local companies and communities. Two particular incentives for localization exist, one being practical necessity arising from within the enterprise and the other the demands of local people and local enterprises. Here let us examine three important areas in which localization develops and the implications of this process for globalization.

Localization in management

At its simplest, localization in management means the delegation of managerial functions to local employees. This is a process in which the management concepts of Japanese companies permeate local staff, while at the same time creating hybrid management through the compromise of both Japanese and local managers as well as workers. Usually, it conforms neither to a typical Japanese nor to a typical local style of management.

Quantitatively the degree of localization in management can be estimated by reference to the number of employees in charge of managerial functions. Levels below top management show an increasing degree of localization. Managerial functions can be classified into:

- top management;
- employment management;
- production management;
- marketing;
- administrative management.

The degree of localization varies widely (Figure 2.5) as follows:

- employment management (85.3 per cent);
- production management (80.2 per cent);
- marketing management (57.4 per cent);
- administrative management (57.2 per cent);
- top management (6.6 per cent).

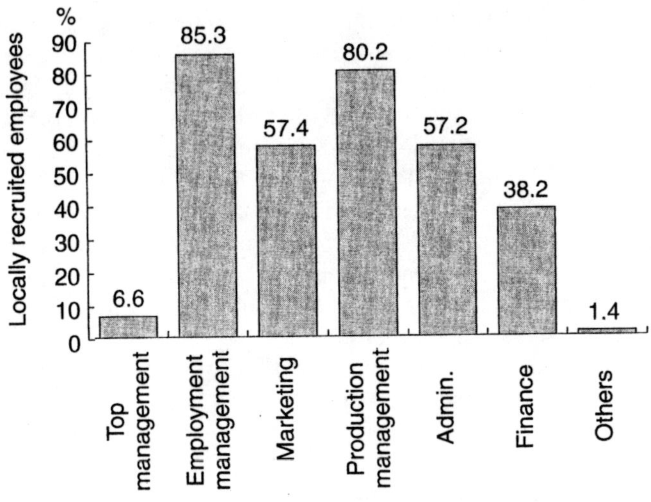

Figure 2.5 Localization of management by managerial function
Source: JETRO (1994a): 76.

In terms of the transfer of authority from the head office in Japan, the above ranking implies that the management functions directly relevant to local employees and production are those delegated to local management at a significant level. Although in administration and marketing the head office in Japan and local management share functions almost equally, the top management function is mostly controlled by the head office in Japan.

The functions of production and employment management are left to the locals, as they are more suitable both in terms of labour cost and culture and existing practices. Delegation of these areas to local staff alleviates friction and conflict in social relations, as a slight and subtle difference in culture may develop into a cause of serious misunderstanding, and for local employees to take over in this area seems a more rational means of management for any multinational operation.

What about the function of top management? A questionnaire to 354 companies (JETRO 1994a) raised the following points as factors preventing localization at this level:

- communication problems (54.0 per cent);
- difficulty in obtaining good top management personnel (50.0 per cent);
- no necessity due to small size (35.9 per cent).

The difficulties of communication involve elements of both language and culture. People in top management in Japan are usually men of 60 or older who are unable to speak English and who hold to traditional Japanese cultural values. British people recruited by Japanese companies for top management jobs are not usually able to communicate in Japanese. Thus from both sides barriers grow, creating problems in discussing important issues affecting local operations and overall corporate strategies. This indicates that communication problems and the difficulty of obtaining good top managers are two major problems hindering localization in this ultimate managerial function. Further globalization of Japanese companies may see more localization in this area and the ideal employee would be someone, either Japanese or local, who can communicate with both top management in Japan and local people. According to the same report, localization in management in general is more advanced in joint venture companies and also in larger enterprises.

Another questionnaire asked 409 companies for their future expectations and received these responses (JETRO 1994a):

- more localization including the chief executive and chairman (46.2 per cent);
- Japanese chief executive and chairman but others of local extraction (44.3 per cent);
- equal levels of both Japanese and local personnel (6.4 per cent);
- Japanese alone (4.2 per cent).

Localization in management also differs according to region. Southern European countries such as Spain, Italy and Portugal have less, registering 27.3 per cent in contrast to the average rate of over 50 per cent in central and North European countries.

One factor for localization in management is practical and short term; it helps reduce labour costs. Japanese employees in Europe, if they are paid in yen, are now relatively expensive due to currency appreciation.[20] The strategy has been to reduce the number of employees as well as to replace the older more expensive employees with younger ones. The other factor encouraging localization is the demand of local management and employees to hand over managerial functions to local recruits. Aside from any normative judgement, such practical considerations come first and localization will inevitably proceed further. This process of localization resolves friction and conflicts arising from cultural and communication gaps. Friction due to cultural difference is more often found between Japanese management and local managers. It is not so obvious between the former and local workers, simply because there is much less cause for conflict at the workplace – production workers do not encounter different cultural predispositions directly in decision-making matters. Further localization in managerial functions, which implies a replacement of Japanese by local management, and in consequence the management of local employees by local managers, may invite a return to traditional British patterns of conflict between managerial and non-managerial employees and management and production workers unless a new framework of industrial relations is created.

Table 2.2 shows the greater spread and depth of localization in managerial function. We can sum up the process in terms of a spectrum of managerial functions, ranging from issues of ownership and control to concerns of the local and regional market and people; in between lies administration. Ownership and control includes the function of top management and finance while local market and people includes employment, marketing and production. The areas of administration seem to reflect the areas where the two cultures meet and reach a degree of compromise.

The difference in the level of localization in administrative function reflects the degree to which a local company or plant is seen as an integral part of a global company and local affairs are considered to be best handled by local staff. On the other hand, the top management functions relevant to ownership and control of the multinational operation will be held by either Japanese or international staff who may be of any nationality as long as they are top management material for a multinational enterprise.

Localization of production

Progress in the localization of production is important to globalization and concerns the amount of production being carried out using materials and parts produced in the country where the investment is made. Its level is reflected in the ratio of locally supplied materials and parts contained in the unit product as expressed by value (price). Conversely this localization is relevant to the local content issue of the European Community Rules of

Table 2.2 Management areas and the degree of localization

Category of management	*Managerial functions*
Top management	Change of capital 0.7% Appropriation of earned capital 8.2% Appointment and dismissal of directors 7.0%
Employment management	Determination of wages 86.1% Employment of administrative staff 74.3% Employment of workers 94.5%
Marketing	Marketing of new products 44.1% Change of buyers 63.0%
Production management	Production/marketing plan 86.4% Procurement of materials 88.0% Change of manufacturing process 70.0%
Administration	Modification of managerial organization 57.7% Decision on publicity strategy 55.5%
Finance	Plant investment 32.0% Borrowing of capital fund 29.1% Borrowing of working capital 53.9%

Source: JETRO 1995b: 84

Origin, which stipulate a 45 per cent added value origin as a guideline for certain representative products such as radios, tape recorders and televisions (JETRO 1994b: 467–85). Not every European country has legislative regulations for the degree of local content but it becomes a trade issue when the products are exported to other EU countries. For this reason, efforts are made by Japanese companies to increase the localization of parts and materials so that they can have greater freedom to sell products anywhere in Europe.

The progress of localization in production, however, differs according to country, industry and type of investment. For some companies, localization of production occurs more naturally, while for others it results from a combination of various factors. On the whole there seems to be an increasing trend towards localization in production. The JETRO survey in 1995 found that a prime incentive is the effective decline of local prices due to the relative increase in the costs of parts and materials from outside the EU, a situation caused by the higher yen and the instability of European currencies since the autumn of 1992. Another incentive is the improvement in quality of local parts and materials, followed by an increased procurement from those Japanese parts and material suppliers that have ventured into Europe.

In contrast to the first incentive, which might change due to macroeconomic conditions, the second concerns a qualitative aspect of localization as part of globalization. In response to the same JETRO questionnaire as to the method of developing relations with local parts suppliers, 91.5 per cent of companies (108 out of 118) stated that 'technical' assistance was most positively employed,[21] with other methods, such as 'personnel' assistance, standing at 11.0 per cent and 'financial' assistance at 10.2 per cent. Technical assistance can create a long-term relationship between the Japanese and local companies. How this relationship develops in future in comparison with the subcontracting relations in Japan will be a matter of interest, but in consideration of other corporate factors, in particular that of the progress in localizing management, the Japanese style of tight relational subcontracting might not develop in Europe, where relations among enterprises rest largely upon market principles. Technical assistance, therefore, seems for the time being to be the limit of relations in subcontracting.

In addition to the above two incentives, localization has developed due to the increase in transplants of Japanese parts suppliers, which must be considered part of globalization rather than localization. The Japanese parts suppliers that have set up their plants in EU countries compete with local parts and material suppliers. In fact, it is harder for them than for large companies such as car manufacturers to be successful, as they face double pressures in price and quality, one from the parent Japanese companies and the other from competing local companies. A JETRO survey (1994a: 29) concerning the profitability of Japanese parts suppliers in Europe in 1992 showed that more than half of those in electronics and car industries ran deficits, while 84.6 per cent of parent companies in the automobile industry reported a profit.

The extent of localization is now quite high. On average 52.1 per cent of all companies surveyed (214 out of 411) claimed localization exceeded 70 per cent. The highest rates are in chemicals/pharmaceuticals (66.7 per cent), raw material acquisition type industries such as pulp/paper, iron and steel, foods, ceramics, stone and clay, and metal products (65.1 per cent), while the assembly and parts supply industries are relatively low at 42.9 per cent on average. But in the last group, the transport equipment industry rates highly at 66.7 per cent for automobiles and 72.7 per cent for transport equipment parts manufacturers (JETRO 1994a: 66).

The degree of localization in production also differs from country to country. The number of companies reporting localization of 70 per cent or over was highest in Italy (78.9 per cent) followed by Holland (58.6 per cent), the UK (56.5 per cent), Belgium (52.0 per cent), Spain (51.3 per cent), France (45.3 per cent) and Germany (44.3 per cent) (JETRO 1994a: 69). The amount of localization in production thus differs depending upon industry and country, but in general it is on the rise and its level is already quite high. This is due to the fact that localization brings economic benefits to multinational companies, but at the same time stimulates the local economy despite remaining within the framework of the corporate strategy of globalization.

Localization of R&D

Another stage of localization occurs when research and development (R&D) activities are set up in the area of local production. This is a relatively advanced stage, as it represents a degree of local autonomy, local management aiming at local and regional markets, and also because such activities will only be initiated when production and other business activities have become successful in both scale of production and profitability. At this point it becomes apparent that local R&D is both more appropriate and more economical than Japan-based R&D.

The amount of R&D transferred to overseas plants has jumped since 1985. According to the 1996 JETRO survey the total number of companies with local design/R&D centres stands at 236 in 1995, not including 71 companies with independent R&D centres. This is equivalent to 42.2 per cent of all the Japanese manufacturing companies in Europe. The number of employees per R&D centre is 38.1 for a plant attached R&D centre and 50.0 for an independent R&D centre. The number of Japanese staff in these centres is 2.5 for the former and 7.6 for the latter. Thus a high localization rate of 93.5 per cent and 84.8 per cent respectively can be identified.[22]

By industrial sector, numbers break down to 74 in electro-electrical, 45 in general machinery, 37 in chemicals, 24 in electro-parts, 25 in auto-parts, 21 in pharmaceutical, 16 in automobile and 16 in precision machinery industries. Thus we can see that design and research/development activities have become an accepted requirement in the process of localization in production in order to meet local and regional demands. It can bring benefits in cost as well as in the recruitment of research staff. It can be taken as a step forward towards organic development of globalization. A more advanced form of this concept is manifest in a series of globalized concepts of R&D operations adopted by major automobile companies like Nissan and Toyota, in which they will aim to establish four R&D centre systems in order to respond to globalization.

The survey by JETRO on the content of R&D activities shows that the objective of attached R&D centres is concerned primarily with product development, product design and change in specifications (Table 2.3). This reflects corporate recognition that people in different countries and regions will prefer goods developed to suit their culture; or at least that some modifications are necessary if the products are to be accepted. In other words, local staff know the nature of demand and the products should be adjusted to local taste.[23] The second highest area is production technology, which concerns manufacturing processes and this suggests that similar changes and new manufacturing processes may become necessary if product development is attended to locally and also if local industrial relations are taken into consideration in work organization and work practices. On the other hand, the importance of basic research is relatively small in R&D centres attached to production plants, which suggests that it is carried out mainly in Japan.

Response to a questionnaire circulated to 260 companies shows that the most commonly given reasons for localization in R&D were: R&D and design 'to meet local needs', 'to be well versed with the local trends' and 'to reduce lead time for products'. The corporate strategy reflected in this survey implies that they have in general no need or capacity to perform full-scale R&D at local level as they are short of capital and human resources. In the process of globalization, a division of labour is carried

Table 2.3 R&D activities and their emphasis, 1995

	Attached R&D centre (221 companies) (%)	*Independent R&D centre (71 companies) (%)*
Basic research	7.0	39.4
Product development	67.6	72.7
Product design, change in specifications	76.8	30.3
Development in production technology	34.5	15.2
Others	7.0	12.1

Source: JETRO 1996: 93

out between overseas R&D centres and those in Japan as well as among themselves, but how they will be done will differ from industry to industry and from company to company. Automobile companies seem to evince the most globalized form of R&D operations in order to deal with their four regional markets, Japan, the USA, Europe and Asia.

In independent R&D centres the basic research rate is quite high, implying that in such centres, independent of the immediate needs of local production, research activities are carried out by scientists and engineers to meet more universal objectives which can be used for broader regional requirements. A typical case of such a centre is Eisai London Research Laboratory, a subsidiary of a Japanese pharmaceutical company, established in 1992 in collaboration with University College of the University of London. It has a total number of 37 staff, including five Japanese. This R&D centre is internationalized with ten different nationalities and regarded as one of the three core R&D centres of this company in the world.

The analysis based upon the JETRO survey (1996) shows that R&D activities of Japanese companies by establishing their subsidiary R&D centres in Europe increased in number from the end of 1994 to the end of 1995 by 15, reaching a total of 307. In terms of ownership of these centres in 1994, 75 per cent of them are solely owned by Japanese parent companies, thus localization in ownership of these R&D centres is not much advanced. In terms of location of these centres, the UK occupies a dominant position by having 34.3 per cent of all centres, followed by Germany (21.4 per cent), and France (13.2 per cent). Thus the UK again plays an important role as a host to the R&D activities of Japanese companies but the percentage of the joint ownership with the UK local companies is much less at 12.6 per cent in 1994, compared with Germany and France with 36.7 and 29.7 per cent respectively. This reflects differences in the kinds of industries and types of operations of the Japanese companies operating in the UK, Germany and France. Japan's direct investment in the UK is represented more by assembly type operations of electro-electrical industry and motor manufacturing industry, and these companies own and develop their R&D activities without relying upon local companies. Germany and France seem to offer opportunities for joint ownership in areas like machine, foods, chemicals and medicines.

GLOBALIZATION, LOCALIZATION AND FORMATION OF REGIONAL MARKETS

Localization was an inevitable process of globalization and through the dynamics between these two processes a concept of regional market is emerging and developing rapidly among Japanese multinationals. Corporate strategy locates design and R&D centres with attention to respective regions, setting a local production site within a regional market for products and parts/materials supplies.

Markets have expanded greatly at regional level over the period 1986–90, as shown in Figure 2.6, and correspondingly the proportion held by the purely local market has declined. Japanese multinationals seem to have anticipated this. The Nissan factory at Sunderland in northern England is a typical case. The plant, which began to produce cars in 1984, produced about 240,000 units in 1994, of which 75 per cent were exported, mainly to the European continent. Nissan has now established four major production sites in the world in North America, Britain, Spain and Mexico, and delivers cars from these plants to 55 sales points worldwide, but mainly in the regional markets to which these production plants belong.

The concept of regional market has thus become an important link between globalization and localization. Honda has also recently reorganized its management structure in order to translate this concept into practice. It began regional operations by dividing the world market into four, with a European headquarters responsible not only for Europe but also the Middle East and Africa (Itō 1994). It aims to develop the dynamics of globalization and localization through this regional operation. The trend of regional operation in 1990 shows that it was already quite a common strategy of Japanese multinationals as indicated by 68 regional headquarters around the world, of which 30 were in the USA, 20 in Europe and 18 in Asia. Regional headquarters in Europe have increased to 58 in 1995, of which 23 were in the UK, 12 in Germany, 11 in Holland, and 4 in Belgium (JETRO 1996).

Regional parts procurement has also developed, and its continuing

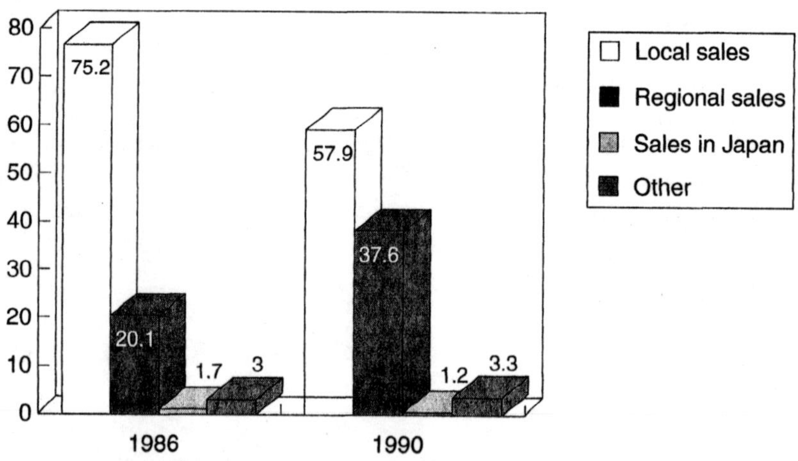

Figure 2.6 Regional markets for product sales
Source: Tsūsanshō 1993: 217

progress is shown in Figure 2.7. Although the percentage of local supplies remains about the same, regional supply has increased greatly over the period of this survey.[24] This shift is mainly due to the reduction of parts/material supplies from Japan, which has significantly affected Japanese parts/material suppliers.[25] Those suppliers, facing a dilemma over whether to remain in Japan and diversify their business or follow their patron companies and invest overseas and compete with local parts suppliers, have experienced more difficulties than the companies they were dependent upon, with small and medium-sized firms being particularly affected by the industrial restructuring of multinational economic strategy.

Large Japanese companies embarked on globalization in response to constrained corporate environments and excess capital build-up, and did so as if their survival depended on it. Their expansion has helped to develop regional economies which straddle the disparity between global and local action. So far, the regions affected are North America, NIEs/ASEAN and Europe. Although these are loosely networked, the Japanese investment in each region is mainly directed at the demand existing within it. According to a survey made by the Japanese Import and Export Bank, the intra-regional trade in each region as of 1992 is 93.8 per cent for North America, 72.9 per cent for NIEs, 63.6 per cent for ASEAN and 94.8 per cent for the EU (Tejima 1993). These figures suggest that in the regions with advanced economies the relation between investment and trade is high, while NIEs and ASEAN function as export bases for other regions. Within zones where the degree of intra-regional trade is high, like the EU, the UK, which can offer relatively better inducements for local production, has emerged as a suitable production base for the whole region. A new development identified in the JETRO report of 1996 is that the Middle and

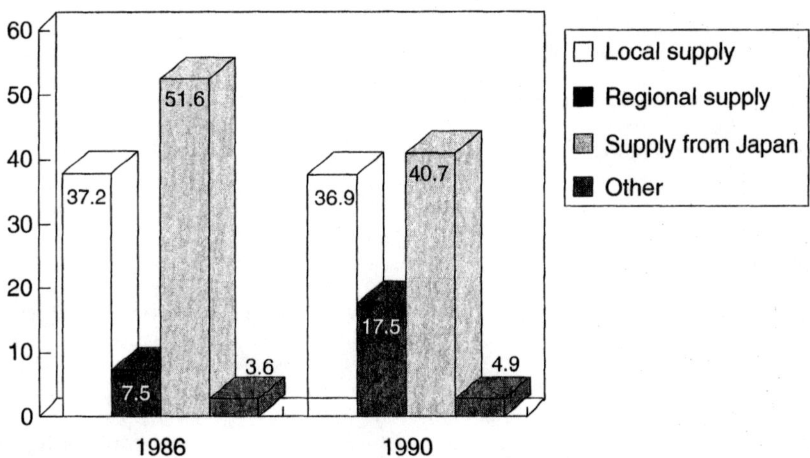

Figure 2.7 Regional markets for parts/material supplies
Source: Tsūsanshō 1993: 217

East European countries have also emerged not only as an attractive market but also as an attractive production base of Japanese multinational companies.

CONCLUSION

The major Japanese companies have transformed themselves into multinational companies in active pursuit of globalization, which itself presupposes localization. This in turn has created regional markets in which major investment and trade are being integrated. In terms of capital accumulation this is a global form of capital concentration; while in terms of management it is a simultaneous process of global centralization and decentralization of management. This whole movement, moreover, is supported by the functions of new technology and internationalized human resources.

Localization and the concept of regional markets will therefore remain important issues in the expansion of Japanese companies. At the same time, they give rise to the potential for meaningful discussion on the global integration of capital and labour by multinational companies, as well as the economic and social issues at local and regional levels consequent upon their influence. In 1995 Japanese foreign direct investment, which began to decrease after 1989, turned to an increase again with a renewed impetus of manufacturing investment in ASEAN and China. The impact of such pro-active globalization upon Japanese domestic employment and small and medium enterprises (examined in Chapter 5) will become more serious, thus creating the possibility of a trade-off in benefits between multinational companies and national domestic economy. Japan may in future have a need for re-active globalization, just as has been the case with the UK.

ACKNOWLEDGEMENT

I would like to thank the Zengin Foundation for Studies on Economics and Finance and Meiji University for support of this research.

NOTES

1 Morris (1991) uses the term 'global localization' as a concept which emerges at the next stage of globalization per se. In this chaper, we use the terms 'globalization', 'localization' and 'regional market' as existing simultaneously in the dynamics of capital accumulation carried out by multinational companies, thus suggesting a globalization of capital accumulation.

2 The opposite side of the same logic is to carry out corporate restructuring in Japan in order to cope with globalization, as discussed in Chapter 5. This restructuring has also been encouraged by imports of parts and goods manufactured in their own overseas plants. Thus, a tendency of 'hollowing out', decrease

in domestic demand, and worsening of working conditions are other consequences of pro-active globalization.

3 Pro-active globalization reflects the interest of capital which carries out overseas investment while reactive globalization reflects that of the politics which receives it. Japan, as a new agent in globalization, mainly stands in the position of pro-active globalization, while the USA and UK hold dual positions. The UK is unique in its sharp contrast, as both a proponent of pro-active and reactive globalization. The pro-active aspect can be seen in its relatively large proportion of overseas capital investment in relation to domestic investment. For example, during the 1980s and the period 1991–3, the UK's percentage of FDI compared to domestic investment was 15.1 per cent and 13.2 per cent, compared to 2.6 per cent and 1.8 per cent for Japan in the same two periods (JETRO 1995a).

4 Localization will not only remain an important aspect of Japanese global operations, but will also become tied increasingly to the socio-economic health of local economies. In other words, localization will be subordinate in the context of the global strategies decided by Japanese companies. This dimension is another important socio-economic issue, although it is not investigated in this chapter.

5 British discussion has largely concerned the 'Japanization' of British industry and the implications of Japanese production systems (White and Trevor 1983; Wickens 1987; Oliver and Wilkinson 1988; Bratton 1992; Elger and Smith 1994), while Japanese academics have discussed the issues in terms of 'universality' versus 'specificity' and the development of hybrid management systems (Sakamoto 1992; Katō and Steven 1993; Abō 1994). Some writers (Morris 1991; Strange 1993, Mason and Encarnation 1994; Sachwald 1995) have raised wider concerns over Japanese overseas investment: these include whether Japanese investment is positive in areas such as the creation of employment opportunities, transfer of technology, enhancement of export potential and stimulation of local economies, as well as considering the outflow of Japanese capital and its effects vis-à-vis deindustrialization in Japan, changes in trade and employment structures, managerial methods and industrial relations.

6 The concept of production system used by the author includes production technology, work practices and working conditions which are intergrated in the system of management (Hasegawa 1996).

7 In Europe export regulations against Japan in July 1991 imposed restrictions until the end of 1999 on car exports from Japan.

8 See Mason and Encarnation (1994: 61–8) for various theories of FDI. Although there exist various immediate and indirect factors for Japanese direct investment, an emphasis is given here to the existence of relative surplus of corporate capital due to the termination of high economic growth.

9 The dynamic operating among them is, however, the rapid increase of Japanese FDI and the gradual increase of German and French, while the large-scale decrease of American and British to the world total from 1980 to 1993.

10 Japan ranked top in the world in overseas investment for three consecutive years after 1989 (Tejima 1993).

11 The increase in the service sector such as real estate, finance and insurance directed at the USA and Europe was one of the major contributing factors for the increase of FDI.

12 Although it is difficult to indicate by percentage, some of non-manufacturing investment has relevance to manufacturing activities. For examples, such investments were for distribution, maintenance, sales and finance which will support and promote manufacturing activities (Mason and Encarnation 1994: 239).

13 In this sectoral distribution of FDI, the USA, Japan and Germany show a similar pattern with a higher percentage of services, while France and Britain show a lower percentage of services than non-service sector (Sachwald 1995: 8).
14 In Britain industrial capital is weaker than in Germany and France as is typically reflected in the investment of the Japanese automobile industry. It is only in Britain that three major investments (100 per cent sole investments by Nissan, Toyota and Honda) were made, while in other European countries they are all either joint ventures or technical affiliations (Toyota 1993: 25)
15 The strategy of the Conservative government was to use FDI as a strategy for industrial regeneration, namely to modernize the ailing manufacturing industry by a new managerial philosophy, industrial relations and technology. Michael Heseltine has said: 'It is of the first priority that we do not undermine the remarkable success we are attracting in bringing all that inward investment. They are coming here because they believe we are the best place in Europe in which to invest. We must not allow doubts to arise about that.' *The Times* (1995), 6 February.
16 The corporate tax in the UK was 33 per cent (maximum), and went down to 31 per cent in 1997, while that of France is 36 per cent (standard), Germany 45 per cent (standard), Italy 36 per cent (flat rate plus 16.2 per cent local tax), etc.
17 See Sachwald (1995: 142–3) for the effects of Japanese FDI on the size and kinds of employment.
18 The percentage share of Japanese cars sales as of 1991 in Europe was 11.6 per cent in the UK, 14.4 per cent in Germany (former West Germany), 4.1 per cent in France, 2.5 per cent in Italy and 3.2 per cent in Spain. The average in the EC is 10.5 per cent. (Tejima 1993)
19 As expressed by S. Itō, President of Honda Europe, in 1994, as part of their corporate approach.
20 In addition to the direct pay the indirect labour cost for overseas employees has become quite high due to various expenses such as travel, insurance, various family allowances and so on (interviews with UK-based Japanese companies).
21 Nissan provides a good example of such technical assistance. Lemmerz of Belgium began to supply wheels to Sunderland for the Nissan Bluebird by effectively using existing Japanese designs. In 1988 the company became more involved in supplying wheels for the new Nissan Primera. Its involvement in product design from an early stage increased ties with Nissan, resulting in them even supplying to plants in Japan (Nissan Press and Public Relations 1993).
22 The relative importance of R&D centres overseas is clearly shown in the result of the questionnaire that R&D activities should be transferred to overseas as globalization proceeds. Only 29.1 per cent of the companies think that R&D should be done solely in Japan, while the remaining 71.9 per cent recognize the importance of R&D activities in the regions they globalize (JETRO 1994a). Nissan, for example, has currently three R&D centres in the world (Japan, USA, Europe) but it plans to create one more in Asia in order to establish a fourth R&D system (Nissan Public Relations Dept 1995).
23 Nissan has three technology centres in the world (Japan, USA, UK), each dedicated to developing products for its local and regional markets; Nissan European Technology Centre Ltd aims to develop European vehicles with a concept of 'vehicles produced in Europe', 'designed by Europeans', 'for Europeans'. The same applies to Nissan Research and Development Inc for the USA.
24 For example, Nissan UK is supplied by 195 European companies, of which 130 are British.

25 This trend has accelerated during 1995 according to JETRO (1996). More than 90 per cent of the 437 Japanese companies in Europe have decreased supply of parts and materials from Japan, while 40 per cent of these companies increased their supply from Asia (JETRO 1996).

REFERENCES

Abō, T. (ed.) (1994) *Hybrid Factory*, New York: Oxford University Press.

Aoyama, S. (1988) 'Nippon kigyō no takokusekika to koyō, rōdō mondai' (Multinationalization of Japanese enterprises and employment and labour problems) in Keizaihenshubu (ed.) *Kaigai Shinshitsu no Jittai* (Reality of overseas advance), Shinnippon Shuppansha: Tokyo.

Bratton, J. (1992) *Japanization at Work*, London: Macmillan.

Elger, T. and Smith, C. (eds) (1994) *Global Japanization?*, London: Routledge.

Hasegawa, H. (1996) *The Steel Industry in Japan: A Comparison with Britain*, London: Routledge.

Itō, S. (1994) 'Gurobaraizeishon' (Globalization), *Temuzu*, London: Japanese Chamber of Commerce and Industry in the UK.

JETRO (1994a) *JETRO Zaiō Nikkei Kigyō no Keiei Jittai* (European operations of Japanese companies in the manufacturing sector), Tokyo: Nihon Bōeki Shinkōkai.

JETRO (1994b) *JETRO Hakusho* (JETRO White Paper), Tokyo: Nihon Bōeki Shinkōkai.

JETRO (1995a) *JETRO Hakusho* (JETRO White Paper), Tokyo: Nihon Bōeki Shinkōkai.

JETRO (1995b) *JETRO Zaiō Nikkei Kigyō no Keiei Jittai* (European operations of Japanese companies in the manufacturing sector), Tokyo: Nihon Bōeki Shinkōkai.

JETRO (1996) *JETRO Zaiō Nikkei Kigyō no Keiei Jittai* (European operations of Japanese companies in the manufacturing sector), Tokyo: Nihon Bōeki Shinkōkai.

JETRO (1997) *JETRO Hakusho* (JETRO White Paper), Tokyo: Nihon Bōeki Shinkōkai.

Kato, T. and Steven, R. (1993) *Is Japanese Management Post-Fordism?*, Tokyo: Madosha.

Mason, M. and Encarnation, D. (1994) *Does Ownership Matter?*, Oxford: Oxford University Press.

Morris, J. (ed.) (1991) *Japan and the Global Economy*, London: Routledge.

Nissan Press and Public Relations Office (1993) *Purchase and Supplies*, London: Nissan Motor Manufacturing (UK) Ltd.

Nissan Public Relations Dept (1995) *Gurobaru Kōzō Kaikaku Hoshin* (Plan for global structural reforms), Tokyo: Nissan Motor Co. Ltd.

Ōkurashō (1996) *Taigai Tainai Chokusetsu Toshi Todokede Jisseki* (Registration of inward and outward investment), Tokyo: Ōkurashō.

Oliver, N. and Wilkinson, B. (1988) *The Japanization of British Industry*, Oxford: Blackwell Publishers.

Sachwald, F. (ed.) (1995) *Japanese Firms in Europe*, Luxembourg: Harwood Academic Publishers.

Sakamoto, K. (1992) 'Nihonteki seisan shisutemuron no kokusaiteki tenkai' (International evolution of the thesis of Japanese-style production systems) in T. Inamura and M. Nakata (eds) *Tenkanki no Keieigaku* (Business management in transition), Tokyo: Chūō Keizaisha.

Strange, R. (1993) *Japanese Manufacturing Investment in Europe*, London: Routledge.

Tejima, S. (1993) 'Genshōkeikō ni aru wagakuni no kaigai chokusetsu tōshi' (Declining Japanese FDI) in *Tekkō Kaihō*, No. 1601.

The Times (1995) 6 February.
Toyota (1993) *Jidōsha Sangyō no Gaikyō* (Outline of the automobile industry) Tokyo: Toyota Motor Corporation.
Tsūsanshō (1993) *Tsūshō Hakusho* (White Paper on Trade), Tokyo: Tsūsanshō.
White, M. and Trevor, M. (1983) *Under Japanese Management*, London: Heinemann Educational Books.
Wickens, P. (1987) *The Road to Nissan*, London: Macmillan.

3 Japanese investment strategy and technology transfer in East Asia

Yamashita Shōichi

This chapter examines the link between Japanese foreign direct investment (FDI) and technology transfer, focusing on the changes occurring in the latter between the 1960s and the late 1980s. These changes resulted from increasing competitiveness in the newly industrializing economies as well as from the decline of Japan's international competitiveness following the yen's appreciation, especially in the manufacturing sector. The emphasis here is on the electrical machinery industry and automobile industry, where in the latter half of the 1980s Japanese corporations introduced the new production systems fully equipped with automated and robotized machines aiming to improve drastically the quality of the products. In this sense, the wave of FDI in Asia following the 1985 Plaza Accord radically altered the pattern of Japanese investment, technology transfer, and education and training in Japanese companies in East Asia. The remarkable growth of Japanese investment in China in the 1990s will also be examined within the context of the changing nature of technology transfers from Japan.

CHANGES IN INVESTMENT STRATEGY: FOCUS ON ASIA

Japanese FDI, which had been declining following a peak of US$67.5 billion in 1989, in 1994 recovered to US$41.1 billion from the trough of $34.1 billion in 1992 (Export–Import Bank of Japan 1995: 158–61). Investment increased in China, the ASEAN 4 (Thailand, Malaysia, Indonesia and the Philippines), Europe, with industries such as electronics, food, finance and insurance once again marking up major increases. A striking feature of the recent flow of Japanese FDI is the increasing focus on Asia, especially China, which is promoting policies of liberalization and reform. Low labour costs make China particularly attractive to Japanese companies. The emphasis on Asian investment is evident in the increasing focus on China and South East Asia in electronics, automobiles, and chemicals, with small and medium-sized enterprises strengthening the supply of parts and materials to local assembly plants.

Figure 3.1 shows the trends in the value of FDI by Japanese companies

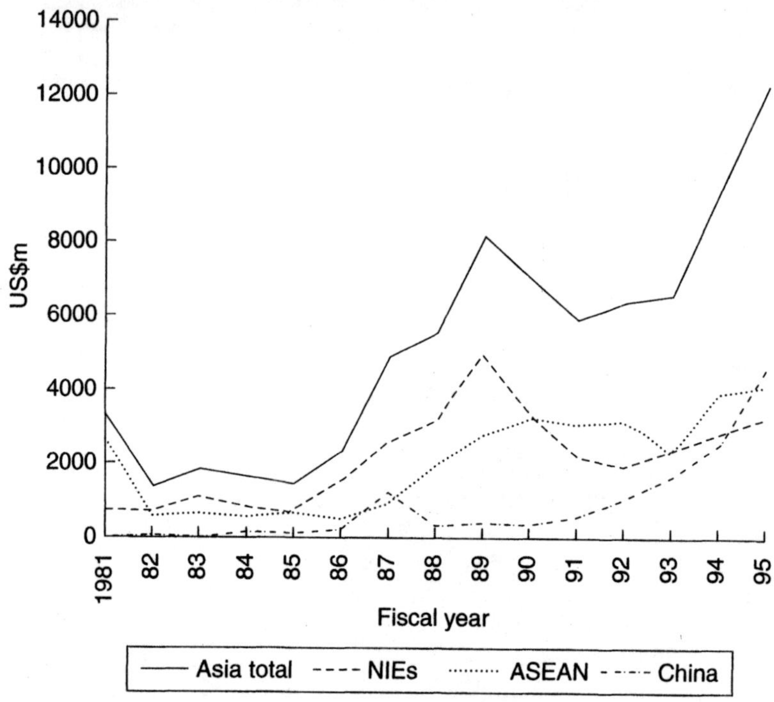

Figure 3.1 Japanese FDI in Asia
Source: The Export–Import Bank of Japan, *Journal of Research Institute for International Investment and Development*: various issues; Ōkurashō 1995, 1996
Note: Asia total includes India, Vietnam, NIEs and Asean.

made in Asia, 1981–95. Although since 1989 the total value of FDI has fallen, this decrease has been small in Asia, with overall Asian investment rising as a proportion of the total. The boom in investment in China in the last few years is especially significant. Investment to China increased by 60 to 80 per cent every year, rising from $349 million in 1990 to $579 million in 1991, and then from $1,070 million in 1992 to $4,473 million in 1995. In comparison, investment in the NIEs (South Korea, Taiwan, Hong Kong and Singapore) is on the relative decline.

Investment in ASEAN declined temporarily, but has now recovered due to the pro-active strategy of Japanese multinationals in strengthening the manufacturing base for electronics and automobiles (including the parts industries) in Malaysia and Thailand. In Indonesia investment is also likely to recover to some extent as a result of progress in deregulation and the adoption of a new foreign investment law (June 1994) which allows the acceptance of ventures with 100 per cent foreign capital.

Various reasons have been put forward in order to explain the increases in FDI in Asia. Salient among those related to Japanese domestic conditions are:

- the decline in international competitiveness due to the appreciation of the yen;
- increased production by parent companies overseas and the resulting sense of insecurity amongst the small and medium-sized companies that supply them with parts;
- domestic recession and falling demand;
- high corporate tax;
- regulations and a high cost economy.

At the same time, changes in local conditions in the host countries have influenced these trends. These include:

- economic growth and the expansion of demand;
- low production costs;
- liberalization and deregulation policies regarding foreign capital (in particular, China has set the lead in allowing 100 per cent foreign capital investment);
- the development of related industries and infrastructure;
- the growth of overseas Chinese capital;
- the increased numbers of middle-ranking managers and technicians;
- political stability.

Due to the end of major investments in the USA and Europe for some industries and the emergence of friction over investment for others, strong reasons exist for companies to reconsider Asia as an investment target.

In the case of China, even though the potential of long-term development is enormous, rapid growth has given rise to inflation and structural distortions. These now require action. Hereafter, changes in economic policy and the strengthening of regulations on foreign capital are likely. We can thus expect Japanese ventures in China to continue to increase, but to become more cautious in their investment and production strategies.

Changes in FDI strategy

Japanese private foreign direct investment has gone through several stages in its development. It began in the 1960s with investment in large machine assembly plants in support of Asian 'import substitution industrialization', and then in the 1970s moved into a phase based on natural resource development and importation. During the period of the yen's high appreciation from 1985 onwards, investment sharply increased in the US and European markets with the aim of alleviating trade friction. At the same time, export platforms were established in Asia, taking advantage of reduced production costs in order to maintain international competitiveness.

This upsurge in corporate FDI following the yen's appreciation began to decline from 1990 onwards. Influenced by the Gulf War abroad and the financial recession brought about by the collapse of the 'bubble economy' at home, corporate investment declined, and the enthusiasm for overseas investment cooled. However, with the further climb in the yen's value after 1993, the FDI strategy of Japanese companies was again revised. At the beginning of November 1994 the value of the yen reached 96 yen to the dollar and in April 1995 broke through 80 yen to the dollar. At these levels small and medium-sized enterprises started to move towards overseas production.

The continued rise in the value of the yen exerted a serious impact upon the international competitiveness of Japanese products. In response, large manufacturing companies in areas such as electronics and automobiles announced plans to strengthen existing production facilities in the ASEAN countries, and to create new facilities in China and Vietnam. Along with the expansion of overseas production by the large parent companies, small and medium-sized subcontractors and allied companies, which were now losing their domestic customers, were forced to consider shifting their own production overseas in order to maintain international competitiveness. Up to this point, the establishment of overseas production facilities had been limited to large manufacturers, but with smaller manufacturers moving abroad, the process of structural transformation within domestic Japanese industry began to intensify with a serious 'hollowing out' of certain industries anticipated in many quarters.[1]

The move towards local production by Japanese affiliate companies has helped to bring about the economic development and industrialization of the Asian countries. From the Japanese perspective, moreover, the phased and chain-reaction-like development of Asian countries with different levels of technology and income[2] has generated beneficial effects both for Japan's growing and declining industries. In planning the expansion of their production facilities in Asia as part of their globalization strategy, Japanese companies at the same time have been able to carry out a restructuring within the company in order to respond to domestic structural changes. Instead of living in fear of the 'hollowing out' of Japan's domestic economy, therefore, Japanese companies are aware of the advantages arising from the cyclical developmental structure in Asia. In this corporate leaders envisage the creation of an 'Economic Co-operation Area', if not a 'co-prosperity sphere', in Asia.

Thus, in addition to the region being considered as an economic growth area and a large potential market, Japanese corporations find Asia attractive as every country is at a different stage of development, and all are involved in a cyclical structure of mutual growth. On top of this, all Asian countries welcome the introduction of export-oriented foreign investment, and provide the necessary conditions for the acceptance of Japanese-style management methods. For Japanese companies, the effect of establishing production facilities overseas is to increase the export of parts, services and associated machinery. Until recently, Japanese exports in terms of value have been highest to the USA, but after 1993 exports to

Asia took the lead. Asia has now become the largest importer of Japanese products, including capital goods, parts and materials for their domestic production.

CHANGES IN TECHNOLOGY TRANSFER

Japanese FDI not only supplemented the shortage of funds needed by high performing Asian economies (World Bank 1993),[3] it contributed to employment creation, export expansion, development of related domestic industries and transfer of technologies. For example, the total direct employment in 6,000 Japanese affiliates in Asia is now 1.33 million in 1993 (Tōyō Keizai Shinpōsha 1994)[4] and if we include indirect employment it is estimated to be 4 million. In terms of the value of exports from Japan to East Asia, it now exceeds North America which includes the USA. As for localization, which suggests domestic industrial linkage, this was 54 per cent for the Thai automobile manufacturing industry already in the mid-1980s.[5] Thus there has been a large-scale contribution of Japanese enterprises to the industrial development of East Asian countries. We should also pay attention to the development of human resources achieved in the process of industrial development in these countries. In the following sections we will examine technology transfer and human resource development, in which Japanese enterprises have played an important role.

Technology transfer before appreciation of the yen

From the beginning of the 1960s, the overseas investments of Japanese companies were centred upon South East and East Asia. At the start, the investment was designed to counter the loss of export markets caused by the national industrial development policies of the Asian countries, and the chief aim was to secure markets rather than profits. Investment was initially centred on textiles, automobiles (including motor cycles) and electronics, and this was then followed by investment in such industries as foodstuffs and furniture, which used locally produced resources. In particular, large Japanese automobile and electronics companies invested intensively in operations in South East Asia.

The distinctive characteristics of Japanese corporate investment at that time were that it was mainly carried out by large companies, and was concentrated in labour-intensive industries which utilized cheap labour. The investment which was designed for import substitution in the domestic market was concentrated in the three industries mentioned above. During this period local Japanese affiliates made a number of changes in their education and technology training.

During the initial period of the advance of Japanese companies overseas, from the 1960s until the 1970s, 'know-how' in such areas as operation technology, machine repair and maintenance, and quality control was taught to local employees by means of on-the-job training (OJT). At this time, seniority-based promotion and lifetime employment were still prevalent, and the education of human resources was carried out under these systems. In other words, systems generally used in Japan were imported unchanged into the plants set up in South East Asia. This meant that operational technology was not just taught by the use of manuals, as was the case in Europe and the USA, but machine repair, quality control and production control were taught directly to local employees (Yamashita *et al.* 1989: 28–45)

The nine-stage hypothesis of technology transfer

In the case of European and other Western companies operating in Asia, company technicians taught the technology, and then returned home. In contrast, the technicians in Japanese affiliate companies stayed on. This was termed the Japanese affiliates 'grudging export' of technology. But in fact, unlike European and US companies, which taught only operational technology as specified in the manuals, Japanese affiliates taught a responsive system, which included along with operational technology the technology it was based upon, such as repairs, quality control and frequent model changes. In order to discover whether the Japanese or the US–European affiliates were the most enthusiastic towards technology transfer and human resource development, a survey of Japanese affiliates was carried out.[6]

The 'nine-stage hypothesis of technology transfer' includes those labour-intensive manufacturing industries, such as automobiles, electronics, and textiles, in which Japanese affiliates are concentrated. It describes the improvement in an employee's technological ability and technological training in industries dependent upon machine processing in assembly, and can be divided into the following nine elements:

1 Operational technology.
2 Repair/maintenance.
3 Quality control.
4 Production control (manufacturing process and parts procurement).
5 Improvement of existing and introduction of new technology.
6 Moulding and the development of tools.
7 Design of technology.
8 Development of new products.
9 Development of manufacturing plant and equipment.

The survey findings revealed that Japanese affiliate companies spent time teaching the nine steps outlined above so that local employees were able to perform these tasks on their own. In the mid-1980s, a large number of managers answered that they had already transferred technologies to employees in stages 1 to 3 and stages 4 and 5 of the technology transfer were underway (Yamashita 1994: 24).[7] These practices were quite different from the way in which European and US companies only taught textbook operational technology to local employees. As a result, if machinery required repair, engineers had to be called out from Europe or the USA, instead of relying upon local employees.[8]

At the same time, however, Japanese managers considered that stages 6 to 9, connected with research and development, could be taught more efficiently at the company headquarters or central research centre in Japan. Even allowing for this, a large number of Japanese affiliates which had been operating in ASEAN countries for around 30 years were clearly working for the technological education of their local employees and the development of their human resources. But with the renewed appreciation of the yen, major changes have appeared in the methods used for technical training and production control in local Japanese affiliates, especially in those companies which have moved overseas in order to construct export platforms.

THE 'BLACK BOX' PHENOMENON IN TECHNOLOGY TRANSFER PROCESS

The construction of export platforms and human resource development

Japanese foreign direct investment increased sharply following the yen's rise after the 1985 Plaza Accord. The biggest difference in Japanese investment in Asia after the yen's appreciation was a shift away from securing markets, as heretofore, towards constructing local production and export platforms. This called for reductions in cost as well as wide-ranging adjustments in quality control. The problem was how to make up for the deficiencies in the technical ability of local employees, as the education of local technicians proved insufficient for the task (compare the Brazilian experience, Schmitz and Cassiolato 1992). The demand for export platforms increased quickly, strengthening the trend towards efficient machine-based production.

As a result, important changes occurred in the production control and technical guidance at local plants. First, automated machinery and robots were introduced into the production line, efficiency greatly improved, and a production system capable of manufacturing high-quality products was established. Second, a training system which simplified and divided the work into small parts, making possible the speedy induction of unskilled employees, was created. This system also served to counter the frequent 'job-hopping' of local employees. Indeed, with two or three days training workers could be put to work on the factory floor.

The 'black box' phenomenon[9]

These changes would seem to contain many drawbacks from the viewpoint of local human resource development and technology transfer. The move towards machine production based upon automated machinery for the purpose of exports certainly allowed the production of high quality goods, but at the same time the level and range of technical skills acquired by local employees was restricted. Even though simple processing and assembly know-how were taught locally, due to the introduction of automated systems incorporating high technology, local staff could not easily acquire high technology skills.

For example, Japanese electronics makers are producing colour televisions in Malaysia. Malaysian models are said to be of higher quality than the Japanese, but this is because state-of-the-art machinery has been installed, and reliance upon human processing and checks has been eliminated. In other words, local employees carry out simple processing assembly tasks, while automated systems carry out the high-level processing and checking. Although product excellence is thereby guaranteed, the skill level of local workers remains lower than that gained under the previous training system implemented by Japanese affiliates. From the viewpoint of the workers, the production process employing high technology machinery 'cannot be seen, touched, or improved'. The structure of technology transfer with these characteristics has been called technological 'black box' in the production process, or 'black box' phenomenon in the process of technology transfer (Yamashita 1992: 126–8; 1995: 347–52).

In the Malaysian colour television plants of Japanese affiliates, key components and materials are imported, mainly from Singapore, South Korea and Japan. The imports are then combined with locally produced components (chiefly from Japanese affiliates), and simple processing and assembly are carried out by local employees on the first production line. Intricate processing is then performed by automated machinery in an order production process, and additional checks and tests are also carried out by automated machinery. Under such a production process, local employees simply operate the machines, double-check the machine tests, package the products which have passed the tests, and then box them for export. In short, the most important parts of the production process and inspection rely upon automated machinery, whereas the checking and operation of machinery, and simple processing and assembly, are in the hands of the local labour force.

Is the 'black box' beneficial or detrimental?

How should we interpret this 'black box' phenomenon, and how should we evaluate the response made by Japanese affiliates to local conditions? Those who take a critical view note that elementary technical training can no longer be carried out as in the past, that a phased introduction to high technology is not possible, and that a delay in the technological learning process occurs as a result.

The traditional view of Japanese technicians suggests an orthodox theory of technology transfer, premised upon the acquisition of basic technology (Hayashi 1990: 50–61, Toyoda 1987: 235–57). In this, the emphasis is placed upon elementary and basic technical training, on acquiring technical expertise that has been present in Japanese technology training up until now. This view is based upon the belief that 'technology does leap ahead' – the normal path of development is from low to high tech, or a progression in accordance with the nine stages outlined above, from operational technology to research and development. As a prerequisite of development this view further emphasizes the acquisition of low and middle levels of education, especially in the sciences.

Nevertheless, we find Malaysia has succeeded in its policy of export-oriented industrialization, and is likely to become the world's leading exporter of both colour televisions and air conditioners. This has been achieved by the government supporting the construction of hi-tech factories without any skilled local workers. Even if this success can be ascribed to foreign capital centred upon Japanese affiliates, domestic industrial production in colour televisions at least has taken off. If the Malaysian government had not adopted a policy of accepting foreign capital, the present development of the television and electronic industries would probably not have occurred. The fast pace of the technological revolution in micro-electronics together with the increased reliance on automation, are natural developments. Even if technology transfer has not gone forward rapidly, the ability to produce and export high-tech products and earn foreign currency has made a major contribution to the domestic economy. Industrialization has shot forward and employment has increased. Over time, moreover, the 'black box' will probably be filled with technology. In fact, the 'black box' phenomenon can also be seen in the existing electronics and electronic machinery plants located in rural parts of Japan. For the economic and technological development of developing nations, both approaches, orthodox and pragmatic, are essential. In order to emphasize the importance of the two operating concurrently, we have coined the phrase the 'pursuit of two hares' (Yamashita 1994: 29–32).

EXPANSION OF JAPANESE AUTO-MANUFACTURERS IN ASIA

The training and technical guidance given to local employees in automobile production plants is different from the cases of the electronics and electrical machinery industries examined above. In the latter industries automation can be used in many areas of intricate assembly and inspection, whereas in the automobile industry reliance upon the skills of the technician is the order of the day. In other words, if care is not taken in the training of local technicians, problems will arise in quality control and in the creation of 'black box' technology. In such a situation, companies can lose competitiveness. A major difference thus exists between the electronic industry and the automobile industry: in the former, even if skilled personnel are absent, high-tech goods still can be produced and an export system set up; in the latter, a lack of skilled personnel can produce a situation in which cars cannot be produced for export. Let us examine the human resource development methods used in Japanese affiliate automobile companies against the background of expansion in automobile production, as shown in Table 3.1.

Localization policies and response of Japanese affiliated automobile makers

Japanese affiliate automobile companies first began overseas production in Thailand, where Nissan set up operations in 1962. This was followed by the construction of Thai assembly plants by Toyota in 1964, Prince in 1965, and Isuzu, Hino and Mitsubishi in 1966. By the end of the 1960s the Japanese car makers were competing for a share of Thailand's 10,000-unit car market (Satō 1993).

Against this background of large-scale moves into Thailand by Japanese automobile makers, the Thai government pursued a policy of domestic industrial promotion. The development of the domestic car industry was regarded as one element in the policy of import substitution industrialization. In line with this policy the Thai government in 1962 revised the law on industrial investment incentives, introducing a policy favouring foreign capital. Japanese car makers were conscious of the need to begin produc-

Table 3.1 Automobile production and domestic sales for Asian countries, 1994

	No. of cars produced (000s)	*No. of cars sold domestically (000s)*	*No. of cars stockpiled* (000s)*	*Population per car* (person)*
Japan	10,554	6,524	63,262	2.0
South Korea	2,311	1,560	6,274	7.2
Taiwan	423	571	4,039	5.3
China	1,339	1,479	8,176	145.6
Thailand	434	486	2,848	20.9
India	487	470	5,203	176.8
Indonesia	325	327	3,231	62.0
Malaysia	216	200	2,884	6.7
Philippines	100	99	1,555	44.9
Vietnam	Not known	6	200	365.5

Source: Information compiled by the author from various sources
Note: *1993 figures

tion in Thailand before the market dried up due to an expected ban on the import of completed cars, and before the favourable terms for foreign capital ran out in 1969.

The local production of Japanese affiliates was based originally on imports of Japanese parts for local assembly. But under new laws passed in 1971, the percentage of domestically produced parts was set at 25 per cent (to become mandatory by 1973), and Japanese car makers had no other choice but to produce parts locally. In 1978, together with a ban on the import of completed cars, the localization ratio was revised, and targets of 30 per cent domestic content by August 1979, and 50 per cent domestic content by August 1983 (a yearly rise of 5 per cent) were made compulsory. In fact, domestic companies were unable to respond at this rate, and the increased local production of parts could only be realized by the overseas expansion of Japanese automobile parts makers. However, as the demand for automobiles failed to increase, the domestic production of car parts did not proceed smoothly.

Despite this, by the latter half of the 1980s the localization ratio had reached 54 per cent, thanks to the efforts of both domestic companies and Japanese affiliates. During this period the number of vehicles produced in Thailand rose from 10,000 to 20,000 in the 1960s to 100,000 in 1977; 300,000 in 1990, 450,000 in 1993, and by 1995 the 570,000 mark had been reached. At present the creation of a production system capable of turning out half a million vehicles for both the domestic and export markets, and the large-scale expansion of plant and equipment centring on Japanese affiliate companies, is now underway. Table 3.1 gives an overview of production and stockpile figures of automobiles in the major Asian nations.

The development of Thailand's automobile industry was thus heavily dependent upon foreign capital and the Thai government's national industrialization policy. Good relations with Japanese affiliates (including parts and raw material manufacturers) are also important. At the same time, as a result of mergers with foreign-owned companies, the numbers of technicians and middle-ranking managers in Thailand increased, raising the stock of management 'know-how'.

Overseas production strategy of Japanese automobile makers

Although the overseas production of automobile assemblers depends upon local conditions, the following four stages are characteristic:

1 CKD (Complete Knock Down) production: more than 60 per cent of parts[10] are sent from Japan, and major components, such as engines, are supplied from Japan.
2 KD (Knock Down) set production: parts supply from Japan is less than 60 per cent with some parts being produced and processed locally and final assembly being carried out locally.

3 Local production: some of the most important parts are supplied from Japan, but the majority are produced locally, and design also is carried out locally.
4 Complete local production: all production, from research to design, is carried out locally.

Having defined these stages in overseas production, the development of Japanese affiliates in the leading Asian countries can be illustrated as in Figure 3.2.

Of crucial significance is the degree to which the transfer to local production has taken place in the overseas expansion and development stage of automobile production. In order to analyse this, the developmental stages of automobile production need first to be introduced. If automobile production is taken as a process from basic research to sales, then seven basic stages can be identified:

1 Basic research.
2 Development (new products, new production technology).
3 Design (products, production technology).
4 Preparation for mass production (manufacturing engineering).
5 Production (sorting, processing).
6 Final assembly.
7 Sales (including servicing).

The transfer of production overseas moves from the technologically easy stage of (7) in the reverse direction. By combining these seven stages of production and four stages of overseas transfer outlined above, Figure 3.3 illustrates the structure of the shift to local production.

Figure 3.3 indicates that Japanese companies are not aiming to transfer basic research to local production areas, and even in areas where complete

	China	*Indonesia*	*Thailand*	*USA/EU*
1 CKD production	*Present* ↓	1970s ↓	1960s ↓	
2 KD set production (transitory period)	Future	*Present* ↓	1970s–1980s ↓ *Present* ↓	
3 Local production		Future	Near future	*Present* ↓
4 Complete local production				Future

Figure 3.2 Stages of overseas operations: Japanese affiliate automobile manufacturers

	Export and services	Final assembly	Sorting and processing	Preparation for mass production	Design	Development	Basic research
1 CKD production (China)	0	+					
2 KD set production (Indonesia)	0	0	+	+			
(Thailand)	0	0	*	*			
3 Local production (USA/EU)	0	0	0	0	*		
4 Complete local production (Future)	0	0	0	0	0	0	0

Figure 3.3 The 'image' of overseas transfer of production process (company M)
Note: 0 Mostly transferred; * Transferred to a fair degree; + Partly transferred

local production has been established, the basic research is carried out in Japan.

Changes in training of local employees

Let us now examine human resource development in the overseas plants of Japanese affiliate car makers, M and T. In company T from the 1960s until 1975, 'knock-down' assembly technology was taught to employees by Japanese personnel by means of on-the-job training. From 1975 onwards, as the move towards national industrial development strengthened, Japanese personnel taught assembly, production technology and quality control, again by means of on-the-job training. During this period local workers began to be despatched to Japan for training.

In the 1980s, due to the rise in local content rates for vehicles (30–54 per cent) automobile makers strove to improve quality control; manufacturing methods such as production control, quality circles, the suggestion system, and employee education were put into effect and worker education reached a higher, more sophisticated level (Satō 1993). Indeed, Japanese affiliates increased the number of employees despatched for training to tailor-made education sections set up at Japanese headquarters, established training centres within the company, provided a system for the acceptance of local employees for training, and carried out the systematic education of their local employees.

For example, company T increased the numbers sent to Japan annually:

in 1990, the company sent 47 technicians and 5 managers; in 1991, 116 technicians and 17 managers. Simultaneously, power was devolved increasingly to Thai employees, and in 1992 a Thai managing director was appointed for the first time. Likewise, in 1990, 140 local managers replaced the Japanese staff transferred from Japan (out of 1,926 total employees, 12 are the Japanese staff) (Satō 1993).

A particular noteworthy feature of the training in Japan was the focus on teaching not just the production system of each company, but also an understanding of the company's way of thinking, Japanese culture, and so on. An example of this is company M's SOMPS (Study of M's Production System) training programme. As a way to cope with understanding basic concepts of manufacturing, quality improvement and productivity improvement, company M has recruited periodically a number of trainees from overseas production bases since about 1986, and put them through the SOMPS programme. There were 39 trainees in 1990, 58 in 1991, 32 in 1992, and 30 in the first half of 1993, who carried out technical support in the local plants.[11]

A salient characteristic of local employee education recently has been improvements resulting from the training combining the despatch of local employees to Japan with the despatch of Japanese technicians of local plants. In the light of previous experience and in response to the various conditions put forward by the recipient countries, the training period has been shortened in cases where a new plant is being established so that local operations can begin relatively sooner, followed by more efficient production methods. At the time company M commenced operation in Thailand (1975), three resident Japanese managers and ten Japanese technicians on six-month postings provided the training for local employees. Two employees were despatched for technical training respectively in body assembly, painting, trim and final assembly, inspections and part supply. These training programmes were carried out after the factory had been completed.

When company M's Chinese plant was established in 1992, however, local employees were trained by local managers and engineers who had been trained in Japan before the factory was constructed. At the time emphasis was placed on a preparatory phase linked to the training programme, with the result that the reception of local staff for training and the despatch of Japanese technicians to the local plants went smoothly. This meant a successful start to the operations.

Table 3.2 highlights the differences between employee training in Thai plants that began operations in 1975, and plants in China which entered the production preparation stage in 1990, before the start of operations in 1992.

We can see that, unlike Japanese affiliates in the electronics and electrical machinery industries, Japanese automobile affiliates enthusiastically embrace the training of technicians and the transfer of technology to local plants. Automobile production is an industry calling for high levels of

Table 3.2 Changes in employee training of company M at commencement of operations: comparison of the Thai plant in 1975 and the Chinese plant in 1992

	Plant in Thailand			*Plant in China*			
	1974	*1975 Commencement of operations*	*1976*	*1990 Preparation*	*1991 Preparation*	*1992 Commencement of operations*	*1993*
(a) Despatches of Japanese technicians to local plants to provide guidance (on the basis of business trips)							
Press	–	–	–	–	4	6	2
Body assembly	–	2	1	–	5	7	1
Painting	–	2	1	–	1	1	2
Trim and final assembly	–	2	1	–	1	1	–
Inspection	–	2	–	–	1	1	1
Parts supply	–	2	–	–	–	–	–
Maintenance	–	–	–	–	–	1	3
New technology response	–	–	–	–	–	1	2
Total	0	10	3	0	12	18	11
(b) Training in Japan							
Press	–	–	–	2	9	3	–
Body assembly	–	–	1	8	7	1	–
Painting	–	–	1	–	5	1	–
Trim and final assembly	–	–	1	–	6	2	–
Inspection	–	–	1	–	5	1	–
Parts supply	–	–	–	–	–	–	–
Maintenance	–	–	–	–	9	–	–
New technology response	–	–	2	–	3	1	–
Total	0	0	5	10	44	9	0

Source: Interview at Company M
Notes: 1 Period of despatch or acceptance varies from one month to one year (average six months)
2 Production scale of the Thai plant was 600 units/year and the Chinese plant was 12,000 units/year

division in the production process, as well as an industry where low-skilled workers are unsuitable for processing and assembly. In producing automobiles under Japanese-style production control methods and concepts like the *Kanban* and 'just-in-time' system (Ogawa 1994), skilled technicians are indispensable, and this need must be borne constantly in mind.[12]

In order to respond to the recent appreciation of the yen and trade friction, moreover, Japanese automobile makers have been forced to consider transferring production to former socialist countries as production costs are low, and in the next few years they are likely to construct assembly plants in China and Vietnam. Similarly, in order to respond to the demands of localization policies, the component and raw material manufacturers of the *keiretsu* will also have to set up overseas manufacturing bases. In this sense, it is not just large-scale manufacturers that are about to face these problems.

Under these conditions, Japanese car makers will advance overseas taking careful account of local conditions. For example, China and Vietnam are still only at the assembly stage, as discussed above. What with a shortage of technical personnel and the risk of changes in policy and restrictions on foreign capital, it is hard to envisage that local production will forge ahead immediately. True, the market in ASEAN countries is expanding, wages are still comparatively low, related industries such as parts manufacturing are expanding, and government policy is becoming more flexible. So if AFTA (ASEAN Free Trade Area)[13] and BBC (Brand-to-Brand Complementation)[14] proceeds, mutual exchange within ASEAN will become freer, and conditions within the region will grow more advantageous.[15] Considering the various stages and conditions of overseas expansion, automobile parts manufacturers and raw materials manufacturers are at present able to devote their main efforts to development in China and Thailand.

CONCLUSION

The prospects for the automobile industry in the high-cost domestic Japanese economy are far from bright. In the light of Asia's rapid economic growth and the emergence of infrastructure support, a situation is bound to develop whereby the overseas expansion of industry embraces related small and medium-sized as well as large companies. In this event 'industrial hollowing out' is likely in Japan's regional economies, such as Hiroshima prefecture, as these are highly specialized and dependent on the automobile industry.

From now on the direction of future policy and co-operation with Asian countries needs to be studied even further. At the same time, we need to put in place a mid to long-term schedule for developing co-operative relations with Asia which takes into account whether industry should remain in Japan or should be shifted to Asia, on the one hand, and whether products and parts should be imported from Asia, on the other. Needless to say, we also need to pay close attention to the trends in overseas Chinese investment, as these are strengthening the economic power of South and South East Asia. In this sense, Japan needs to respond in both areas of co-operation and competition.

NOTES

1 Harrison and Bluestone (1988) have analysed the 'industrial hollowing out' in the USA since the 1970s. Japan is now facing the relocation of industry overseas and closing down of domestic plants. The impact is rather serious in regional economies, such as Hiroshima, whose economy heavily depends on the automobile industry. The value added share of the automobile industry in the manufacturing sector in Hiroshima is about a quarter. The *keiretsu* and the small and medium-sized subcontract companies face a fear of bankruptcy.
2 Japanese economists sometimes call this pattern of development the 'flying geese pattern of development', following Prof. Akamatsu's observations (see Akamatasu 1956).
3 'High Performing Asian Economies', a definition given by the World Bank (1993).
4 Tōyō Keizai Shinpōsha, *Kaigai Shinshitsu Kigyō Sōran 1994* (List of overseas Japanese companies 1994): 95–8. This figure is based on a questionnaire survey and does not cover employment of all Japanese affiliated companies.
5 See later section of this chapter.
6 To do this, we drew up a 'nine-stage process of technology transfer', and by using a questionnaire of Japanese affiliates that had set up operations in four ASEAN countries (Thailand, Malaysia, Singapore and Indonesia), and by making company visits, we surveyed the actual situation of technology transfer (Yamashita 1991: 16–20).
7 By our survey carried out during 1987 and 1988, 74 per cent of Japanese managers among 132 answered our questionnaire by saying that they had already transferred the operational technology to locals, 57 per cent the repair and maintenance, and 50 per cent for quality control; however, only 28 per cent had transferred production control and 11 per cent technical improvement. Stages 6 to 9 were not so active.
8 Japanese affiliate companies in ASEAN countries utilized various methods for training, i.e. manuals in both English and local languages, OJT by locals, QC circle activities, seminars and personnel despatch to Japan for training. The applications of each method are illustrated in Yamashita (1995: 345–9). Skill formation at Japanese companies in Japan and South East Asia has been studied by Koike and Inoki (1990).
9 When there is an advanced technology which 'cannot be seen, touched, or improved' at the local level we call this an example of the 'black box' phenomenon of technology in the production process'. In essence, the basic pattern of technology transfer is to progress from lower level technology to a higher level. This phenomenon emerges when, in spite of the large gap in technology between advanced countries and developing countries, the latter countries embark on the production of high technologies such as electronics equipment. This tends to emerge when the developing countries seek to introduce a production system which narrows this 'technology gap' through the machine production by attracting foreign direct investment. There are two views on this point: one is that local

production is possible even if there is a gap, while the other is that it is impossible and that it is necessary to have a learning process to narrow this gap.

10 FOB price of supplied parts divided by FOB price of all parts per one car ≥ 60 per cent.

11 Interviews with company M's managers.

12 The Indonesian government has hastened to promote their 'national car project' which will be carried out within 1996. However, it is wise to take into consideration this aspect.

13 Member states of ASEAN have agreed to lower the common tariff within the region from 0–5 per cent by 2003.

14 ASEAN member countries agreed in 1988 to promote localization of automobile production and mutal complementation of auto-parts in the region.

15 We should pay attention to the aspects of technology diffusion (Ōkawa and Ōtsuka 1994) and technology blending (Bhalla and James 1988) in the development process.

REFERENCES

Akamatsu, K. (1956) 'Wagakuni sangyō hatten no gankō keitai: kikai kigu kōgyō ni tsuite (A flying geese pattern of Japanese industrial development: machine and tool industries), *Hitotsubashi Review*, vol. 6, no. 5, 68–80.

Bhalla, A. S. and James, D. (eds) (1988) *New Technologies and Development: Experiences in 'Technology Blending'*, Boulder/London: Lynne Rienner Publishers.

Export–Import Bank of Japan (1995) *Journal of Research Institute for International Investment and Development*, July.

Harrison, B. and Bluestone, B. (1988) *The Great U-turn: Corporate Restructuring and the Polarizing of America*, New York: Basic Books.

Hayashi, T. (1990) *The Japanese Experience in Technology: From Transfer to Self-Reliance*, Tokyo: United Nations University Press.

Koike, K. and Inoki, T. (eds) (1990) *Skill Formation in Japan and Southeast Asia*, Tokyo: Tokyo University Press

Ogawa, E (1994) *Toyota Seisan Soshiki no Kenkyū* (A study of the Toyota production system), Tokyo: Nihon Keizai Shinbunsha.

Ōkawa, K. and Otsuka, K (1994) *Technology Diffusion, Productivity, Employment, and Phase Shifts in Developing Economies*, Tokyo: University of Tokyo Press.

Ōkurashō (1995, 1996) *Taigai Tainai Chokusetsu Tōshi Todokede Jisseki* (Registration of inward and outward investment), Tokyo: Ōkurashō.

Satō, I. (1993) 'Japanese-style management and technology transfer', in Tran Van Tho (ed.) *Japanese Management Style and Technology Transfer in Thailand*, Tokyo: Japan Centre for Economic Research.

Schmitz, H. and Cassiolato, J. (1992) *Hi-Tech for Industrial Development: Lessons from the Brazilian Experience in Electronics and Automation*, London: Routledge.

Toyōda, T. (ed.) (1987) *Vocational Education in the Industrialization of Japan*, Tokyo: United Nations University Press.

Tōyō Keizai Shinposha (ed.) (1994) *Kaigai Shinshitsu Kigyō Sōran* 1994 (List of overseas Japanese companies 1994), Tokyo: Tōyō Keizai Shinposha.

World Bank, (1993) *The East Asian Miracle*, Oxford: Oxford University Press.

Yamashita, S. (ed.) (1991) *Transfer of Japanese Technology and Management to the ASEAN Countries*, Tokyo: University of Tokyo Press.

Yamashita, S. (1992) 'Gijutsuiten ni okeru black-box ni tsuite' (On the black-box phenomenon in technology transfer), *Journal of International Development Studies*, vol. 1, no. 2, 121–30.

Yamashita, S. (1994) 'Foreign direct investment and the process of technology transfer', *Hiroshima Economic Studies*, 15, 15–44.

Yamashita, S. (1995) 'Japan's role as a regional technological integrator and the black box phenomenon in the process of technology transfer', in D. F. Simon (ed.) *The Emerging Technological Trajectory of the Pacific Rim*, New York: East Gate Books, M. E. Sharpe Inc.

Yamashita, S., Takeuchi, J., Kawabe, N. and Takehana, S. (1989) 'ASEAN shokoku ni okeru nihonteki keiei to gijutsu iten nikansuru keieisha no ishiki-chōsa' (Survey of Japanese managers on Japanese-style management and technology transfer in ASEAN countries), *Hiroshima Economic Studies*, vol. 10, 1–89.

4 Changes in Japanese automobile and electronic transplants in the USA

Evaluating Japanese-style management and production systems

Abō Tetsuo

This chapter appraises, analyses and seeks to understand changes in Japanese management and production systems in light of their transfer to the USA. It is based on the results of surveys of Japanese automobile assembly and associated component plants, and semiconductor factories, as carried out in 1989 and 1993. In the following analysis, some significant changes are identified in the transfer level of Japanese production techniques at the Japanese transplants in the US, compared with the period of 1986–1989, when our first research was carried out (Abō 1990). Although the details are not given in this chapter, an interesting implication of the change in direction is its similarity with the pattern of transfer by Japanese firms in the East Asian region (Abō 1995a). In the context of the globalization of the Japanese economy, management/production systems have come to be used not only by Japanese companies involved in local production, but also by non-Japanese companies in every region of the world. In this sense, the Japanese economy can be said to have entered a stage of 'globalization'.[1]

INTERNATIONAL TRANSFER OF JAPANESE MANAGEMENT AND PRODUCTION SYSTEM: A MODEL

The comparative superiority of the Japanese production system is evident from the remarkably high standards of work efficiency and in the quality of the goods produced. This results from a 'manufacturing workplace-centred' style of management which attaches great importance to human resources. If it is assumed that this style of management depends heavily upon the specific systems and customs unique to Japanese society, then problems are bound to arise when the strong points of the Japanese system are introduced to foreign societies, which differ in terms of their historical and cultural environment. It will naturally call for the amendment or 'indigenization' of the foreign system (Abō 1994a). In comparison with western companies, Japanese manufacturers were 'reluctant' to move production overseas, not merely because they started later, but also because of this need to amend the Japanese production system.[2]

In order to take these theoretical points into account, an 'application and adaptation (hybrid) model' was constructed. While, on the one hand, US-based Japanese transplants seek to import the superior element of the Japanese production system – the 'application' aspect – on the other, some adjustments must be made in order for the system to fit local conditions – the 'adaptation' aspect. This produces a dilemma. In order to resolve this dilemma, in our study performance was also taken into account and various 'hybrids' of both aspects were created.

Taking into account the changing direction in transfer of the Japanese production systems at the factories of Japanese and American companies, it seems more appropriate to use our 'hybrid' approach, which lays emphasis on the situation in the combination of application and adaptation rather than one-sided evaluation of the degree of application. And this would also be true in research on Japanese foreign direct investment (FDI) in Europe, and so on. For example, the 'Japanization' approach which is popular in Europe, is more likely to be a uniform approach that assumes the one-sided spread of Japanese-style practices emanating from a single source.[3]

In our research, the basic elements constituting the Japanese production system were broken down into 23 categories in 6 groups. Next a five-stage measurement method was introduced in order quantitatively to measure the level of 'application–adaptation'. If the systems in place at the parent company are also in place at the point of local production, the degree of application is 5 (this produces the figure 1 for the degree of adaptation in the American system). If no systems are in place at all, the degree of application is 1 (accordingly, the degree of adaptation is 5). The factory is then regarded as being administered almost entirely in the American way. In reality, of course, values from 2 to 4 are more common, suggesting the degree to which the American and Japanese methods and systems have been combined.

As we will see below, the degree of transfer of the 23 categories/6 groups has been evaluated in accordance with the organic relationship within the Japanese management production system. This is the orthodox approach, looking at performance in terms of the quality of goods and efficiency from the perspective of the parent companies and factories (see Chapter 3). In addition, we will focus here on the substantial content and nature of the international transfer of technology, using a four-point method of evaluation as, so to speak, an approach from the viewpoint of the adopting country.

In the 1986 survey, 14 out of the 15 factories were Japanese, in 1989, 34 out of 49 were Japanese; and in 1993, 10 out of 14 (see Table 4.1).[4]

CATEGORY AND GROUP EVALUATION

Table 4.2 shows the combined contents of the 23 categories/6 groups and the 1989 and 1993 results. The numerical values of Table 4.2 compare the hybrid evaluation of the 10 Japanese factories of the 1993 survey (5

Table 4.1 List of plants surveyed

Plant name	*Start of plant operations*	*Number of employees (1993)*	*Number of employees (1989)*	*Location (state)*	*Principal products*
Japanese affiliate (automobile assembly plants)					
AA	1982	10,000	6,500	Ohio	Automobiles, motorcycles, Automobile/motorcycle engines
AB	1983 (June)	5,806	3,294	Tennessee	Automobiles, pick-up trucks
AC	1984 (Dec)	4,250	2,800	California	Automobiles, pick-up trucks
AE	1988 (May)	4,685	2,950	Kentucky	Automobiles, key components (engines, transmissions, etc.)
AF	1988 (Sept)	3,100	2,300	Illinois	Automobiles
MA	1986	292		Tennessee	Construction machinery
(Auto-parts)					
AJ	1984 (Feb)	819	663	Tennessee	Air-conditioners, radiators
AV*	1988 (Apr)	301		Kentucky	Auto-wheels
(Semiconductors)					
SB	1978 (Dec)	1,400	750	California	4M/16H-DRAM, 256K-SBAM
SC	1979 (May)	550	318	Texas	4M/1M-DRAM, 256K-SRAM, MPU
SF	1984	494	400	North Carolina	1M-DRAM, SRAM, 4M-DRAM assembly
SG	1988 (Oct)	532	355	Oregon	1M-DRAM, 256K-SRAM EP-ROM, memory
(US automobile assembly plants)					
AUA	1947	2,684		Georgia	Automobile
AUB	1992 (Jun)	3,026		Ontario, Canada	Automobile
(Semiconductors)					
SUA	1984	3,500		Texas	16/32 Bit MPU, RISC MP, CSIC, DSP
MUA*		3,170		Texas	Printed wire board

Note: * These results are taken only from the latest survey, and therefore are not part of the evaluation

Table 4.2 The 'hybrid ratios' of Japanese production systems in the USA, 1989, 1993

	Japanese Plants								US Plants		
	Automobile		Auto-parts		Semiconductor		Average all Jpn plants		Auto	Semiconductor	Average all US plants
	1993	1989	1993	1989	1993	1989	1993	1989	1993	1993	1993
G1 Work organization/admin.	**3.3**	**(3.4)**	**3.8**	**(3.3)**	**3.7**	**(2.7)**	**3.5**	**(3.0)**	**2.3**	**3.7**	**2.8**
(1) Job classification	4.0	(4.8)	4.0	(3.0)	4.3	(2.3)	4.1	(3.6)	2.0	4.0	2.7
(2) Job rotation	3.6	(3.4)	4.0	(3.5)	3.3	(2.3)	3.5	(2.8)	3.5	4.0	3.7
(3) Training	3.8	(3.4)	4.0	(3.5)	3.5	(3.0)	3.7	(3.1)	3.0	4.0	3.3
(4) Wage	2.0	(2.2)	3.0	(2.5)	3.8	(3.0)	2.8	(2.6)	1.5	3.0	2.0
(5) Promotion	2.8	(3.2)	4.0	(3.5)	3.8	(3.0)	3.3	(3.2)	2.0	4.0	2.7
(6) Supervisor	3.6	(3.2)	4.0	(4.0)	3.3	(2.5)	3.5	(2.9)	2.0	3.0	2.3
G2 Production control	**3.8**	**(3.6)**	**4.3**	**(4.3)**	**3.6**	**(3.3)**	**3.7**	**(3.5)**	**2.9**	**4.0**	**3.3**
(7) Equipment	4.0	(4.0)	4.0	(5.0)	4.0	(5.0)	4.0	(4.5)	2.5	3.0	2.7
(8) Maintenance	3.4	(3.0)	4.0	(4.0)	3.3	(2.5)	3.4	(2.9)	2.0	4.0	2.7
(9) Quality control	3.8	(4.0)	5.0	(4.0)	3.5	(2.5)	3.8	(3.4)	3.5	5.0	4.0
(10) Operation control	3.8	(3.2)	4.0	(4.0)	3.5	(3.0)	3.7	(3.2)	3.5	4.0	3.7
G3 Parts procurement	**2.4**	**(2.9)**	**2.7**	**(2.0)**	**3.1**	**(3.6)**	**2.7**	**(3.1)**	**2.0**	**2.0**	**2.0**
(11) Local content	1.8	(2.0)	2.0	(1.0)	2.8	(4.0)	2.2	(2.8)	2.0	2.0	2.0
(12) Suppliers	2.8	(3.6)	2.0	(3.0)	3.8	(4.8)	3.1	(4.0)	2.5	2.0	2.3
(13) Methods	2.6	(3.0)	4.0	(2.0)	2.8	(2.0)	2.8	(2.5)	1.5	2.0	1.7
G4 Team spirit	**3.7**	**(3.9)**	**4.7**	**(4.3)**	**3.4**	**(2.8)**	**3.7**	**(3.5)**	**2.0**	**4.7**	**2.9**
(14) Small group activity	3.2	(2.8)	4.0	(4.0)	3.8	(2.0)	3.5	(2.6)	1.5	4.0	2.3
(15) Information	3.8	(4.4)	5.0	(5.0)	3.3	(3.3)	3.7	(4.0)	2.5	5.0	3.3
(16) Unity	4.2	(4.4)	5.0	(4.0)	3.0	(3.0)	3.8	(3.8)	2.0	5.0	3.0

(continued)

Table 4.2 (continued)

	Japanese Plants								US Plants		
	Automobile		Auto-parts		Semiconductor		Average all Jpn plants		Auto	Semiconductor	Average all US plants
	1993	1989	1993	1989	1993	1989	1993	1989	1993	1993	1993
G5 Labour relations	**4.1**	**(4.2)**	**4.8**	**(4.0)**	**3.4**	**(3.8)**	**3.9**	**(4.0)**	**2.4**	**4.0**	**2.9**
(17) Employment policy	3.8	(4.2)	4.0	(3.0)	3.3	(3.5)	3.6	(3.8)	1.5	2.0	1.7
(18) Job security	4.2	(5.0)	5.0	(4.0)	2.8	(2.8)	3.7	(4.0)	3.5	4.0	3.7
(19) Union	4.2	(4.4)	5.0	(5.0)	3.8	(5.0)	4.1	(4.7)	2.5	5.0	3.3
(20) Grievance	4.2	(3.2)	5.0	(4.0)	3.5	(3.8)	4.0	(3.5)	2.0	5.0	3.0
G6 Parent–subsidiary relationship	**2.9**	**(3.0)**	**2.3**	**(3.7)**	**3.6**	**(4.1)**	**3.1**	**(3.5)**	**1.0**	**1.0**	**1.0**
(21) Jpn ratio	2.4	(2.8)	2.0	(4.0)	3.5	(4.5)	2.8	(3.6)	1.0	1.0	1.0
(22) Power of delegation	3.2	(3.0)	2.0	(3.0)	3.8	(4.0)	3.3	(3.4)	1.0	1.0	1.0
(23) Local managers	3.0	(3.0)	3.0	(4.0)	3.5	(3.8)	3.2	(3.4)	1.0	1.0	1.0
Total Average	**3.4**	**(3.5)**	**3.8**	**(3.6)**	**3.5**	**(3.3)**	**3.5**	**(3.4)**	**2.2**	**3.3**	**2.6**

automobile assembly plants, 1 associated parts plant and 4 semiconductor factories) with the 1989 survey of the same factories. The table focuses on the changes since 1989 and also puts forward an account of a 'hybrid evaluation' of the US factories.

Taking into account the relatively small number of factories for evaluation, especially in the case of auto-parts (only one), we need qualifications in order to draw any general conclusions. However, since these ten Japanese factories are among the most important and representative ones in the USA, it can be assumed that there is basic relevance to our results.

Overall evaluation

Table 4.2 indicates that the general average of the hybrid ratio for each category is 3.5 for all Japanese factories. Rather than a 50–50 relationship between the Japanese methods and American methods this indicates a small degree of 'Japanization'. In the 1989 survey the figure for the same factories was 3.4, indicating almost no change over the four-year period as far as the general average is concerned. By comparing each of the values in the groups and categories, changes occurring in opposite directions can be seen between values. An offset of such changes accounts for an approximation of all averages. Let us here examine the difference and changes in each item and group.

Group evaluation

First if we look at the 1989–93 change in the hybrid ratio in the group for the Japanese plant average in the three industries as seen in Table 4.2 or Figure 4.1, the rise in values for G1 (work organization/administration) from 3.0 to 3.5, G4 (team spirit) from 3.5 to 3.7, and also the fall in values in G3 (parts procurement) from 3.1 to 2.7 and G6 (parent–subsidiary relationships) from 3.5 to 3.1 stand out as contrastive movements. No large change can be seen in G2 (production control), which rose from 3.5 to 3.7, or G5 (labour relations) which remained fairly stable, falling slightly from 4.0 to 3.9. Such changes in the hybrid ratio between groups signifies that, during the first few years of the 1990s, the constitutional make-up of the production system at local production plants has gone through major changes.

The reduction in the hybrid ratios of G6 (parent–subsidiary relationships) is a particularly important change. For the local adaptation of personnel as represented in the drop from 3.6 to 2.8 in the ratio of Japanese workers, resulted from an increase in the degree of application (hybrid ratio) of the Japanese method in the core section, related to the personnel of G1. In essence, this trend is in a desirable direction. Of course, our model hypothesizes that it is when the operating conditions of a parent Japanese company are applied directly as a standard that the efficiency of a factory's manufacturing activities and the quality of its goods achieve the highest

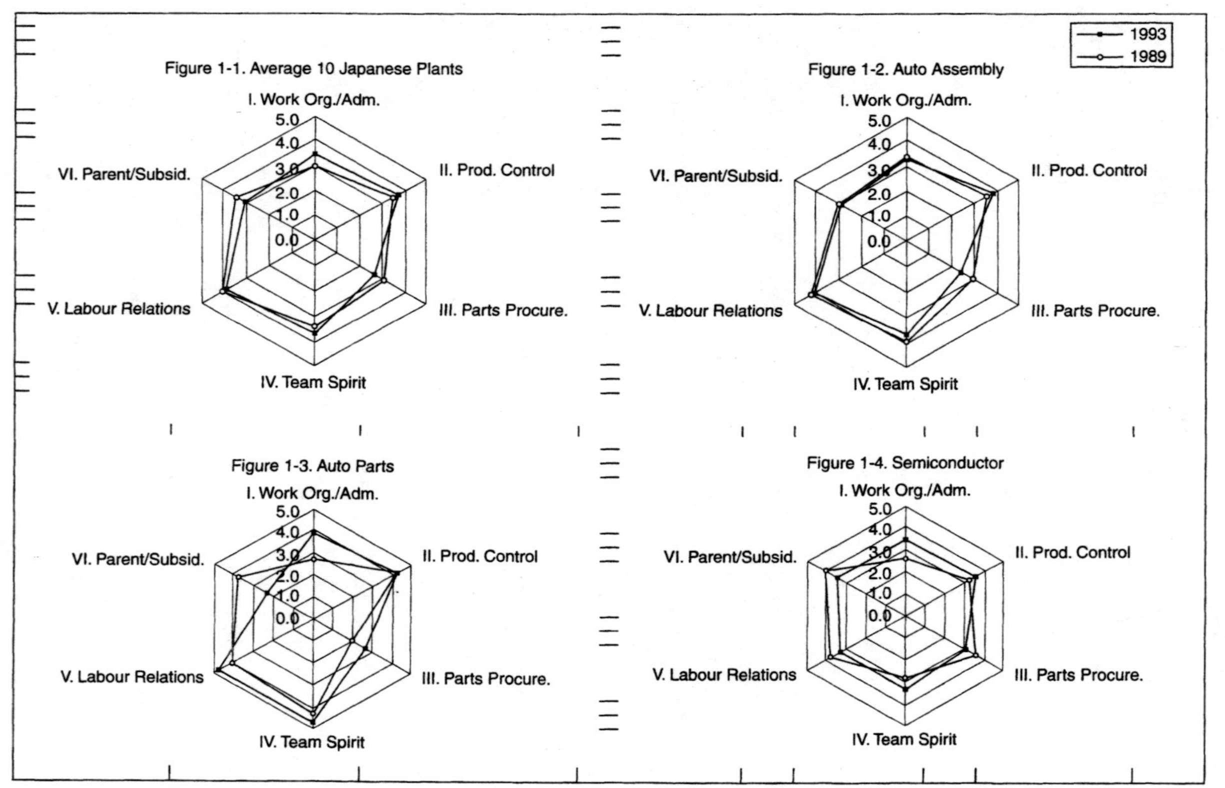

Figure 4.1 Hybrid ratios of 6 groups

level. In this sense, so long as we examine the efficiency of transferring the system theoretically this kind of standard must first be decided and fixed. Moreover, it is necessary actually to examine the transfer from the perspective of the system's relationship with the local society; that is, as an easy to accept and an essentially easy to establish technical transfer (refer to four-perspective evaluation on p. 101). From the practical standpoint of a company, therefore, ultimately the construction of a long-term and stable management system contributes and is linked to a reduction in costs through the appointment of local managers who understand the Japanese system.

It may safely be said that, in the light of the nature of the Japanese system already discussed, the large number of Japanese personnel in overseas operations is a straightforward feature of multinational companies. True, within Japanese enterprises employees share a wide range of responsibilities and respond flexibly to different circumstances. However, in many western countries, whenever Japanese-style management is introduced, gaps tend to emerge in the vague areas of overlapping responsibilities. In directly communicating the detailed accumulation of local skills and know-how, as well as in technical activities such as the introduction of new machines or changes in models, the removal of Japanese personnel covering these gaps becomes progressively difficult.

According to our standards the 1989 hybrid ratio of 3.6 for the 'Jpn ratio' represents an all-employee ratio of 2–3 per cent. This contrasts sharply with the 1 per cent figure for American multinationals. The 1993 value for the 'Jpn ratio' was 2.8, an all-employee ratio of 1–2 per cent. To put this more concretely, a 1 per cent difference is equivalent to 30 Japanese at a factory with 3,000 employees. In this sense, even though the labour costs for workers in the USA are two to three times greater than those incurred by working in Japan, this development allows a fair reduction in personnel expenses. As long as other core elements like the hybrid ratio for G1 do not fall, and especially as long as rises in values are accompanied by other changes which compensate, this kind of drop in the category and group hybrid ratio is an important element in determining the system's efficiency.

Category evaluation

There follows a detailed examination of the contents of the 23 categories/6 groups of Table 4.2 and Figure 4.2.

G1 Work organization/administration

One of the features which can be recognized in changes in each category constituting G1 is that while categories in which the hybrid ratio has increased by a wide margin (job rotation 2.8–3.5, supervisor 2.9–3.5, job

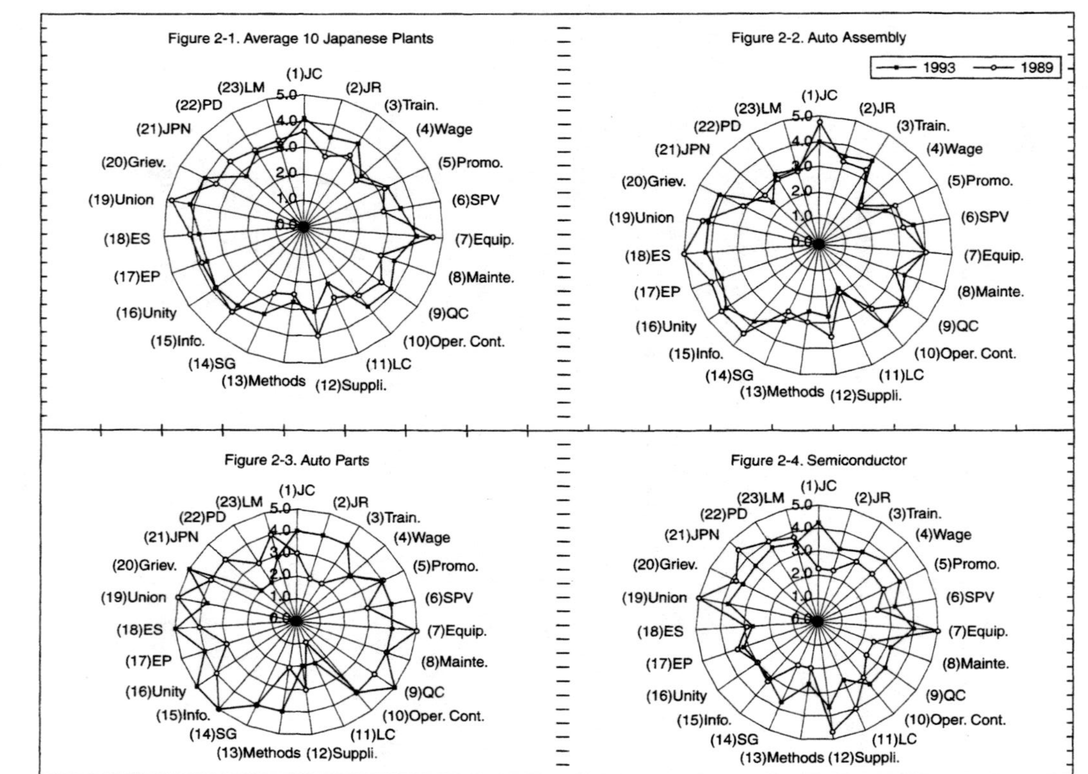

Figure 4.2 Hybrid ratios of 23 items

classification 3.6–4.1, training 3.1–3.7) are common, there are also categories such as wage (2.6–2.8) and promotion (3.2–3.3) which do not exhibit such obvious rises. Over the last few years, at the workplace on the management side the development of long-term workers, who become the core of the workplace, has been fostered. These long-term workers can respond in a fairly flexible way with respect to the posting of employees and work practices, and this is clearly shown by the development of 'application' in the categories representing job rotation (multi-functional skills), 'education training' and 'supervisor'.

One of the features of the 'supervisor' category is that it sums up all of the levels of the elements of G1. This function is broadly divided into two – work management and personnel management – and in Japan is considered as the area in which these two aspects can be maximized. However, at the time of the first survey, at many local production plants the supervisor role was close to that of an American 'first-line supervisor', responsible only for the personnel management side. Specifically, a method of division of labour involving one worker fulfilling one role was being used – the team leader and group leader were responsible for the work sphere and personnel management respectively. In this case, the group leader was either a graduate or a person with outside experience or expertise and concentrated on personnel management, leaving work practices to work-experienced team leaders or following the directives set out in a manual written by an 'industrial engineer'.

However, according to the latest survey, this method of division of labour has not disappeared as a system but, as a result of the increase in numbers of team leaders becoming group leaders through either internal promotion or a certain level of accumulated experience, it appears that conditions enabling the creation of leadership, based on an understanding of the contents of the job, have been to a certain degree provided. In response to such things as the quality and range of goods manufactured, line speed, and especially to the situation of delivery of parts at a factory, supervisors of required ability have appeared. They post team members to each line process, restrict laxness during work time and problems in the quality of goods (such as defects due to inexperience and the occurrence of breakdowns) and also adjust work standards. Also, the supervisors themselves initiate the necessary technical training for employees so that these kinds of adjustments can be made. In this way, if every team member's ability can be controlled, manpower which can be diverted to other jobs is created because, in each process, time can be economized. Several cases of this 'line balance' were discovered.

Able supervisors have thus appeared and, as a precondition for the fulfilment of this function, a certain level of 'job rotation skill' is needed at the workplace. At the time of the first survey, the training for this kind of 'job rotation skill' was at the level of having just been introduced as a programme in only a few of the factories.

'Multi-functional skill' is a basic concept involving the organization of flexible personnel in Japan's 'workplace-centred' production system. It is not as simple as technical training at a training establishment. As a process within the company (on and beyond the line) it implies gaining expertise, experiencing many different related processes and jobs, increasing knowledge and mastering a wide and varied range of skills (Koike 1988). To these ends, the concept of 'our' company spirit, is necessary. Employees need to think not only of their immediate work but also of the performance of the whole company – in what ways are they directly concerned with their own interests?

In Japanese factories, those workers who are able to master ten kinds of job within one group are promoted to group leader or team leader. Management ability aside, all at least must be able to cope with these ten jobs. In the latest survey, there were some group leaders who had been promoted through the internal promotion system. Even though on a different level from the Japanese parent factories, among these personnel there was also the appearance of those group leaders who had mastered several jobs outside the aforementioned system of a simple division of labour.

At many factories, the basic introduction of a special apprenticeship programme for industrial skills training, centring on essential maintenance workers, stood out as the most salient feature in promoting job rotation (3 Japanese automobile assembly plants, 1 semiconductor factory and 1 US factory used the actual term 'apprenticeship programme', but also a few other factories employed a substantially similar training method). The method of this programme involved adapting the application of the 'logic' and 'spirit' of Japanese-style training techniques to the systems and shape of American industrial society, thus becoming an easy-to-understand system to Americans. This is termed 'revised application' (Abo 1994a: 30). At the time of the first survey, one advanced factory had just instituted a larger scale programme and we were looking forward to investigating the results (see the explanation given later by the automobile union).

The hybrid ratio value for 'job classification', representing a departure from the system's preconditions for a flexible work organization/administration, rose from 3.6 to 4.1. Given the full set of trends within G1, however, this upswing is unsurprising. Still, as will be argued more concretely later, when different industries are examined this trend appears to be most obvious at the semiconductor factories. The limits and contents of jobs are clearly prescribed, and employees who have the ability and specific skills are assigned to the jobs. This way of organizing the division of labour to get the job done is American in construction. If authority and responsibility are divided up in this way, jobs become subdivided, job numbers rise and a tendency emerges for the system to become inflexible. In response to this kind of job demarcation, wage and promotion systems based on assessments and rewards become the order of the day.

This demarcation problem lies at the root of the division between the Japanese and American systems (Abō 1994a: Chs. 1 and 2). Therefore Japanese automobile companies from the start have been strongly against a large number of job demarcations. The hybrid ratio figures were already uniformly as high as parent factories.[5] This is shown symbolically as a rise in the operation figures of these semiconductor factories and automobile parts plants reflecting the smooth development in overall management.

In addition to examining the various large rises in the hybrid ratio for G1 categories, we must also investigate the meaning of changes in categories which exhibit smaller rises, such as wage systems. The conspicuously low value in this category arises from a particular interesting set of circumstances related to job demarcation. While somehow implementing a guarantee of institutional preconditions, the corresponding Japanese reward system based on wages and promotion was not introduced. In the case of automobile assembly, while US plants have over one hundred job classifications, Japanese plants have only two or three. With wages and promotion fixed according to the American system, the 'job-centred' system cannot be changed so there are only two or three ranks of blue-collar workers.

In short, it is impossible simply to import alien concepts into something like a reward system which is deeply connected with a society's value system and lifestyle. Even presuming that the strategy to destroy American-style job classification was appropriate, there was no switching around of system arrangements to allow the new foundations to be laid.

At factories with a long history, there are blue-collar workers who over a period of more than ten years have only experienced promotion or a pay rise once (excluding inflation adjustment). At constantly expanding new factories, first promotions to management positions have been successively provided for group and team leaders, contributing to a fairly high level of morale. However, as factory expansion has almost come full circle, it was hoped that an investigation into how long this unnatural system would continue could provide an important checkpoint for the latest survey. But again, the hybrid ratio for the wage system exhibited no significant change and stayed around the two point level, although on the management side two out of five plants were involved in a rethink on this matter and two more admitted the need for change.

Nevertheless, even if the factories had begun a rethink, as above arguments illustrate, the issue is not straightforward. Assuming that the rethink would not move away from the premise of a simple job demarcation system, in order to enhance the chance for the promotion of blue-collar workers, the only viable solution is a 'promotion on qualification rank' system. Like the Japanese system this would combine a 'person-centred' inhouse qualification system (rank classification) and a personal evaluation system, regardless of job duties. This kind of Japanese-style concept is difficult for westerners to understand. Of course, even in the

USA assessments of white-collar workers are carried out, and in unionless hi-tech companies, such as semiconductor manufacturers, processes similar to the performance evaluation system do exist. However, these evaluations are basically just attachments to a reward system corresponding to certain job duties. In the case of the UK, quite a large number of Japanese automobile and electronic plants have introduced an inhouse qualification system and a personal evaluation system, which have met with some success. This is an interesting theme requiring further investigation (Wickens 1987; Abō 1992)

G3 Parts procurement

According to the previous survey, in line with G6 (parent–subsidiary relationship) one other group, G 3 (parts procurement), exhibited a large drop in the hybrid ratio (3.1 to 2.7). This change, as seen from the host-society side, is needed, so it is a development in a desirable direction. Here, rather than focusing merely on the fact that the group average hybrid ratio has fallen, it is necessary to concentrate on the changes in the categories comprising the group. First, if we check the combined results of the first survey, the group average hybrid ratio of 3.1 is made up of the relatively low 'local content' ratio (2.8), an extremely high ratio for suppliers (4.0) and an extremely low ratio for supply methods (2.5). This average is an offset figure gained from the high ratio of suppliers calculated on the basis of the country of origin of the parts (high ratio of Japanese suppliers) and the low level of Japanese methods of supply assessed with JIT (just in time) as its criterion.

With respect to this, not only had the 'local content' hybrid ratio fallen to 2.2 (close to 80 per cent), 'suppliers' also experienced a large drop (4.0 to 3.1) and 'methods' rose from 2.5 to 2.8. In other words, while greatly lowering dependence on the country of origin (Japan), Japanese style long-term, co-operative dealing relationships were formed between local suppliers (including Japanese). This kind of development is not only a mere localization of parts suppliers; it also points to the steady formation of a stable local production system, coping with the age of 'unstable foreign exchange' and raising the quality control development (QCD) level and thus the local supply rate.

During this time, of course, the localization of Japanese supplies continued and even though many difficulties were faced localization was able to overcome them. The level of American company suppliers also marked a large increase. These companies are competing with US-based Japanese suppliers and have developed a process which requires dealings with Japanese assemblers and American companies. Further, it is clear that this is becoming an extremely important factor in the 'rebirth' of the American assembler.

G2 Production control

G2 (production control) experienced little change in general average hybrid ratio (3.5 to 3.7) compared to the above three groups, but there are some obvious opposing rises and falls in value which make the general average a mere result of their cancelling each other out. The value for 'equipment' dropped from 4.5 to 4.0, but is offset by 'maintenance' (2.9 to 3.4). These were due to rises in 'quality control' (3.4 to 3.8) and 'operation control' (3.2 to 3.7). These changes can be seen as comparatively important.

First, it is possible to assume that the fair drop in the values for 'equipment' are natural considering that the first survey's value of 4.5 indicated that almost all the imported equipment was identical to that of the parent plant. But so long as the import of Japanese style 'software' relevant to an organization and its operation is difficult, it is also not so easy to control the way that the standards of efficiency and quality of goods are ensured by introducing already-made hardware (machines and equipment).

The localization of equipment and the matching rise in the hybrid ratio of the 'maintenance' category is a change in an extremely desirable direction. This is because, as seen in the first survey, the maintenance and presentation of Japanese equipment according to American techniques, when considered as a method of introducing a Japanese system, is the worst of combinations. There has been no change in the American method of clearly classifying specialized personnel according to duty and, as ever, it remains at the level of maintenance. Still, the following developments are important.

First, the introduction of inhouse training systems through apprenticeship programmes ties the personnel to the workplace and so acquired skills are fairly 'firm specific'. In other words, they provide a continuity with respect to skills between each factory process and each level of personnel. Second, and related to this kind of continuity, as the years of experience are added, even in the semiconductor industry where hi-tech automation is common, general employees check in detail the condition of machinery within their own sphere of work, concentrating on preventative maintenance. In this way, they contribute to rises in rates of operation. Of course, considering the difference in reward systems, it is necessary to refrain from putting too much emphasis on evaluating this kind of movement.

Clearly, movements in 'quality control', as the direction of change with respect to equipment, are the same as those in maintenance. Techniques of quality control are basically American style in that they mostly depend on specialized staff or a specialized section. However, the system of assigning personnel to each process, and thus to the greatest possible extent attempting checks during the process, is different from the traditional American approach of checking the results at the end of the line. As a result of the increases seen in small group activity and employee participation activities, it appears that the commitment of general workers to quality control has been improved and co-operation with specialized staff has progressed. The effects on costs of this kind of 'general participation' are considerable. According to an American manager responsible for quality control who moved from a typical American semiconductor manufacturer, the number of quality control staff in US factories is presently about four times that found in Japanese factories.

G4 Team spirit

Making up the slight rise of 3.5 to 3.7 in the general average hybrid ratio in G4 (team spirit), the conspicuous rise in 'small group activity' (2.6 to 3.5) is especially noteworthy. As the low value in the first survey indicates, small group activity in local production plants is lagging compared to the categories of 'information' (4.0) and 'unity' (3.8) in the same group. While the latter two categories occur as one-sided activities on the management side at all kinds of meetings, in open-style cafeterias and at all office functions, small group activity is more or less independent on the employee side. It is fair to say that the extremely large difference in small group activity between overseas factories and parent factories is normal and is an element which is strongly influenced by the differences in social and cultural background.

At the time of the first survey, these were elements which had not yet been introduced and participation rates, as usual, stopped at around 20 to 30 per cent, but according to the latest survey, at a large proportion of factories, group activities were being enthusiastically carried out. Recently, in the parent factories in Japan, too, the subject has, so to speak, turned full circle. With the influence of automation, and general change, this element has been unexpectedly sluggish. Workplaces starting such a system since 1989 are large in number and there were at least five places with a volunteer participation rate of over 50 per cent at the time of the latest survey. In addition, proposal activities have always been quite widespread in the USA and, with slightly more money used than in Japan, it appears that these activities continue to be lively.

G5 Labour relations

There was no change in the general average hybrid ratio for G5 (labour relations). It is possible that the values for the categories comprising G5 were high from the start so little room remained for change. At a relatively early period in the factory's start of operations, the introduction of various groups and categories which relate to the system's core is not easy. This group at first provides the external conditions and environment surrounding the systems of groups IV and VI and thus supports the core, but during the last few years the introduction of difficult elements of the system continued, while the preceding factors supporting a high level of application, as is the case in this group, remained constant.

Within this group, only the value for the 'grievance' category showed a large rise (3.5 to 4.0) and this in itself has substantial significance. Dealing with grievances at traditional American factories is an important activity carried out by the local labour unions. Any bad conditions at the workplace are usually dealt with through the unions. If the problem cannot be resolved at the union level, the matter is taken to local arbitration bodies. This American system is quite different from the Japanese way of dealing basically with problems inside the company through the group leaders. In fact, for this survey we were unable to collect sufficient data related to this issue, but the majority of cases gave the strong impression that, to a fair extent, problems were being dealt with on the level of the experienced group leader.

ASSESSMENT ACCORDING TO INDUSTRY

The above evaluation and analysis examined the state of and changes in general application and adaptation of Japanese factories in the USA using as a base the averaged values for three industries, but important differences also can be seen between the three industries. As space is limited only the most salient features of these industries are addressed.

Automobile assembly plants

Comparing the hybrid ratios of automobile assembly plants, no great change was seen between 1989 and 1993. However, this is perhaps due to the fact that even from 1989 fairly developed levels of application and adaptation were already in place. On close examination, the elements making up these developments clearly have been advancing. The following points deserve attention.

As mentioned above in the section on general evaluation, there was the issue of introducing an apprenticeship programme. At AE factory, where a programme started at the time of the first survey, the first three-year stage of the programme had finished by 1992. However, from the 170 carefully selected participants, only 19 had achieved the aims and had been given job assignments. At the time it was hoped that together with these 19 personnel a further supplement of 20 trainees would finish the second stage at the end of 1995. But even if all the trainees graduate to provisional posts, only a handful would have been ready in time for the opening of a second factory in the spring of 1994. These results, considering the original aims, are poor. An analysis of the various technical skills necessary for maintenance at Japanese parent factories would turn up a few thousand elements. These elements were reconstituted within the programme, so from the beginning the aims were extremely ambitious. It can be said that the concept of inserting one section of the Japanese system into the American system ('amending application') is a new, fresh idea. However, the practical process is fraught with difficulty.

The issue of amending wages systems was already mentioned, in that the studies aimed to produce opportunities for wage rises and promotion based on simple job demarcation. In fact, at factory AE, the opposite is occurring. At this factory in 1989, the introduction of a prudently investigated and individually based 'personal evaluation' system was scheduled. However, according to the latest survey, this plan has not in any way been put into action. This can be taken as an indicator of how serious a problem the issue is for automobile factories in the USA.

The drop from 2.8 to 2.4 in the category of 'Jpn ratio' (ratio of Japanese personnel to local personnel) stands out among those categories which evidenced little change. Japanese auto-assembly plants are outstanding among those manufacturing industries operating in the USA with regard to the extent of transfer and scale. From the stamping process to final assembly, an entire line is provided and there is also an extra subline for times of high demand. If the import of conceptually different parent company management skills and know-how into an environment of unaccustomed Americans is attempted, it becomes necessary to dispatch a large number of Japanese personnel to the factory. This situation has over the last few years influenced the values gained in our results. Moreover, it is important not to forget that during these last few years, many factories expanded the scale of their operations and that the number of car models also increased (Table 4.1). Whenever a basic model is divided into two types, then further model changes occur. Even in Japan nearly all basic design and model changes mean an almost geometric rise in the number of local workers needed.

However, on the other hand, there is one interesting case of a factory exhibiting a kind of 'retrogression' as opposed to the tendency described above. Factory AB had an original workforce of 3,000 with less than 20 Japanese (a 0.5 per cent ratio), so naturally the hybrid ratio was 1. All important posts below the president were occupied by Americans. This means that, compared to factory AA, AB had undergone a thorough localization with respect to personnel. Still, problems arose with models and types of cars, and performance was poor. From around 1992, though, the number of Japanese personnel had been increasing gradually. Posting to management positions basically remained the same but the role of the Japanese personnel changed. From behind the scenes, so to speak, many began to function more in the role of co-ordinator, constructively leading and supporting line work through planning, improving skills and purchasing. The plants gave us quite a different impression. A vigour and nervousness could be seen in the employees' attitudes and it appeared that their 'look' had changed. Actually, this factory had been favoured with a new model and a new plant and truck line also had been added. Moreover, when this company built a factory in the UK based on its American experience, a higher proportion of Japanese employees and a Japanese president were introduced.

The 'parts procurement' group showed a clear fall in hybrid ratio, but the 'supplier' category experienced a more dramatic decrease from 3.6 to 2.8, representing a significant development in localization. In almost all plants, the relationships with suppliers were strengthened and the conditions for co-operation, quality of goods through assistance, and prompt delivery of goods were improved.

Although little change was observed, it is necessary to discuss the tendency for small drops in the values for 'labour/management relationships' (there are, however, mistakes in the evaluation standards). First, rather than the UAW becoming institutionalized, it has been, rather, floundering at large factories. At exactly the time of the 1989 survey, it became clear that at factory AB the UAW large-scale institutionalization strategy had failed after an employees' ballot. Since then, it appears that this type of basic activity has not been seen at large factories. Once or twice annually circulars are distributed, but according to one investigation, almost 90 per cent of workers are satisfied so no further action is taken. It looks as if middle-scale suppliers have been targeted instead.

At unionized factories, and clearly in relation to this, we found several cases where influence on the construction of operational and management systems was evident. For example, although one factory is said to be the most highly automated factory in the world at present, over the five years since operations began, its production quota has not exceeded 200,000 units (this is also related to sales). Of course, just because a factory is unionized does not mean that it will have this kind of problem on its hands. Even though factory AC is unionized, its 200,000 unit quota system was realized in a comparatively short time.

Automobile parts

The only automobile parts factory assessed in the latest survey was factory AJ. Therefore, there must be a certain qualification in generalizing the result of this analysis. Yet as a case study this is still effective, judging from the similar situation of the AV case, which was not part of evaluation in this chapter as we had not visited it in 1989 (see Table 4.1) and from other related information. The changes themselves are interesting but of greater importance is the way in which the changes occurred. First, the way in which the general usage hybrid ratio clearly rose from 3.6 to 3.8 is unusual (Table 4.2). Moreover, as is shown particularly clearly in Figures 4.1 and 4.2, the combined rises and falls in hybrid ratios of both groups and categories are almost all in desirable directions.

Looking at the groups in Figure 4.1, the combination of a large rise in value for 'works organization/administration' and a drastic fall in 'parent–subsidiary relationships' is typical. In addition, the values for 'team spirit' and 'industrial relations', which were originally high, rose even further. The shape of this six-cornered radar chart is a more complete directional shape than that of the aforementioned automobile assembly plants and the same pattern also can be seen for Japanese factories in Taiwan and Korea (Abō 1995b). It is fair to say that it is close to an 'ideal shape' for the current level of overseas factories of Japanese companies.

Corresponding to the remarkable fall in the ratio of Japanese personnel, the position of local managers and the competence of the local production plant is high. A high standard is required of the parts supplied to automobile assembly plants, but against the background of advances in the skills of general workers and local engineers following the accumulation of systematic training and large-scale automation, the last few years have seen the number of Japanese being controlled in relation to corresponding expansions in scale.

What makes this factory particularly stand out is the strikingly high hybrid ratio value for 'team spirit' (4.7). From the beginning this factory has been tackling seriously issues such as this and has achieved a participation rate as high as 85 per cent for a 'small group activity' (hybrid ratio 4). This could even be felt in the atmosphere surrounding the way in which employees greeted visitors.

In this way, when considering the transfer of systems, factory AJ can be said to be heading for an extremely positive hybrid situation. It seems that the results of this can also be seen in the factory's performance. Even in the face of the slow recovery of the US economy, the balance has been in the black since the start of the 1990s.

Semiconductors

As has already been indicated, the four semiconductor factories evidence the general changes in manufacturing observed in the latest survey. In the first survey, an imbalance could be seen in the application and adaptation of the semiconductor factories. However, this has changed considerably.

Although it is possible to almost ignore the change in the general average hybrid ratio (3.3 to 3.5), there was an extremely important change in the constituent groups. According to Figure 4.1, in 1989 the values for 'parent–subsidiary relationships', 'parts procurement' were high (along with labour relations) and those for 'work organization/management' and 'team spirit' were low. Particularly when considered using the four perspective evaluation, this was quite an imbalanced combination. However, in the latest survey, everything had moved in the opposite direction, the six corners approached a perfect shape and in a certain way had become a balanced pattern.

Among these kinds of changes, the most important are those large rises in hybrid ratio in the various categories of 'work organization/ management' (Figure 4.2). At every factory, the number of job classifications had been reduced and a system of promotion, not directly connected to duties and similar to the Japanese system, had been instituted. However, in new hi-tech fields like electronics, the number of job classifications is comparatively low even in American companies. A substantially different promotion system based on a personal evaluation system is employed and the Japanese semiconductor industry in the USA has learned from this (Abō 1994a: Chs 5–6).

At present, even in factories where automation concentrating on 1–4 mega pre-process and based on this fairly simplified system has progressed, the issues of quality control skills, staff maintenance, education and training (centring on job rotation) are being enthusiastically tackled. At this kind of factory, the job of the general manufacturing core workers is mainly to keep an eye on screens and metres, and occasionally in supply. Even so, because of differences in their levels of job mastery, breakdowns in machinery range widely in frequency from once every six hours, every thirty hours or once every week. At factory SF, principally because of this method, the number of employees could be reduced from 525 in 1990 to 495. Also, at factory SC, the number of maintenance personnel and core personnel for quality control was as few as one-quarter of the number employed in American companies.

However, there is a difference between factories like SC, which produce a wide range of goods including memory, ASIC (Application Specific Integrated Circuit) microprocessors and design systems, and those like SB which concentrate on 4 mega memory production. SB is also said to be the world's largest scale semiconductor factory, employing 1400 staff.

This kind of change, however, did not occur in all factories and in all fields. The more complicated and precise the automated equipment produced, the greater the tendency for the responsibility for its operation and maintenance to be passed to the machine maker. Most Japanese makers taking on this responsibility have branches in each area of the USA and also provide service to American semiconductor factories.

Related to this kind of change in the workplace, the conspicuous rise in the hybrid ratio for the 'small group activity' category of the 'team spirit' group (2.0 to 3.8) must be noted. This rise occurred because the three factories discovered in the last survey to be making an effort had all started their activities since 1989. At factory SF, from the spring of 1993, the old 'duty order method' was reviewed and made voluntary. Nevertheless, the participation rate exceeds 70 per cent.

The localization of personnel is quite advanced in this industry and is illustrated by the drop in value for the 'Japanese ratio' category (4.5 to 3.5). The old image of the semiconductor industry, with automated machinery from Japan being operated by Japanese personnel, has changed and this drop in the 'Japanese ratio' category is an important illustration of this change.

With respect to machinery and equipment, while dependence on Japan is still high, the localization of 'parts procurement' has progressed in its own way. In particular, the supply of silicon essential for the manufacture of silicon wafers has almost all been switched to Japanese suppliers in the US – a kind of 'local supply'. This has had its effect, and although assembly parts are not truly supplied locally, a drop in the 'local content' hybrid ratio became possible (4.0 to 2.8). (two factories moved most of their assembly processes to various ASEAN countries and have been re-importing manufactured finished goods from these overseas factories).

As illustrated above, changes in the semiconductor industry over the last few years have been considerable. It suggests that the temporary production as evidence of 'domestic' production induced by the semiconductor trade conflict at the end of the 1970s, has evolved into a sturdier manufacturing system. Eventually, while being 'compelled' over the last ten years, a certain kind of experience has been accumulated and, keeping an eye on different factors and costs, the know-how to import Japanese methods has to a certain degree been created. In the meantime, market trends after the Japanese bubble burst have begun to favour America. It was not easy for factories to recover their accumulated losses, but there remain prospects for them to settle in the US market.

FOUR-PERSPECTIVE EVALUATION

The above results were based on the 'hybrid ratio' analysis of the local application of Japanese systems, using the 23 categories/6 groups and considered from the parent company's perspective. Using a four-perspective evaluation method to look at the degree of transfer of the Japanese systems into local societies, these results will be reassessed. As dealt with in Table 4.3(b), the four-perspective evaluation reclassifies 21 of the hybrid ratios of the 23 categories into four perspectives – methods or results (mode) and human or material (nature of elements). This perspective is an attempt to evaluate the nature of the transfer of the systems and, for instance, technical skills.

The organizational structure of the Japanese parent factory, and such things as the movement of personnel and materials, are transferred through the 'invisible logic' and know-how of the local personnel. 'Methods' means the substantial transplantation of the techniques of the Japanese systems into the context of a local society. Opposed to this, 'results' is the transfer of parts and manufacturing equipment (materials) and Japanese overseas personnel (humans), i.e. 'ready-made' visible elements, through relations with the Japanese parent factory or related suppliers. These 'results' are the fruits of Japanese-style techniques and although there are problems concerning costs, the transfer of these techniques has an

Table 4.3(a) Four-perspective evaluation, 1989, 1993.

	Average for 10 plants		*Auto assembly*		*Auto-parts*		*Semiconductors*	
	1993	*1989*	*1993*	*1989*	*1993*	*1989*	*1993*	*1989*
Methods								
Human	3.6	3.4	3.6	3.7	4.3	3.5	3.5	3.0
Material	3.3	2.9	3.3	3.3	4.3	3.3	3.2	2.3
Results								
Human	3.0	3.5	2.7	2.9	2.5	4.0	3.5	4.2
Material	3.1	3.8	2.9	3.2	2.7	3.0	3.5	4.6
Average	3.3	3.3	3.4	3.3	3.5	3.5	3.4	3.5
Methods: results ratio %	113.1	86.3	123.2	114.8	165.4	97.1	95.7	60.2

Table 4.3(b) Perspective evaluation model

Element mode of transfer	*Human*	*Material*
Methods	*G1 (work organization and administration) -All elements: (1)~(6) *G4 (team spirit) -All elements: (14)~(16) *G5 (labour relations) -All elements: (17)~(20)	*G2 (production control) -(8) Quality control -(9) Maintenance *G3 (parts procurement) -(13) Methods
Results	*G6 (parent–subsidiary relations) -(21) JPN expatriate ratio -(23) local manager	*G2 (production control) -(7) equipment *G3 (parts procurement) -(11) local content -(12) suppliers

immediate effect on the performance of local factories. It could be said that this transfer is the quickest way of improving performance. However, if the systems/techniques are withdrawn, none of these results may remain.

Table 4.3(a) is a reconstitution of the degrees of application and degrees of adaptation of the first and latest surveys, using the four-perspective evaluation.

First, if the ratios for method/result in Table 4.3(a) are examined, according to the ten factory average a large change occurred from 86.3 per cent in 1989 to 113.1 per cent in 1993.

The reason the ratio for the first survey was well less than 100 per cent was that, concentrating on 'results', the direct transfer of equipment, parts, and Japanese personnel had an immediate effect on local factory efficiency and the standards and quality of goods. However, the ratio exceeding 100 per cent in the latest survey indicates that the import of work organization systems and equipment, methods of dealing with parts and goods – in other words, elements connected with the administration and management of personnel and materials – came to predominate.

The results of the four-perspective evaluation do not show the make-up of performance as seen at once from the parent company side. Looking at this more concretely and in the long term, it is thought that whether or not the systems and techniques of the parent company will be absorbed and take root in the organization of the local factory will become a valuable benchmark. Therefore, just because 'methods' exceed 'results' according to the latest survey, this does not necessarily mean that a favourable turn in the productivity and profitability of local factories is secured. However, in general it could be said that the change towards a method-centred transfer is a landmark for Japanese overseas factories. This has already been made quite clear through the evaluation of the 6 groups/23 categories. Now using Figure 4.3, the contents and nature of these changes will be explained.

Figure 4.3 is a representation of the evaluation, on horizontal and vertical axes, of the Japanese overseas factories with regard to combined averages for personnel and materials. First, the feature which stands out the most is the lengthening of the vertical axis against the shortening of the horizontal, a development also reflected in the aforementioned changes in ratios. 'Method/human' and 'method/material' have both improved while at the same time 'results' have decreased. In short, in the latest survey, 'method' improved on all counts and results were reduced. It can clearly be seen that at local factories as a whole, there has been a movement in the direction of the Japanese systems taking root. This does not just relate to the substance of transfer, it also contributes to a reduction in costs at this time of a strong yen.

If we look at the different industries, in the case of automobile assembly plants, changes in 'method-results' ratio figure have not been great. The nature of progress in this industry, which was illustrated earlier, is also shown here. Changes in the automobile parts plant were striking. The 'method-results' ratio increased steeply from 97.1 per cent to 165.4 per cent. In Figure 4.3, the 'method/human' and 'method/material' axes lengthened, the 'result/human' and 'result/material' axes shortened. These changes are neatly balanced and could be said to exhibit an 'ideal model'. If this kind of shape pattern continues, the transfer of systems and techniques will probably advance steadily. In the semiconductor industry, too, the 'method-results' ratio rose from 60.2 per cent to 95.7 per cent, but only in this industry did the latest survey turn up a value of less than 100 per cent. As in Figure 4.3, the horizontal axis at the time of the first survey was extremely long and the shape was resultingly poor. However, according to the shape of the 1993 survey results, the lengths of both axes are almost balanced and the degree of improvement significant.

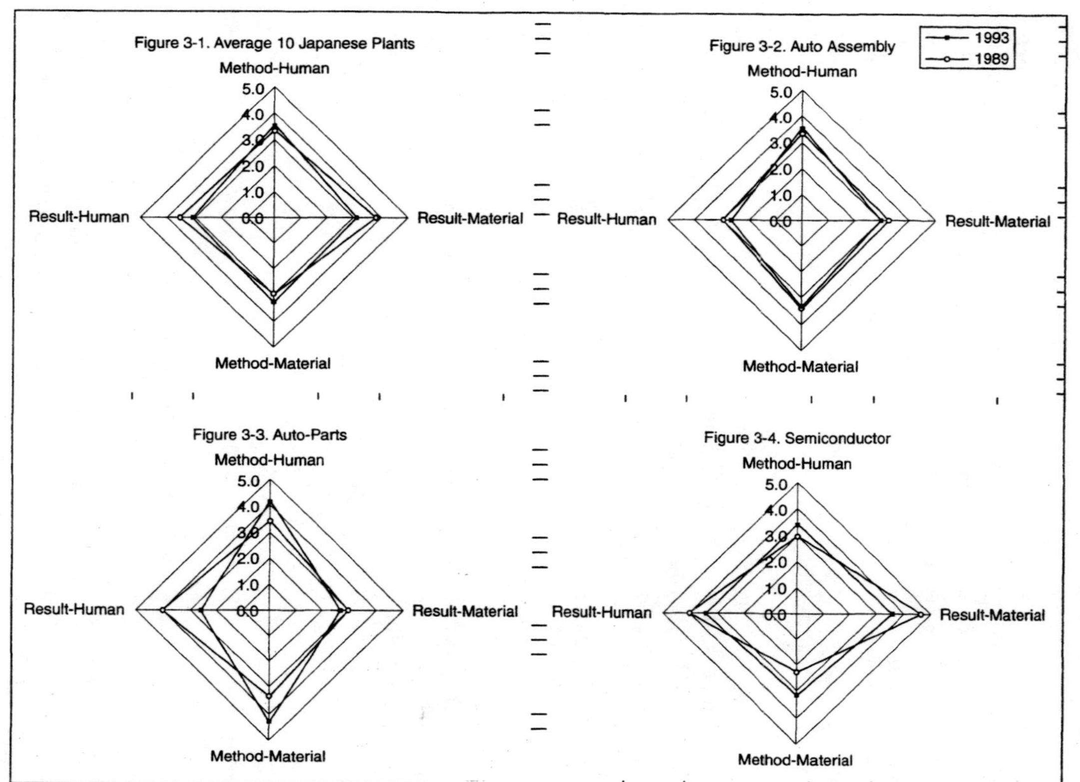

Figure 4.3 Four-perspective evaluation

CONCLUSION

The most important result of this analysis/evaluation is that it allowed us to confirm the fairly large changes in Japanese local production taking place in the few years since 1989. These changes involved the 'result' preference approach which imports personnel and equipment already completed in Japanese parent companies being gradually replaced by an approach by which the 'logic' of the Japanese system takes root accommodating local elements. This is perhaps a sign that local factories have entered a new stage of development.

Local supervisors and management have been improved and in consequence this has reduced the number of Japanese personnel and broadened the sphere of local purchase of equipment and materials. It has also become clear that there is a movement towards managing and educating the workforce so that the organization of people and materials becomes more flexible. This could be called a movement towards an 'ideal shape' for a certain type of local production factory and, according to our recent survey, is similar to factories in NIEs such as Taiwan and Korea (Boyer and Drache 1996; Abō 1995a).

However, the above only emphasizes the importance of the 'direction' of the changes. The 3.5 value for the general average hybrid ratio itself indicates among other things a fair distance from Japan. Also, if we look at the difference in ratios of Japanese personnel (2.8) against that of Korea/Taiwan (1.5), there seems to be a distance from Taiwan/Korea, and it is also certain that a convergence will not happen in these circumstances. But it can be easily confirmed that the changing direction, which is supported by provisional results, coincides with the 'hybrid' situation which exists in the major regions of the world including ASEAN and Europe (Abō 1995a, b).

In any case, local production plants are firmly sinking roots into American industrial society, and while continuing at a slow pace, helped along by the recovery of the American economy and the high yen, steady increases and production and expansion are occurring. Rather, for the time being, the most crucial problem concerns the production adjustment with Japanese parent companies which have been overproducing. Without such adjustment problems, of course, further increases in production would be possible.

An appraisal of performance was not fully carried out in this survey. However, all of the three industries investigated were successful in manufacturing systems and operations, and during recent years many plants have had accounts in the black on a year-to-year basis.

NOTES

1 The surveys began with the USA because, as its social and cultural environments differ significantly from those of Japan, it was assumed that the introduction of the system into a country such as this would prove quite difficult and therefore serve as an important test case.

2 As for the related issues of the characteristic features of Japanese management and production systems and problems with their local adaptations, see Dore (1973), Yoshino (1976), Ozawa (1979), Trevor (1983), which are the earlier milestones, and also Abō's publications, Aoki (1988), Cole and Deskins (1988), Koike (1988), Oliver and Wilkinson (1988), Kenney and Florida (1993) Nishiguchi (1994) and Fujimoto and Tidd (1994).

3 See Oliver and Wilkinson (1988), one of the most representative of the 'Japanization' approach. For a similar but more insightful review on the above issue, see Bonazzi (1995, 1996).

4 The author of this chapter and other group members formed the 'Japanese Multinational Enterprise Study Group' (JMNESG) during the 1980s and since then have been conducting investigations to clarify the state and nature of the international transfer of the Japanese system. The JMNESG members in 1993 (Abō Tetsuo and Yoshida Toshiaki, and Hirano Yoko from the Japan Centre for International Finance) prepared detailed company records in which the data of each local production factory to be investigated were recorded. Checking these data against the criteria for application and adaptation (Abō 1994a: Table 4.2), and with respect to the 23 categories, a grading took place. Further, for every industry the grades were averaged and a general table was completed (Table 4.2). As for the main English publications related to the above research, see Abo's publications in the References.

5 The reason that the figures fell in the latest survey was because of a mistake by the assessor.

REFERENCES

Abō, T. (1990) 'Local production of Japanese automobile and electronics firms in the United States', *Research Report*, no. 23, Institute of Social Science, University of Tokyo.

Abō, T. (1992) 'Overseas production activities of Nissan Motor Co.', in S.J. Park (ed.) *Managerial Efficiency and Co-operation*, Frankfurt/New York: Campus Vertagand Westriew.

Abō, T. (ed.) (1994a) *Hybrid Factory: The Japanese Production System in the United States*, New York: Oxford University Press.

Abō, T. (1994b) 'Amerika ni okeru nihonteki keiei seisan sisutemu iten no dōkō' (Recent trends of the Japanese hybrid factories in the US), in *Taibei Tōshi no Saihyōka*, Tokyo: Japan Centre for International Finance.

Abō, T. (1995a) 'Technology transfer of Japanese corporation: "application-adaptation" of Japanese production system in North America, NIEs, ASEAN and Europe', in M. Yunshi and H. Mannari (eds) *Comparative Studies between Chinese and Japanese Management*, Zhongshan University.

Abō, T. (1995b) 'A comparison of Japanese "hybrid" factories in the US, Europe and Asia', *Management International Review*, Gabler Verlag, vol. 35, 1995/1: 79–93.

Aoki, M. (1988) *Information, Incentives, and Bargaining in the Japanese Economy*, Cambridge: Cambridge University Press.

Bonazzi, G. (1995) 'Discovering the Japanese model', in S. Bacharach and P. Gagliardi (eds) *Research in the Sociology of Organization*, Greenwich, Conn.: JAI Press.

Bonazzi, G. (1996) 'New development in the debate on the Japanese model', in S. Bacharach and P. Gagliardi (eds) *Research in the Sociology of Organization*, Greenwich. Conn.: JAI Press.

Boyer, R. and Drache, D. (eds) (1996) *States Against Markets*, London/New York: Routledge.
Cole, R.E. and Deskins, D.R. Jr. (1988) 'Racial factors in site location and employment patterns of Japanese auto firms in America', *California Management Review*, Fall: 9–22.
Dore, R.P. (1973) *British Factory–Japanese Factory*, London: George Allen & Unwin.
Fujimoto, T. and Tidd, J. (1994) 'The UK and Japanese automobile industry: adoption and adaptation of Fordism', Actes du GERPISA, 11, *Histoire Et Hybridation Du Fordisme*, November: 69–108.
Kenney, M. and Florida, R. (1993) *Beyond Mass Production System*, New York: Oxford University Press.
Koike, K. (1988) *Understanding Industrial Relations in Modern Japan*, London: Macmillan.
Nishiguchi, T. (1994) *Strategic Industrial Sourcing: The Japanese Advantage*, New York: Oxford University Press.
Oliver, N. and Wilkinson, B. (1988) *The Japanization of British Industry*, Oxford: Blackwell Publishers.
Ozawa, T. (1979) *Multinationalism, Japanese Style*, Princeton: Princeton University Press.
Trevor, M. (1983), *Japan's Reluctant Multinationals*, London: Frances Pinter.
Wickens, P. (1987), *The Road to Nissan: Flexibility, Quality, Teamwork*, London: Macmillan.
Yoshino, M. Y. (1976), *Japan's Multinational Enterprises*, Cambridge, Mass.: Harvard University Press.

Part II
Restructuring in management

5 Globalisation's impact upon the subcontracting system

Ikeda Masayoshi

The impact of the strong yen, which in 1995 broke through the 100 yen to the dollar barrier, in conjunction with the protracted economic recession, has deprived Japan's automobile industry of its international competitiveness, and confronted it with problems that are without precedent.

In May 1994, nine car manufacturers – excluding Toyota and Isuzu – disclosed their accounts for March of that year. All had experienced falling revenues due to the declining value of exports as a result of the yen's strength, and because of the decline of domestic sales (*Nikkei Sangyō* 1994: 8 June). In particular, Nissan had suffered a deficit of some 47.3 billion yen, its financial situation worsening considerably in comparison to the same period in 1993. Mazda's sales had also fallen by 19 per cent over the previous year, which translates to a fall of 55.1 billion yen on its operating account.

In order to extricate themselves from this desperate situation, all these companies have undertaken thorough restructuring (Ikeda 1993c). The clarion calls have been efficiency and effectiveness. Product development has been restructured, exports have been scaled down and global strategies accelerated, with growing emphasis on overseas production. What is more, co-operation has increased among auto-makers in a strategic programme of rationalisation covering the whole industry.

Inevitably, this ongoing restructuring by large manufacturers has set in motion a ripple effect within the *keiretsu* system, with component makers and successive layers of subcontractors all being involved. It is in effect a wholesale programme of reorganisation and consolidation initiated from the top.

During the period of rising growth in the automobile industry, the reorganisation of subcontracting went ahead slowly. Now that the market for cars has reached maturity, with little prospect for further growth, the process of rationalising subcontracting companies – both those within the *keiretsu* and those outside – is moving ahead far more ruthlessly. Let us consider some of the specific measures now being adopted in order to reorganise the subcontracting system in the context of ongoing globalisation.

PRICE CUTTING BY AUTO-MANUFACTURERS

In October 1994 Nissan unveiled a 'new pricing system'. By 1996 it plans to be selling new cars at prices 10 to 20 per cent lower than current models. From 1997 the pricing of new cars will be reduced by another 30 per cent (*Nikkei Sangyō* 1994: 6 October). Nissan's commitment to producing cheaper cars can be seen as a last-resort pricing strategy to turn around depressed sales. In August 1994 the retail price of the modified 'Cefiro' was on average 5 per cent lower than that of previous models. This reduction effectively boosted sales, and with orders for 26,000 vehicles by October, the 'Cefiro' has been a great success. At the end of September the same year, the 'Laurel', which had undergone many minor changes in design, such as fitting air bags as standard and making improvements to the exterior for a more luxurious finish, was nevertheless sold at an average 24,000 yen cheaper than the previous model. This, too, was successful and resulted in an increase in orders exceeding all expectations.

Here we see at work the effort to make substantial reductions in the price of new vehicles. Co-operation with part suppliers made it possible for Nissan to scale down the number of models, reduce the number of components (many of which have been standardised) and, through attention to Value Analysis (VA), Value Engineering (VE) and such like, price cuts in the range of 1 to 1.5 per cent have been achieved. In 1994 Nissan raised by 0.5 per cent the target for reduction, aiming at a 2 per cent or 40 billion yen reduction in costs per year. The cost reduction campaign which Nissan is promoting with the companies in its 'Part Co-operation Group' (*Nishōkai*) has been termed officially Parts Price Improvement Action (PIA).

Since the cost reduction programme launched in autumn 1994 aimed at a fundamental rationalisation of costs amounting to a more than 30 per cent reduction in the price of current models, a vastly more effective system than previously existed was called for. To this end Nissan put together the Vehicle Innovation Programme (VIP) which embraces twelve principal component manufacturers and aims at achieving deep cuts in prices. These companies, which are organised into various groups, such as air-conditioner manufacturers, dashboard manufacturers, and so on, have adopted an organised approach to tackling the problems of cutting costs through the standardisation of models and components, and have created conditions favourable for mass production. As yet only twelve component makers are involved in the VIP at Nissan, but already they are being asked to reduce costs by 30 per cent over the next three years.

This demand for drastic cuts of 30 per cent is not confined to Nissan: the same approach to developing new vehicles also has been adopted by Honda, only whereas in Honda's case the demand is for a 30 per cent reduction in costs, Nissan has set an upper target of 40 per cent for its own cost reductions. In comparison with Toyota and Nissan, moreover, far fewer component manufacturers make up Honda's *keiretsu*. To compensate for this, Honda is pressing these companies to set up operations overseas. By establishing production sites in South East Asia or China, for example, where labour costs are lower, substantial cost savings can be achieved by exporting back to Japan.

In comparison with Honda, Nissan has made a more concerted effort to cut costs. The roots of this programme are in the 1990s. As early as 1993, in what also was called the VIP, Mazda sent eight-man teams of management specialists to twenty-two of their component manufacturers that were either making a loss or were otherwise in need of special support. These teams promoted improvements in the workplace and simplification of ancillary functions (*Nikkei Sangyō* 1994: 4 April). Of these twenty-two companies some seventeen were operating at a deficit, but within a year, as a result of their visit, ten companies looked set to go back into profit in March 1993.

Mazda judged these results to be impressive. In 1994 it therefore extended the programme to include more companies and planned to target sixty of its principal suppliers in 1993. With the co-operation of component manufacturers, the VIP programme escalated VA activity. At the same time, because of the management downturn among component manufacturers, administrative reforms were also implemented. In 1993 Mazda's rationalisation brought total savings of 80 billion yen, and of this some 2.8 billion yen was accounted for by VA. Rationalisation of parts procurement was expected to bring a further saving of 3 billion yen in 1994.

This outline of Mazda's VIP programme shows that ultimately, Mazda too is engaged in extending managerial support to its component manufacturers. In this respect, Nissan's VIP work is similar, inasmuch as the key to its success is the firm guidance provided by the company's advisory teams.

Toyota has also responded to the fierce competition launched by other Japanese auto-makers with its new strategic low-cost model known as the 'World Car' (*Nihon Keizai Shinbun* 1994: 25 October). This has involved a fundamental reappraisal of parts procurement and design concepts, and with new investment in production lines, production costs have been reduced by 30 per cent compared with existing models (Sei 1995). The launch on domestic and foreign markets is planned for 1998. The new car is the same size as the 'Corolla', Toyota's leading model, and has the same displacement. But whereas the Corolla retails in Japan at between around 900,000 yen and 1,000,000 yen, the 'world car' will rival the kind of low-cost vehicle exemplified by the American Chrysler 'Neon'. Even if the yen reaches an exchange rate of 80 yen to the dollar, the new model is still claimed to be able to maintain international competitiveness, although this car is manufactured in Japan. Toyota is aiming at maintaining price competitiveness in export markets, in particular, as a strategic vehicle for the Asian market.

In the lead-up to the production of this new car Toyota is calling on 113 component manufacturers to realise a 15 per cent reduction in costs by 1997. In the production of internationally competitive small vehicles, however, limits exist as to how far present techniques can be improved. Hence a re-examination of design concepts from first principles has been undertaken. In particular, new production methods are under investigation whereby various components are combined to form Toyota-dedicated units. Through the promotion of 'unitisation', cost reductions may reach as much as 30 per cent over existing practices involving the assembly of around 20,000 components. On production lines, savings will not be made by improving existing equipment; rather, the objective is to replace this with simplified and more efficient lines based on new concepts.

Nissan, Honda and Toyota, then, are all grappling with cost cutting. As this translates into stepping up pressure on their component manufacturers, all the signs are that, from here on, the movement to achieve 30 per cent cost savings will spread to embrace the whole industry. The signs are that component manufacturers in the automobile industry will stand or fall according to their ability to clear the 30 per cent cost reduction hurdle.

COST CUTTING AND RATIONALISATION BY FIRST-TIER COMPONENT MANUFACTURERS

The pursuit of drastic price cutting for new vehicles by all car manufacturers between 1993 and 1994 has had a dramatic impact on component manufacturers, forcing them to establish their own targets for cost cutting and to adopt specific practices to achieve these targets. Table 5.1 illustrates the cost-reduction targets and practices of eight selected companies.

Clearly, starting in the financial year 1993–4, first-tier component manufacturers adopted a policy seeking an annual cost reduction of between 5 and 10 per cent. The four pillars of this cost-cutting campaign are:

- cost cutting through rationalisation of production practices;
- reduction in ancillary staff;
- a shift to production overseas;
- a review of purchasing strategies.

The efforts of selected companies and the progress made in each of these four areas is examined below.

Cost cutting and rationalisation of the production site

With the onset of economic recession, parts manufacturers for some time have been promoting broad cost reductions in response to the demands of the car manufacturers which they supply. However, with the dollar at less than 100 yen, the automobile industry is now facing a critical situation, forcing an unprecedentedly high cost-reduction target in the order of 30 per cent. The circumstances are such that nothing but a single-minded pursuit

Table 5.1 Cost-cutting targets and measures for first-tier component makers

Company name	*Cost-reduction targets*	*Cost reduction/rationalisation*
Company M (carburettor maker)	1994: 10% cost reduction	(1) Automatisation of design and production: review of functions at 3 plants (2) Reduction in ancillary staff: 30% reduction, including direct secondment to other sections (3) Shift of production overseas: use of 'M Thailand' as an export base to reduce costs
Industrial Plant I (piston maker)	1994–7: 10% cost reduction every year	(1) Review of purchasing: 10% reduction per year (2) Reduction of ancillary staff: 20% reductions compared to 1993 (3) Shift of production overseas: expansion of plants in Indonesia and Thailand; setting up of joint ventures in China
Factory O (door parts producer)	1993–5: 15% cost reduction	(1) Reduction of ancillary costs: rotation of 910 staff to other departments (2) Reduction in product costs: suggestions received from factories (3) Reductions in material purchases: requests to 90 companies participating in co-operative groups, and to other subcontractors, to cut costs
Industrial Plant N (brake system producer)		(1) Introduction of new assembly lines: sixfold increase in productivity (2) Shift of production overseas: expansion of factories in Indonesia and Thailand; parts factories in China (3) Reduction in scale of satellite factory system in Japan
Company Z (producer of jet devices for diesel engines)	1994–6: 15% cost reduction	(1) Reductions through VA, VE, etc. (2) Reductions of ancillary staff: 20% cut in white-collar employees (3) Cost cutting promoted among co-operating employees (4) Shift of production overseas: tenfold increase in imports in 1993 (16 billion yen)

(continued)

Table 5.1 (continued)

Company name	*Cost reduction targets*	*Cost reduction/rationalisation*
Company U (producer of electronic control parts)	30% reduction in costs over 5–7 years	(1) Decreased assembly lines by one-third, leading to increases in productivity; standardisation of components (2) Cuts in the workforce: reducing the total workforce by 20% over 5 years (3) Review of purchasing: switch from outside suppliers to inhouse component manufacture
Factory H (producer of engine parts and electrical components)	1993–6: substantial increases in productivity through the introduction of just-in-time methods	(1) Enhanced factory productivity by introducing just-in-time systems (2) Staff reductions (3) Promotion of just-in-time among co-operating companies. Just-in-time guidance to these companies
Company T (seat maker)		(1) Reductions in production costs (2) Staff reductions: cuts particularly in the number of foreign workers; workforce cut by 0.6% through suspending contracts mid-term, natural wastage, etc. (3) Shift to production overseas: substantial expansion of production abroad

Sources: Survey by the author and information collected from newspapers

of cost cutting can hope to achieve these targets. Along with the expansion of sales during the heady days of the bubble economy, manufacturers diversified their product ranges and introduced a wide variety of options to their vehicles in the name of consumer demand. Around this time a seat manufacturing company, company T, was producing 30 to 40 different kinds of seats, with up to 200 seat variations for any one car. Since each seat requires in the region of 900 parts altogether the company had to make use of about 20,000 components (*Nikkei Business* 1993: 28 June).

This proliferation of components, along with their increasing complexity, hindered effective large-scale production and resulted in escalating costs. Under the direction of company T's president a full-scale appraisal of its stocks and component range was conducted. This was a cue for the efforts made to control components diversity through 'parts standardisation'.

The result was the standardisation of more than 30 per cent of components making up the frame, 53 per cent of the bolts and 37 per cent of the parts contained in the sliding mechanism. Thus in the period between

March 1987 and March 1990, when recorded profits reached a peak, company T increased profit margins by more than 1 per cent, from 1.46 per cent to 2.71 per cent. Without a root-and-branch review of equipment and the production process, however, this practice of standardising similar components will inevitably run up against limits. This is because 70 per cent of production costs are entailed at the design stage. Even if improvements move ahead through standardising the production of parts, if these have passed through the design stage already, the result can be no more than superficial.

Realising that the standardisation of components was yielding diminishing returns and, in the face of the deepening recession, in 1992 company T was forced to redouble its efforts in cost cutting and entered on the second stage of its programme. Since that time it has gone right back to the source of components. Recognising that they could not go so far as reorganising the whole earning structure, the company called for an airing of complaints and ideas for improvements from staff at eight factories across the country. In the end, some 1,600 suggestions for improving production were forthcoming.

All aspects of product development were thoroughly investigated. In March 1993 the company launched a new technology centre at Akijima, bringing together some 230 members of the Research and Development unit that had been carrying out work at Aoume. Although company T is part of the Nissan *keiretsu*, it supplied seats to eight car manufacturers, including companies not in the group, such as Toyota and Honda. Of all the interior fittings, the design of seats is particularly important, and this has made a vertical relationship with suppliers unavoidable. In turn, this has complicated development in the company and hindered full rationalisation.

Along with research and development, co-operation with other departments has also been stepped up. In the past, only the planning and sales department followed up customer orders. Now, however, staff from production control are also involved. Indeed, from the moment customer requirements are known research product feasibility is undertaken. They assess orders in terms of ease of production and against criteria contained in the 'production manual' put together by the technical planning office.

In addition, the 'primary processing control department', a special unit with responsibility from the planning to production stage, runs on-site checks, and cost cutting is being promoted even further through a support system which tackles problems with components. It is clear from the efforts of company T to standardise parts that the most effective companies in reducing costs are not those who passively design and produce parts exactly as requested. Companies must be more forthcoming with suggestions, positively putting forward ideas to customers for low-cost, high-performance components right from the development stage. Parts manufacturers unable to do this will not survive in what is becoming an intensely competitive market.

The movement towards rationalised production lines has also attracted attention as a way of pursuing cost reductions in plants. Company C is an influential component manufacturer within the Nissan *keiretsu* and produces exhaust systems and pneumatic products like air-conditioners and compressors. Since 1994 it has been carrying out a three-year plan to rationalise the lines at all stages of production, matching the pace of cost reduction among car manufacturers. At company C this is known as 'line correction' (*Nihon Kōgyō* 1994: 4 April). The review of the production process aims to cut down the amount of work in progress. Until now, production lines have been arranged around vehicle models, and compared with the final assembly line, preceding lines have involved too many production processes. This has brought about an accumulation of work-in-progress inventory.

The current rationalisation of manufacturing processes enabled the company to integrate lines which were originally divided into processes and models on the production line. By scaling down inventory, striking cost reductions of 15 per cent have thereby been achieved. The Gunma factory, for instance, has reduced around 180 production lines by half. The number of lines producing mufflers has been cut by one-third, from 68 to 47. Air conditioning lines have been scaled down from 19 to 15.

Due to this kind of integration, multiple production processes have now been amalgamated. What is more, significant savings have been achieved in the fork lifts and transporter vehicles used for conveyance between lines. This has also allowed a large reduction in the staff involved in conveyance from seventy to forty five. The build-up of work in progress is checked by 'line correction', but also achieved by operating the equipment at higher levels because production with standardised components means increased output for each line.

As a result of automation, we can find large savings in production through introducing 'just-in-time' (JIT) methods with 'U'-shaped production lines as well as cost cutting through more orthodox improvements. The example of a braking system manufacturer, company N, can be cited. The company's third factory at Tōbu-chō in Nagoya produces components for a four-wheel braking system. Through the introduction of a new production line at this factory, worker productivity shot up sixfold (*Nikkei Sangyō* 1994: 4 April). The new set-up allows a low-cost, flexible response to alterations in components resulting from car model changes. Machinery is combined in such a way that standard parts are manufactured by specialist equipment, with parts requiring change being handled through the 'Flexible Manufacturing System' (FMS). Whereas it formerly took six workers to produce 20,000 pieces a month, with this new production line two operatives can manage 40,000 pieces, representing a sixfold increase in productivity per worker.

Three to four years ago company N completely switched to this new style production line at its main plant, achieving substantial productivity growth as a result. In the wake of this success, the vehicle project department of H plant introduced U-shaped production lines. Under the guidance of just-in-time consultants this department switched to U-shaped production lines in the sections producing starters and alternators. Between 1992 and 1994 these sections aimed to improve productivity by 160 per cent and 120 per cent respectively. They also set staff reductions target of 40 per cent and 30 per cent.

Reduction in ancillary staff

The auto-makers that boosted productive capacity in the period of the bubble economy were urged to make serious reductions in production. Component makers that were obliged to introduce new equipment and expand employment in response to the demands of car manufacturers were also in the same depressed situation.

With the principal aim of reducing costs all component makers have now set their sights on realising a slimdown in sections of the company. Company Z, an important producer of jet equipment for diesel engines as well as air conditioners, is carrying out a complete restructuring because of the serious deficits experienced by Nissan, Isuzu and Mazda, which together account for more than 60 per cent of its sales. As part of its rationalisation of support sections, from 1994 it undertook reform among its white-collar workers (Ikeda 1993c), as described below.

Of the company's 2,600 white-collar employees, 300 have been transferred to new duties, dealing with domestic air conditioners or navigation systems, for example, or seconded to subsidiary or related firms, which have burgeoned with the break-up of companies; natural wastage has taken care of another 200 employees. As a result of these measures ancillary workers have been reduced by 20 per cent. In addition, as part of the review of existing work practices, eight project teams have been organised around department and section chiefs, and they are working to revamp all areas, including purchasing, sales and development.

Company U, an important manufacturer of parts for Nissan, has made the paring down of core staff central to the restructuring programme now underway (*Nihon Kōgyō* 1994: 9 December). Although 7,600 employees are currently employed by the company, in the five-year period from 1993 the plan is to reduce substantially staffing by 1,600, leaving a workforce of 6,000. These targets for rationalising the workforce will be achieved through natural wastage and limiting new recruitment. The company's annual wastage is around 300. From 1994 recruitment of new graduates was restricted to 56 a year. An increasing number of employees is also being seconded to related companies. Finally, apart from one section of part-timers, more than 1,000 extra workers who were used at peak times have already been laid off.

Company M, a carburettor manufacturer, has increased its cost-cutting targets from the 10 per cent set in 1994 to 15 per cent. One of the three objectives in this cost-cutting programme is a 30 per cent reduction in ancillary workers (*Nikkei Sangyō* 1994: 8 June), which will be achieved partly by the direct secondment of workers to departments. By 1995 the productivity of its ancillary workers should have been raised by 30 per cent. In order to reduce labour costs the same company has fixed recruitment for 1995 at about half the number of technicians appointed in 1994. Alongside this scaling down of support sections, company M also has plans to restructure eight related companies in Shizuoka and Kanagawa prefectures. These companies, which produce components for carburettors and such devices, will be merged into two or three companies by 1996 (*Nihon Keizai Shinbun* 1994: 27 April). Since it judged the overlap of production with the group's principal affiliated companies to be inefficient, the company's manufacturing base is being shifted overseas. In essence, this is in response to the long-term decline in demand for cars. With subsidiary companies being reorganised in this way, the problem of reducing the 800-strong workforce in related firms seems to have become even more acute.

In this way, component makers have considered various measures to rationalise the company's ancillary workers. Clearly, even if rationalisation of the ancillary sector does go ahead, it may involve restricted recruitment, direct secondment to related companies or other departments, but not voluntary redundancies or lay-offs. It cannot be concluded, however, that no possibility exists for car manufacturers increasingly to press demands for cost reduction by imposing such severe measures on parts manufacturers.

Shifting production abroad

As the yen approaches an exchange rate of around 90 yen to the dollar, it has become more evident that Japan's electronics and car manufacturing companies will shift production abroad and that the consequence will be a 'hollowing out' of the Japanese economy. Although car component production has shifted overseas, these producers are not equally developed in terms of the scale of their foreign operations or the level of technology that they employ. Let us examine the situation facing each component manufacturer.

Among the component manufacturers operating in South East Asia, company M, I Industries, J Industries and J Electric recently have been switching part of their production to their overseas operations because of the high yen, with the aim of exporting back to Japan. This move of production overseas has accelerated the hollowing out of industry in the area around the component manufacturers and has had a direct impact on some small to medium-sized subcontractors and satellite plants in rural areas.

Company M carries out aluminium stamping and hole-punching processes for carburettors. It has a production centre in Thailand (M Thailand) which produces carburettors for two-wheel and four-wheel drive vehicles. M is an important trading partner for Suzuki and Yamaha. The sudden rise in the value of the yen and car manufacturers' insistence upon dramatic cost reductions have precipitated company M's plan to export carburettors made in Thailand to Japan (*Nihon Keizai Shinbun* 1994: 9 August).

In 1993, the year after the company was set up, M Thailand produced 780,000 carburettors, an increase of 56 per cent over the previous year. In 1994 the plan was to increase production by a further 70 per cent to 1,300,000 units. The export total for 1993 was around 100,000 carburettors, of which about 10,000 went to Europe and around 90,000 went to Japan. In 1994, exports to Europe were expected to increase by around 20,000 and exports to Japan by more than 200,000. At the same time 300,000 units were expected to be sent to China.

In 1994 company M established companies in Shanghai and Chengdu as well as a joint venture business to manage the production and sales of carburettors in China (*Nihon Keizai Shinbun* 1994: 27 April). The companies will begin full operation in 1996 and between them plan to produce a total of 3,500,000 carburettors for use in two-wheel drive vehicles by the year 2000. M Thailand will also supply the Chinese joint venture with sets of carburettor parts to enable it to start production.

At the same time, the Chinese operation will take on some of the functions of three factories located in Japan. Henceforth, the carburettors for two-wheel drive vehicles hitherto produced at the Kikukawa plants will be manufactured in China. Production in Japan will be concentrated at the Sagara factory, while the plant at Odawara will become a technical centre.

I Industrial, a piston maker which carries out the same aluminium cutting as company M, is shifting production overseas, principally to South East Asia. Federal I Production, based in Indonesia, will increase the present production capacity of 400,000 to 500,000 pistons to 1,000,000 units in 1994 (*Nikkei Sangyō* 1994: 21 January). With this increase in productive capacity the prospect of Federal I Production being able to clear accumulated debts of 1.7 billion rupias (around 80 million yen) appears possible. Elsewhere in the company, Thai I Pistons is planning to expand its annual production of 1,200,000 by 20 per cent. Up until now the company has supplied other Japanese factories located in the country, but from 1995 aims to start exporting to Japan. I Industrial also plans to set up a joint venture in China in the autumn and in future it is assumed this will produce diesel engine pistons for export to Japan.

Company N is a component manufacturer that produces brake systems for Honda. The company's exports, which comprise supplies of brake components for subsidiary companies in the USA, Britain, Thailand and Indonesia, now amount to some 6 billion yen. Because of the build-up of local orders, however, there are plans to limit this to 3 billion over the next four to six years (*Nihon Keizai Shinbun* 1994: 9 August).

Even taking all the various costs into account, the import of components has become increasingly attractive. There are plans to increase the value of imports from the current 100 million yen to 300 million yen by the year 2000. So far, the company's overseas subsidiaries have been working flat out to meet local demand, and exports to Japan have been impossible. The company's plants in the USA, Thailand and Indonesia are each undergoing expansion, however, and when this is completed the new productive potential will be exploited fully to produce goods destined for Japan. For example, from March 1994 the two-wheel drive brake components factory in Indonesia expanded production and a new aluminium casting plant was set up. Although this factory had only just started its machining and assembly processes, an expected expansion of the market prompted a change of plan and moves towards equipping an integrated component system. The investment in capital equipment needed by this factory was limited to 50 million yen since it received surplus equipment from the company's second and fourth factories in Ueda and Jōetsu, Niigata.

During the 1960s, company N located strategically about ten companies as satellite factories in the rural towns around the main plant. The current developments of a manufacturing base in Indonesia, Thailand and China can be seen as gradually supplanting this former strategy. The movement of surplus equipment from Japan to the expanding factory in Indonesia is occurring at the same level as the previous movement to the rural satellite factories. What is occurring now is not simply a transfer of surplus equipment, however, but a shift of the entire manufacturing base, which implies a shift of labour power. For the factories around Ueda and Jōetsu this has meant a rapid contraction, a process confirmed by their gradual integration with the main plant, which has itself been modernised.

Car manufacturers will probably continue to press component makers to make dramatic reductions in costs. If this does occur, a proportion of work will be relocated; that is, away from the satellite factories of parts specialists scattered through all rural areas and away from the small to medium-sized subcontractors, towards South East Asian countries and China. This relocation began one or two years ago and as yet is only occurring on a negligible scale. But the pace of expansion observable in Indonesia or Thailand, for example, suggests that the process can be expected to accelerate. In particular, with the development of production in China, the relocation of manufacturing bases may outstrip all expectations.

Reviewing purchasing costs

The review of purchasing costs is moving forward in a number of different areas, including an increase in procurement from abroad, a switch to inhouse production of parts rather than external orders, and a more selective approach to suppliers. Let us now focus on this review of purchasing, which is based on the selective rationalisation of second and third level subcontracting companies.

At company Z, an important manufacturer of air conditioners and fuel-jet equipment, selected subcontracting companies have been organised into a co-operative association known as the *Shin Eikai* (Ikeda 1991). The company relies on outside suppliers for more than 60 per cent of parts requirements, just under 70 per cent of these being purchased from members of the *Shin Eikai*. With the current rise in demand for cost cutting by car manufacturers, the company regards the rationalisation of its activities with second level subcontractors to be essential. Therefore it has taken steps to do so throughout the group, with the aim of being awarded a prize for Production and Maintenance (PM) which is sponsored by the Japanese Plant Maintenance Society (*Nikkei Sangyō* 1993: 3 March).

By March 1994 the company had secured a 50 per cent increase in productivity compared with the figures for 1990. Defective goods were also reduced to less than one-fifth. Moreover, by eliminating technical malfunctions and industrial accidents, by the end of the year more than five members of the co-operative association were displaying standards which qualified for the PM prize.

Of the forty-five member companies making up the *Shin Eikai*, however, wide differences exist in the scale of members' operations and in their respective levels of technology, many being small to medium-sized businesses. For this reason, company Z established an inhouse plant maintenance award aimed at those businesses that in the short term could not hope to win the national prize. The company's own PM award promotes a standard of 30 per cent increased productivity and a halving of the rate of defective products.

It is important to note that in this example of group-wide rationalisation, the parent company Z is administering a system of direct guidance for participating companies. The company has organised a support section comprising twenty personnel, half of whom are engaged on guidance in production and maintenance, with the rest working on improving company structures – that is, on cost-cutting activity. In April 1992, the department set up to support 'co-operating companies' was made independent from other company sections. Then, in April 1994, it was incorporated within the newly established Purchasing Head Office.

N Industrial, which manufactures brakes, is following a similar course. While developing plans to procure parts from abroad, the company is encouraging the restructuring of chosen satellite factories and other co-operating companies (Ikeda 1993a). The company formerly had ten subsidiary companies (satellite factories) engaged in casting, cutting, processing and assembling brake cylinders for two- and four-wheel drive vehicles. These have now been integrated to form five companies operating out of six factories (Ikeda 1993c).

As mentioned previously, the surplus equipment from these factories has been dismantled and is in the process of being relocated, just as in the 1960s satellite factories were sited in rural and mountain districts to exploit the cheap labour in those areas. In this way, the strong yen has proved to be the cue for the continuing relocation of the company's manufacturing base to South East Asia and China (Ikeda 1995a).

As many as thirty small to medium-sized companies organised by N Industrial were subject to a process of gradual weeding out; only the top subcontractors, such as those which are able to manage the high precision processing required for anti-locking brake system (ABS) parts, now remain. The co-operative association has been disbanded, but the companies, though not numerous, have adapted to the new situation and formed a small group for the mutual exchange of information.

STAGNATION AT THE LEVEL OF SECOND- AND THIRD-TIER SUBCONTRACTORS

Finally, let us focus on the northern region of Ibaraki prefecture in order to analyse the structural changes which are occurring among the second- and third-tier subcontractors of principal car component manufacturers.

In 1985, the automobile machinery and parts division at factory H in this area had built up production around four major specialisms: engine components, electrical fittings (starters, alternators, etc.), electronic devices (micro-computers, etc.), and pneumatic equipment (Ikeda 1988). At the time, it was operating with a monthly turnover of 16.5 billion yen and a 4,900 – strong workforce. By 1993, however, after the bursting of the 'bubble economy' and the rapid appreciation of the yen, operations at the pneumatic section had been suspended. What is more, because of production in the USA going forward, particularly in electronics, monthly turnover had fallen to 14 billion yen and staff levels to 2,500.

The stagnation affecting parent companies has exerted a dramatic and immediate impact on the second- and third-tier subcontractors in the area and is threatening the economy of the region as a whole. This is particularly noticeable in the case of electrical fittings, such as starters and alternators, which were produced by second-tier subcontractors that supported the parent company's assembly processes. One of these, an alternator producer, had all its components returned as a result of increased production in the USA. It has now withdrawn entirely from the *keiretsu* and is dealing instead with a smaller office automation equipment manufacturer.

Another alternator assembly business has gradually seen orders decline and, having suspended production of finished goods, has returned to parts assembly – namely, winding coils. Thus, assembly of alternators by subcontractors has been reduced to just one company, with the rest being produced either at the parent company or at a subsidiary.

The three companies that assemble starters have also been affected seriously by falling production and are now forced to cut back their own operations. The largest of them, company K, had to close down three of its provincial factories as a result of the suspension of canister production. A total of sixty employees was laid off. Although eighty workers are still on the payroll, the prospect of a reduction to around sixty employees as a result of further changes still remains.

Parent factories have used the space created through the introduction of just-in-time systems to switch to inhouse production of parts, rather than ordering from outside, and this has exerted a particularly severe impact on the second-tier subcontractors that produce electrical components. Parent factories also are promoting the introduction of JIT methods among subcontractors within their *keiretsu*. Under the guidance of JIT consultants, participating companies are doing their utmost to follow the lead set by their parent companies. For those companies without the production techniques required to upgrade tools and other equipment, however, improvements in processing and rationalisation are extremely difficult to achieve. For this reason the introduction of JIT systems has prompted increasing stratification among subcontractors.

Before the recession there were about seventy companies co-operating with the motor vehicle machinery and parts division at factory H; now the number has been reduced by half. Since 1993 factory H has initiated projects at every plant to assist co-operating companies in converting their operations. The motor vehicle machinery and parts division has also created two five-man outside supplier advisory teams which are seconded to companies for a month at a time to help with improvements (Ikeda 1993a). In addition, a 'caravan group' has been organised using converted buses and centred on the outside supplier co-ordinating division. This has set about trying to revive co-operation between companies (Ikeda 1993b). In this way, factory H, which once boasted strong ties with its subcontracting companies, is at last concentrating on rebuilding these connections through intensive and large-scale restructuring.

What effect has this kind of restructuring had on the third tier of small to medium-sized subcontractors that are employed by second-tier suppliers, either in towns or rural areas? Let us now focus upon the process of change that is occurring at the bottom end of the subcontracting structure.

The example to be considered here is a producer of starters which is used as a supplier for the second-tier company K. Company K has about ten companies as regular suppliers. Table 5.2 illustrates the activities of five of these companies (Ikeda 1993b), and shows that these very small subcontracting businesses employ about ten people at most. Although they continue to receive work from the parent companies, they are affected by changes in production practices and the work that these companies are required to do also changes frequently. Apart from using some simple general purpose mechanical equipment, then, the overwhelming bulk of the

Table 5.2 Outside suppliers for company K (second-tier subcontracting companies)

Business no.	*No. of male employees*	*No. of female employees*	*No. of outworkers*	*Degree of dependence on parent company*	*Job specifications*	*Changes caused by the recession*
(1)	1	13	Previously 7, now 0	100% on Company K	Hoist assembly; low skill assembly	At the peak point 17 employees and 10 outworkers
(2)	2	4	Previously 1, now 0	100% on Company K	Press processing and assembly	2 years ago the company employed 13 people, but reduced numbers due to lack of business
(3)	5	3	0	40% of business with Company K, 10 companies dealt with altogether	NC machine processing; small piece cutting	3–4 years ago, 5 NK machines; 2 machines still not paid for
(4)	2	2	Previously employed outworkers, now 0	50% on Company K, 50% on other companies	Cutting on NC lathes; metal pressure tapping	10 people employed before recession; presently looking for new business
(5)	1	5	0	50% on Company K, 50% on other companies	Tap assembly and screwdriver assembly; drilling holes	50% of boring lathes now idle; 5% cut in processing costs

Source: Ikeda 1993b
Note: Employees includes managers and family members

work undertaken is done by hand and the nature of the work is labour intensive.

These third-tier subcontractors respond to fluctuations in their workload by either increasing or reducing the amount they send to outworkers. It is noticeable that, with the current recession, these companies have been dispensing with outworkers altogether in order to preserve jobs for regular employees. Since the tasks given to outworkers were typically low paid and involved only a small amount of work, even by moving away from outworkers and switching to inhouse production it has been difficult to stabilise the business.

Similarly, in order to preserve their own jobs the parent companies of second-tier subcontractors increasingly are producing components themselves rather than ordering them from outside. This compounds the problems faced by third-tier companies. Under such difficult conditions third-tier subcontractors will take on any kind of work requested by the parent companies, and this increasingly involves small quantities of different types of components, all of which need to be finished very rapidly.

Naturally, parent companies also have increased pressure on subcontractors to reduce processing costs. Because of the strong yen, one company has demanded an across-the-board 5 per cent price cut by subcontractors. Since minimum wage legislation makes pay cuts difficult, managers are forced to find savings in processing costs. In response to this managers are concerned increasingly with how to improve the consistency of their operatives' work, and how to be able to respond quickly to frequent changes in plans. Some smaller companies have been remarkably effective in these areas.

A brief review of the results of the above rationalisation is given in Table 5.3 based upon the financial statement in March 1996 of the major automanufacturers. The results of rationalisation which began in either 1994 or 1995 aiming at 30 per cent cost reduction brought about huge cost savings, as typically represented by Nissan. Nissan, which suffered from the largest deficits in the entire company history, in the last financial period achieved cost savings of 140 billion yen, surpassing those of Toyota whose sales are double those of Nissan. Mazda, which welcomed a new president from Ford in 1996, also achieved 120 billion yen of savings.

Table 5.3 Financial statement for March 1996 of the five major car manufacturers (100 million yen)

	Sales	*Recurring profits*	*Effects of rationalisation*	*Effects of foreign exchange*
Toyota	79,571 (−3.2)	3,407	1,300	−200
Nissan	35,181 (+3.2)	324	1,400	−500
Mitsubishi	25,225 (−4.9)	553	417	−270
Honda	24,475 (−0.9)	471	440	−340
Mazda	12,222 (−15.1)	12	1,100	−270

Source: *Asahi Shinbun* (morning edn) 30 May 1996
Note: ( ) percentage of increase and decrease compared to the previous financial period

On the other hand, the number of parts suppliers that have begun cost reduction along with the parent companies has begun to increase. We may envisage that, in the future, the gap between the suppliers who succeed in rationalisation and those who fail will become larger.

CONCLUSION

This chapter has analysed the way in which Japanese car manufacturers have been forced to undertake thorough-going rationalisation and substantial cost cutting in response to the sudden and dramatic rise in the value of the yen. Since no prospect of an expansion in the market exists, the stratified structure of subcontractors has had to absorb the costs. This has made it increasingly difficult to function effectively. In the long term, all these companies will be forced to carry through a process of restructuring and change.

In response to the efforts made by car manufacturers to slash costs by 30 per cent, first-tier component makers are promoting cost cutting in parts production. As a result, there have been changes in the way that these companies deal with car manufacturers. On the whole car manufacturers may come to regard the subcontractors more highly, in their roles as system suppliers with their own particular technology and expertise (Ikeda 1992). On the other hand, the efforts of many small to medium-sized component makers to cut costs have had disappointing results. Car manufacturers are being highly selective in weeding out subcontractors, and an increasing number of these companies is being relegated to second- and third-tier contractor status (Ikeda 1995a).

At the same time, this selective and intensive restructuring initiated by Japanese car manufacturers has extended beyond the limits of the *keiretsu*, and is fostering new ties with non-*keiretsu* component makers through mergers, tie-ups, and the like. As it involves the small to medium companies that comprise the second and third tiers of the hierarchy, this will undoubtedly produce a leaner, streamlined subcontracting structure with the car manufacturers at its head (Ikeda 1995b).

The low-wage economies of South East Asia and China are being integrated as part of an international subcontracting network, supplanting the rigid stratified structure within Japan. The shift of production overseas is bound to play an important part in the future development of the Japanese automobile industry. Although this shift is still in its early stages, it can be expected to accelerate rapidly into the twenty-first century.

REFERENCES

Asahi Shinbun (morning edn) (1996) 30 May.

Ikeda, M. (1988) 'An international comparison of subcontracting systems in the component manufacturing industry', in *Keizaigaku Ronsō* (Chūō University) vol. 29. no. 5–6: 62.

Ikeda, M. (1991) 'Endaka de kitaerare ō-bei no reberu kōeta shitauke' (Bolstered by the strong yen, Japanese subcontractors surpass competition in Europe and the U.S.), *Ekonomisuto*, 11 February: 69–70.
Ikeda, M. (1992) 'Henbō suru nihongata shitauke shisutemu' (Transformation of Japanese-style subcontracting system), *Kōsei Torihiki*, no. 505, 30 November: 18–20.
Ikeda, M. (1993a) 'Haigyō tsugu shoreisai kigyō' (Very small enterprises in successive closing down), *Ekonomisuto*, 8 November: 55.
Ikeda, M. (1993b) 'Tōta ga susumu jidōsha shitauke kigyō' (Auto-subcontracting firms in the process of weeding out), *Ekonomisuto*, 30 November: 44.
Ikeda, M. (1993c) 'Jidōsha sangyō ni okeru bungyō seisan shisutemu no henbō' (Transformation in the system of division of labour in the automobile industry, *Keizaigaku Ronsō* (Chūō University) vol. 34, no. 1: 195–6.
Ikeda, M. (1995a) 'Hokubei ni okeru nikkeijidōsha meika no seisan kakudai to buhin gyōkai e no eikyō' (The expansion of Japanese makers in North America and its influence on parts makers in the domestic market), *Survey Report*, Medium and Small Enterprises International Centre, 30 March: 92–5.
Ikeda, M. (1995b) 'Sanwari nesage o semaru buhingyokai e no aranami' (30 per cent reduction activity spreading across auto-parts makers), *Ekonomisuto*, 11 July: 66–7.
Nihon Keizai Shinbun (morning edn) (1994) 27 April.
Nihon Keizai Shinbun (morning edn) (1994) 9 August.
Nihon Keizai Shinbun (morning edn) (1994) 25 October.
Nihon Kōgyō (1994) 4 April.
Nihon Kōgyō (1994) 9 December.
Nikkei Business (1993) 28 June.
Nikkei Sangyō (1993) 3 March.
Nikkei Sangyō (1994) 21 January.
Nikkei Sangyō (1994) 4 April.
Nikkei Sangyō (1994) 8 June.
Nikkei Sangyō (1994) 6 October.
Sei, S. (1995) 'Tototsu na endaka wa nihon meika no genkai o koeta' (The sudden appreciation of yen reached the limits of Japanese auto and parts makers' patience), *Ekonomisuto*, 11 July: 50.

6 Ownership and control of large corporations in contemporary Japan

Nakata Masaki

The debate over the ownership and control of large corporations began with the establishment of the categories of majority control, minority control and management control, which were utilised by Berle and Means in their own analysis (1932). In this debate, control was originally understood to be based on the power of shareholders, who decided the composition of the board of directors. Basically we would like to follow this view in respect of the concept of control.[1]

First of all, the category of majority control describes a situation whereby the make-up of the board of directors can be decided by individual shareholders possessing a majority of the shares issued. This is a mode of control that arises from an insufficient distribution of shareholdings. Next, minority control describes a situation whereby, under conditions of broadly spread shareholdings, large shareholders wield power which is held either individually or jointly even when their shareholdings is less than 50 per cent. This is a mode of control which is seen in large sized joint-stock corporations. According to Berle and Means, minority control can be established wherever large shareholders possess more than 20 per cent of the issued shares, whether jointly or individually. But later research indicates that because share ownership has advanced so much, it is actually possible to establish minority control with less than 20 per cent of shares (Larner 1970; Herman 1981). The view which currently prevails in both the business and academic communities is that minority control is possible if more than 10 per cent of the issued shares are held (Scott 1986: 50).

At the present stage, the participants in the debate have reached a similar understanding in terms of examining the 250 largest enterprises in Japan, and considering the relations between the distribution of shareholding (the decrease in the percentage of shares held by the biggest shareholder) and modes of control (majority control, minority control, management control). These opinions concern whether or not management control can be established in companies in which large individual shareholders possess less than 10 per cent of the shares, and how the interests of shareholders are secured under this type of system (Maekawa 1993; Sutton 1993). These questions are also related to the recent debate on corporate governance.[2]

In the large corporations of the leading capitalist nations, through the development of intercorporate shareholding and interpersonal relations between members of boards of directors, ownership and control have shifted from a system of individual and familial control to one based on collective and impersonal control. Scott named this 'the system of impersonal possession' (Scott 1986). This system has become predominant in those large corporations in which management control is regarded as having been achieved. In these corporations the composition of the board of directors is decided in practice, not by the individual shareholders, but by a coalition of the top major shareholders. Under this type of control structure, top management within the board of directors carries out strategic decision-making based on the information channelled through intercorporate personal relations. In addition, all the executive directors can carry out their duties as members of the management structure (Scott *et al.* 1993).

The purpose of this chapter is to focus upon the system of impersonal possession in six large enterprise groups (or business combines) in relation to the points made above, and then to elucidate the various new features observed in these companies.

OWNERSHIP AND CONTROL

Characteristics of impersonal possession in Japan

The system of impersonal control is predominant within the following six large Japanese enterprise groups: Mitsubishi, Mitsui, Sumitomo, Fuyō, Sanwa and Dai-ichi Kangyō (hereafter DKB). Each group has organised a presidents' club, and using these as an 'interest group', are creating intercorporate relations in various areas. At times they have even established joint companies together. The first three are those companies which before World War II existed as *zaibatsu*; after the war the system of individual and family control of such organisations was broken up, and they were then reorganised as enterprise groups. These are termed former *zaibatsu* enterprise groups. The second three are new groups organised after World War II. They are all termed corporate banking groups. In 1992, the total number of corporate members of the presidents' club among these groups was 189. These companies are the focus of this chapter.

First of all, it is important to consider how much economic power is held by these groups within the total body of corporate enterprises. In this instance, the financial organisations of the six enterprise groups and the total body of corporate enterprise are excluded. By doing so the number of companies in the six enterprise groups is reduced from 189 to 164. These 164 companies only account for 0.007 per cent of the total number of corporate enterprises, but in terms of capital funds they account for 15.29 per cent, 12.52 per cent of total assets, 13.79 per cent of sales, and 16.52

per cent of profits (Kōsei Torihiki Iinkai, 1994). These figures do not include subsidiary companies (companies under majority control) or associated companies (companies under minority control), but after figures for these are included, the economic power of the six enterprise groups becomes even greater.

These enterprise groups are called *kigyōshūdan* in Japanese, and share common characteristics. They form integrated enterprise groups through reciprocal shareholding, the presidents' club, interlocking directorships, credit relations, and dealing relationships (Scott 1986). Such common attributes establish particular social relations, which structurally characterise the strategic management and corporate control of the companies belonging to the enterprise groups.

The recent trends in the impersonal system of possession in contemporary Japan will be examined by dividing them into two main issues. The first issue is to what degree the structural changes in the balance of mutual shareholdings have affected corporate control in the enterprise groups. The second issue is what kind of influence have recent trends in presidents' clubs, executive director responsibility, financial relations and dealing relations, had upon strategic management and/or corporate rule.[3] In this section, corporate control will be examined, and strategic management, or corporate rule, will be examined in the next section.

Japanese corporate finance has for long relied upon loans from government financial institutions or banks within the enterprise group, rather than securities markets in the post-war period. In the UK and USA around 50 per cent of corporate finance is derived directly from the issue of shares. In contrast to this, in Japan up until the first half of the 1980s close to 70 per cent of corporate finance was indirectly obtained from banks. For Japanese enterprise groups, capital obtained from the issue of shares only accounted for a small percentage of the total. Instead of this, credit relations with financial organisations inside the enterprise group, and especially with banks, performed an important role. However, this meant that enterprise groups, through the device of intercorporate mutual shareholding, usually retained a fixed percentage of shares in each company and across the whole enterprise group. This percentage rarely fell below the 10 per cent cut-off point of minority control.[4] Therefore, within the structure of corporate finance created by the great reliance upon indirect finance and mutual shareholding, the balance of mutual shareholding exerted an important impact upon corporate control. In turn, this can be seen as the foundation for the system of impersonal possession in Japan.

Recent developments in control by enterprise groups

The system of impersonal possession in Japan has been supported by the unique structure of corporate finance, based upon the balance of mutual shareholding and bank finance. This structure has in recent years been shaken by various changes in social, economic and financial conditions which began in the 1970s, and which include the end of high economic growth, the liberalisation of finance, and the deregulation of corporate finance which promotes equity finance. According to a survey of companies listed on the Tokyo Stock Exchange, since the latter half of the 1980s the percentage of finance obtained from banks has declined, whereas the procurement of equity finance has increased. In particular, the procurement of capital from the offering of shares to the public at market prices has increased, and reached a peak in 1989. During this period, the procurement of capital from equity finance increased sixfold, from 4.1 trillion yen in 1985 to 26.4 trillion yen in 1989. However, not all of this huge amount of capital was invested in fixed assets. A large part of it was used for land speculation, the purchase of bonds and shares of other companies and foreign securities (Sakurai 1994). This was a product of what is now known as the 'bubble economy'. But whichever way it is looked at, the increase in equity finance did effectively lead to the increased procurement of capital from the issue of shares. In fact, most companies obtained close to 50 per cent of the capital they required from the issue of shares. Even though this occurred during the 'bubble', it did produce long-term changes in the structure of corporate finance.

The point to note here is that if it can be accepted that the expansion of equity finance raised the percentage of capital procured from the issue of shares, then this stagnated mutual shareholding in enterprise groups, and furthermore reduced the dependence upon capital obtained from member banks in the group. The situation of bank finance will be examined in the next section. At this stage the actual trends in shareholding within enterprise groups in the 1990s, and their special characteristics, will be examined.

Table 6.1 shows the average percentage of shares held in one company within the enterprise group by each corporation within the same enterprise group. Each figure is the shareholding percentage of one corporate member in another. The same table demonstrates that during the 1980s the average percentage balance of shareholding declined across all enterprise groups. This supports the notion that the decrease in shareholding within the enterprise groups has been due to an increase in equity finance. The trend of decrease is more apparent in banking groups than in the former *zaibatsu* groups. However, according to Table 6.1, from around 1990 onwards the average rate of shareholding within enterprise groups increased in 1991 in the Mitsubishi, Sumitomo and Fuyō groups, and in 1992 it also increased in the Mitsui group.

During this period, what kind of changes occurred in the structure of shareholding? Basically, one of the chief causes for the increase in the rates of shareholding in the 1990s was the expansion of share ownership, not only by non-financial business enterprises, but also by financial organisations, such as life insurance and non-life insurance companies. At this point

Table 6.1 Average percentage rates of shareholding per company in groups

Enterprise groups	*1977* %	*1981* %	*1987* %	*1989* %	*1991* %	*1992* %
Mitsui	2.08	1.77	1.58	1.42	1.33	1.34
Mitsubishi	2.10	2.20	1.85	1.75	1.81	1.81
Sumitomo	2.30	2.17	1.68	1.54	1.56	1.56
Average rate for former *zaibatsu* groups	2.16	2.05	1.70	1.57	1.57	1.57
Fuyō	1.96	1.47	1.28	1.30	1.31	1.29
Sanwa	2.51	1.68	1.55	1.43	1.43	1.41
DKB	2.18	1.39	1.16	1.08	1.04	1.03
Average rate for the banking groups	2.22	1.51	1.33	1.27	1.26	1.24
Average rate for the six large enterprise groups	2.19	1.78	1.52	1.42	1.41	1.41

Source: Kōsei Torihiki Iinkai 1994: 122
Note: Average rate of shareholding equals total rate of shareholding by each company within same enterprise group, divided by total number of shareholding relationships within same enterprise group, multiplied by 100

it is sufficient to state that the decline in the rate of shareholding has come to a halt.

Table 6.2 has been created in order to show the rate of reciprocal shareholding. Intercorporate reciprocal shareholding within the enterprise groups increased throughout the 1970s, and reached a peak in 1981. However, from 1980 onwards, the rate of reciprocal shareholding within the enterprise groups declined, due to the expansion of equity finance based on

Table 6.2 Percentage rates of intercorporate reciprocal shareholding

Enterprise group	*1981* %	*1987* %	*1989* %	*1991* %	*1992* %
Mitsui	23.13	21.35	19.45	19.28	19.29
Mitsubishi	36.93	36.04	35.45	38.12	38.21
Sumitomo	36.57	29.40	27.46	28.02	27.95
Average rate for former *zaibatsu* groups	32.21	28.93	27.46	28.47	28.48
Fuyō	18.80	17.11	16.39	17.06	16.88
Sanwa	19.95	17.05	16.46	16.77	16.88
DKB	17.50	14.92	14.60	14.59	14.24
Average rates for the banking groups	18.75	16.36	15.82	16.14	15.93
Average rate for the six large enterprise groups	25.48	22.63	21.64	22.31	22.21

Source: Kōsei Torihiki Iinkai 1994: 122
Note: Rate of intercorporate reciprocal shareholding equals total percentage of shares held by every company in same enterprise group, divided by number of companies within enterprise group, multiplied by 100

the social, economic and financial changes already outlined, and due to an increase in the number of shareholding relationships between enterprise members which will be examined later. However, even allowing for the fact that the figures for the rate of reciprocal shareholding vary for each enterprise group at the beginning of the 1990s, overall the change was negligible. This demonstrates that with the end of the 'bubble economy' and the recession, reciprocal shareholding remained as strong as ever, and was beginning to be revitalised.

What kind of influence did this have upon company control within the enterprise groups? In order to examine this, it is necessary to look at the cohesive strength through shareholding of enterprise groups and the state of share ownership by top shareholders in every company during the 1990s. First of all, the cohesive strength of enterprise groups can be measured by the density of cohesiveness in the group.[5] In order to measure this, the survey data of the Kōsei Torihiki Iinkai (Fair Trade Commission) on the degree of enterprise shareholding is useful. This is calculated by the following equation as is the same with social network density measurement. The rate of shareholding relationships can be utilised as one method for measuring the cohesiveness of enterprise groups.

$$\text{Rate of shareholding relationships} = \frac{\text{Total number of enterprise group members in which every company holds shares}}{\text{Total number of shareholding relations possible within same enterprise group}} \times 100$$

When the cohesiveness of enterprise groups between 1977 and 1992 is measured using this equation, differences in each enterprise group can be seen, with 75.26 per cent for Mitsubishi, 94.46 per cent for Sumitomo, 46.81 per cent for Fuyō, and 27.47 per cent for Sanwa in 1992 (Kōsei Torihiki Iinkai 1994). However, from 1977 onwards, the density value for all enterprise groups has slowly increased. This figure demonstrates in quantitative terms that the cohesiveness of enterprise groups is increasing. Therefore, the rate of shareholding relations signifies that enterprise groups from the 1980s until the present have been strengthened rather than weakened.

Lastly, corporate control of the groups in the 1990s will be examined. As already discussed, under the system of impersonal possession no individual shareholder possesses more than 10 per cent of the shares necessary to establish minority control. Thus, in this situation the composition of the board of directors is decided by a coalition of the major shareholders. Whether or not the major shareholders can be seen as the top ten or twenty shareholders varies depending on the situation. In the case of large corporations in the USA and UK, the major shareholders are regarded as the top twenty shareholders. But in the case of the six large enterprise groups, because the ownership and distribution of shares is concentrated in the top ten shareholders, it is reasonable to regard those ten as the major shareholders.[6]

Table 6.3 illustrates the average rate of shareholding by the top ten in the listed companies of the six large enterprise groups, and changes in the total percentage of shares held in members of the same enterprise group by these same ten shareholders. According to this table, the average across the whole enterprise group of the percentage of the total shares held by members of the same enterprise group was 14.33 per cent in 1989, even under 'bubble' conditions. This figure means that if those group members constituting the top shareholders formed a coalition, then they would be able to establish minority control in the enterprise group. In addition, the percentage of shares held by the same group members in the top ten shareholders, even at its lowest point in 1989, was still 43.55 per cent. This is the typical pattern of the system of impersonal possession in Japan, and it shows that the structure of control in the enterprise groups through mutual shareholding still exists. In turn, it is necessary to note that, entering the 1990s, the structure of control is again beginning to strengthen.

CORPORATE RULE AND INFLUENCE OF COMBINED INTERESTS

Changes in mechanism of corporate rule

The full-scale introduction of the management system characteristic to modern corporations really took place after World War II. This system, known as 'the management system characteristic to modern corporation', was one in which the highest levels of management within the headquarters

Table 6.3 Rates of shareholding by the top ten shareholders

	Total percentage of shares held by top ten shareholders as an average across the enterprise group %	*Total percentage of shares held by top ten shareholders within same enterprise group* %	*Percentage of shares held by enterprise group members in top ten shareholders* %
1977	40.20	20.55	50.02
1981	39.02	19.89	50.97
1987	38.87	18.12	46.60
1989	32.91	14.33	43.55
1992	38.37	18.53	48.30

Source: Kōsei Torihiki Iinkai 1994: 130
Note: This table displays the values for every company within the enterprise group listed on the stock market

(referred to below as top management) carried out centralised corporate rule through functionally organised departments, such as purchasing, manufacture, marketing, accounts, personnel and finance, and through divisional departments that integrated these either by products or areas. This kind of management system was typically developed in the USA.[7]

Under this system, the board of directors, or the executive committee which was its representative body, undertook strategic decision-making and administrative decisions. The responsibility for carrying out these decisions was then given to executive directors selected by the board of directors and officers employed by the board of directors. Then, in order to counsel and advise top management, staff departments, such as survey, corporate planning, evaluation, personnel and development sections, were created within the company's headquarters. Therefore, in the company headquarters there is a level of top management which directly carries out corporate rule, and below them managerial staff who are engaged in management and staff functions.

Between top management and managerial staff there is the 'economic and accounting' distinction between those who receive part of the company profits as directors' rewards, and those who receive wages, although both share the function of responsibility for the operation of capital. There is therefore a functional difference between the two types of management. Top management is chiefly responsible for strategic decision-making, such as the procurement of capital, investment decisions, the promotion of senior management, labour relations, work composition, production targets and price; whereas managerial staff are involved in providing support to top management, involving supervision of operations, surveys, corporate planning, personnel and technology development.

This management system was partly introduced into Japan before World War II, but in the main came into practice after the war as part of the economic reforms which broke up the *zaibatsu* and, in the 1950s, through revised commercial laws. Specifically, the revision of commercial law established for the first time the board of directors responsible for decision-making and a representative director as chief executive officer. A distinctive feature of Japanese top management thus lies in that it was introduced by the revision of laws. Consequently, the mechanism of corporate rule in Japan was established in the period of high economic growth from 1955 to 1973 through the spread of divisional organisations and creation of functionally organised departments, together with the formation of *Jōmukai* (a committee of executive directors and above) which is similar to the executive committee in the USA and the formation of various types of staff section at company headquarters.

During the period of low growth, from 1974 until the present, in order to respond to the sharply changed conditions, alterations have been made to the structure of corporate rule (Scott *et al.* 1993). These changes can be broadly divided into the two areas in which they appeared. First, the functions of top management, especially strategic decision-making and administrative decisions which had previously been carried out by the deliberations of the board of directors, now passed to policy-making meetings composed of higher ranking executive directors. This implies decision-making by a much smaller number of top executive directors, thus establishing a system of corporate rule suitable for decision-making quickly responding to the changes in corporate environment. As a result, in contemporary Japan the board of directors has now effectively become a body which merely rubber-stamps decisions. This situation led to the creation of a hierarchical structure within the directorship, consisting of the president, vice-president, managing directors, executive directors, and non-executive directors. This is an important characteristic of Japanese top management.

The second alteration in the structure of corporate rule was that various staff departments within company headquarters, which handle managerial corporate planning, technology development, human resources, subcontracting and external supplier relations, greatly increased the ratio of their staff in comparison with other departments. This brought about a cumbersome system of corporate rule and an increase in management costs.

In the 1990s, with the collapse of the 'bubble economy' and the continuing recession, the structure of corporate rule has given rise to a number of serious problems. One of the greatest of these is the fact that corporate decision-making and operations have been concentrated in a small number of managing directors. In a situation where the board of directors ceases to function, it is doubtful whether the social responsibilities of the corporation, the development of the company itself, and the benefits of the shareholders can be achieved. In fact, in Japan during the period of the 'bubble economy', executive directors carried out activities such as the improper and illegal acquisition of capital, real estate deals which harmed the interests of the company and shareholders, bribery of local government officials, and illegal donations of money to politicians. The issue then arose of how the activities of executive directors could best be regulated. In order to deal with this problem, in October 1993 Japan's commercial laws were revised. An auditing council was set up in order to strengthen control over large corporations. Moreover, so that greater executive director responsibility could be pursued, the cost of a legal action by representatives of shareholders was dropped to 8,200 yen. Subsequently, on 22 December 1994, a judgment was given in court on legal action by one shareholder. This judgment declared that an executive director had improperly and illegally bribed a high local government official, and that this had harmed the interests of the company; the court then ordered that he pay compensation of 14 million yen to the company. Two more legal actions similar to this are now pending in court.

Changes which improve the process of corporate governance have also appeared in the 1990s. These are connected with the progress of the recession and the transfer of plants overseas due to the appreciation of the yen (Ōnishi 1994). The continued recession and transfer of plants have led to a 'hollowing-out' of Japanese industry. Therefore, many corporations are reducing the structure of corporate rule, and in order to achieve reductions in management costs are moving towards the creation of smaller company headquarters and 'flat' management structures (Maekawa 1993; Mizota 1994, Tsūsanshō 1993). These various trends in corporate rule in the 1990s mean that, in order to create front-runner companies in Japan, the debate on corporate governance needs further development.[8]

Constraints upon strategic decision-making

What should be clear by now is that the system of impersonal possession in the large Japanese enterprise groups has institutionalised corporate control through intercorporate reciprocal shareholding, and upon this basis top management has been carrying out corporate rule. The top management of every company has carried out strategic decision-making in the areas of corporate finance, senior management personnel, labour relations, business structure and marketing, while execution of these decisions has been the responsibility of executive directors. This type of structure of control and mechanism of corporate rule is not based upon power belonging to an individual or family, nor is it based on the power of a specific firm. Therefore, the top management of every company in the enterprise group has taken over autonomy in strategic decision-making from individuals and from individual companies. In this result, the Japanese model of strategic decision-making under impersonal possession resembles the Anglo-American model. However, a difference exists between the type of corporate control as seen in the Anglo-American model, which is based on 'control through a constellation of interests', composed of the leading shareholders of rival financial institutions, and the Japanese model, which is based on 'control through a coalition of interests', or control by enterprise groups. As a result of these different types of structures, differences similarly emerge in the structure of constraints upon the strategic decision-making of top management. As has been made clear by Scott, the structure of constraints upon decision-making in the USA and UK is a 'bank-centred sphere of influence', but in Japan it is interest groups composed of the members of enterprise groups or interest groups (Scott 1986: 3–5).

The decision-making of top management in the member companies of Japanese enterprise groups has secured autonomy from individuals and individual companies, but it is influenced by the overall interests of the enterprise group. The interests of the whole enterprise group and of individual member companies are achieved and adjusted through various intercorporate relations. These intercorporate relations consist of personal, credit, and trading relations. Now let us turn to the ways in which intercorporate relations have changed in the 1990s.[9]

Intercorporate personal relations

The intercorporate relations of the six large enterprise groups are formed through the presidents' club, the dispatching directorships (see below) of managing directors or auditors, and interlocking directorships. The member companies of the presidents' club are large banking, finance, trading, real estate, and manufacturing corporations. Meetings of the club are held once a month (or once every three months for DKB group) and are attended by the presidents of the corporate members, or the chairmen of the board. The purpose of the presidents' club is to share information on economic conditions and other business matters. The agenda does not include the organisations or the operation of individual companies (Kōsei Torihiki Iinkai 1994). However, according to research and the evidence of former company presidents (Gendai Kigyō Kenkyūkai 1994: 134–5), the exchange of opinions and information shared between company presidents is carried out in regard to the break-up or merger of companies, the establishment of new enterprises, and high-level personnel matters in the member companies. Therefore, even allowing for the fact that the presidents' club does not interfere directly in the strategic decision-making of top management, it still fulfils an important role in decision-making related to the interests of the enterprise group.[10]

The 'dispatching directorship' is an intercorporate relation by which personnel from a specific company, who are neither managing directors nor auditors or who have less than two years until retirement, are recruited by the managing directors or auditors from another company within the same enterprise group. The persons taking up such positions are called dispatched directors. This is one more method of personal intercorporate relations in Japan. In the six large enterprise groups, seldom does a managing director from one specific company hold an additional managing director post in a different company. According to the Fair Trade Commission, the percentage of member companies which accepted dispatched directors from other companies in the same group decreased slightly in all groups between 1977 and 1992, with the exception of Mitsubishi, which increased from 93 per cent to 100 per cent. As a result, the average rate for the six large enterprise groups fell from 64 per cent in 1977 to 60 per cent in 1992. But when recent trends from 1989 until 1992 are looked at, we should note that the figures for the Mitsubishi, Sumitomo, Fuyō, and Sanwa groups have begun to rise. Moreover, the same survey revealed that the order of origin of dispatched directors for all enterprise groups is as follows: banks, general trading companies, trust banks, and manufacturing companies (Kōsei Torihiki Iinkai 1994: 135–6). This demonstrates that the channel of information which influences the strategic decision-making of top management is formed around and centred upon the various financial institutions and trading companies of the six large enterprise groups, and these can be seen as the nodal points of adjustments in company interests.

Intercorporate credit relations

Intercorporate credit relations within the same enterprise group are chiefly:

- relations between financial institutions;
- relations between the financial institutions and trading companies or manufacturing companies;
- relations between trading companies and manufacturing companies.

The influence of these relations upon the strategic decision-making of top management will be investigated. In this case, long-term credit relations, rather than short-term ones, probably exercise a greater influence upon strategic decision-making. Table 6.4 has been constructed in consideration of this point. According to this table, the rate of long-term loans obtained from financial institutions within the enterprise group has increased consistently, even during the 1980s, which saw the greatest expansion in the procurement of funds from the issue of new shares in Japan's history. This demonstrates that the influence of financial institutions upon the corporate rule of top management has strengthened in the 1990s. Moreover, it is notable that this influence is stronger upon the enterprise groups related to the former *zaibatsu* than upon the enterprise groups related to the banks.

From the above observations it can be said that top management decision-making in every company in an enterprise group is influenced by the general interests of that enterprise group (in the case of Japan, centred upon banks and trading companies) through personal and credit relations.

Table 6.4 Average percentage rates of long-term finance procured from group member financial institutions

Enterprise group	*1981*	*1987*	*1989*	*1992*
Mitsui	17.77	18.70	22.07	22.87
Mitsubishi	23.19	21.82	21.03	25.11
Sumitomo	26.52	24.99	25.50	25.65
Average for former *zaibatsu* groups	22.07	21.60	22.26	24.26
Fuyō	14.83	16.56	16.93	16.73
Sanwa	17.64	15.95	15.50	17.62
DKB	8.57	9.34	10.79	11.09
Average rate for banking groups	13.10	13.00	13.59	14.39
Average rate for six large enterprise groups	16.57	16.05	16.68	17.82

Source: Kōsei Torihiki Iinkai 1994: 153

Note: Average percentage rate for long-term financial procurement, equals total amount of long-term finance procured from enterprise group member financial organisations, divided by total amount of long-term finance for enterprise group member companies, multiplied by 100

CONCLUSION

This chapter has explored the most recent trends in the corporate control and corporate rule of six large enterprise groups in Japan in which the system of impersonal possession has become predominant. The Anglo-American model of corporate control takes the form of 'control through a constellation of interests', and corporate rule is restricted by a sphere of influence centred upon the banks. In contrast to this is the system of impersonal possession in the six large enterprise groups, in which corporate control is dominated by enterprise groups, and corporate rule is restricted by the personal and credit relations of interest groups within the enterprise group.

In the latter half of the 1980s, the *keiretsu* relations of the six large Japanese enterprise groups were seen to weaken. However, as we make clear, in the 1990s the system of impersonal possession in the six large corporate groups has reasserted itself. This is one of the main conclusions of this chapter.

Although we focused upon the six large enterprise groups in which the Japanese system of impersonal possession is dominant, there are other companies which have a system of 'control through a constellation of interests' and which account for close to 30 per cent of the 250 largest enterprises. From now onwards the collection of data and detailed examination of these companies will be necessary. In addition to this, during the 1990s the percentage of intercorporate shareholding by financial institutions other than commercial banks, such as life insurance mutual companies, indemnity insurance companies and pension funds, is increasing.

What kinds of impact will this bring to impersonal possession in Japan? Does this lead to an increase of corporate control of the Anglo-American type? Space did not allow discussion of this point nor the impact of recent globalisation upon ownership and control. Internationalisation of business tends to be understood as a move overseas but in the 'bubble economy' period in the late 1980s, shareholding by foreign financial institutions increased. This dimension of internationalisation will continue to develop. If the percentage of foreign shareholders continues to increase throughout the 1990s, then this will probably become one more factor for change in corporate control.

NOTES

1 There 'control' is used as a technical term which describes the 'actual power to select the board of directors', as defined by Berle and Means (1932: 66–7). The power which is used to select the board of directors and to achieve majority control is formally and legally exercised through the general shareholders meeting, but in practice it is exercised through an informal process of mutal understanding and information exchange between the major shareholders. The results of this process are summarised in the general shareholders meeting prospectus.

2 For articles which briefly summarise the recent state of the debate on corporate governance in the UK, USA and Japan, see Bishop (1994) and Charkham (1994).

3 The term 'corporate control' is used by managerialists to refer to corporate decision-making. In order to avoid confusion over terminology, the term 'control' will be taken as a social relationship which determines the origin of share ownership rights, and will be defined as in note 1. In turn, management power which carries out corporate decision-making will be termed corporate rule. These are concepts developed by Scott (Scott *et al.* 1993).

4 The total shareholding of group member companies among the six groups did not go below 10 per cent before 1992 except in the case of DKB, which happened in 1989 with a return to 11.45 per cent in 1992, which was the next survey year (Kōsei Torihiki Iinkai 1994: 131).

5 Density can be measured by the techniques of social network analysis. Social network analysis is a technique which applies the graph theory of mathematics to social structure analysis. Fore more details see Iwanami (1994), Wellman and Berkowitz (1988), Scott (1991) and Wasserman and Galaskiewicz (1994).

6 The distribution of the rate of share holding by the top 20 shareholders in the 250 largest enterprises in the UK and USA, is about the same as for the top 10 shareholders in Japan. Therefore, in order to ascertain the true situation in Japan and to make comparison with the UK and USA it is sufficient to examine only the top ten shareholders in Japan.

7 For a detailed explanation of this point, see Scott *et al.* (1993).

8 The key point in the current debate on corporate governance seems to have begun with the need to remind executives in order to improve management not paying due attention to the interests of the enterprise's stockholders. See Prentice and Holland (1993), Dimsdale and Prevezer (1994).

9 The intercorporate trade relations within the six large enterprise groups are recorded in the Kōsei Torihiki Iinkai survey (1994). According to this survey, the percentage of total sales accounted for by the corporate members of the enterprise groups was on average 6.85 per cent in 1992. The rate for corporations which run manufacturing operations was 12.58 in 1992 (Kōsei Torihiki Iinkai 1994: 41–54). These figures continued to fall from 1989 onwards. As yet there has been insufficient discussion on how to evaluate this decline, and further examination will be necessary.

10 It is difficult to determine the exact role which the presidents' club fulfils in practice. Up until now it has been pointed out that the role of the club has been in the adjustment of the interests and the exchange of information within the corporate group; the employment of top personnel; the establishment of joint investment companies (Gendai Kigyō Kenkyū Kai 1994).

REFERENCES

Berle, A. A. and Means, G. C. (1932) *Modern Corporation and Private Property*, New York: Macmillan.

Bishop, M. (1994) 'Corporate governance', *The Economist*, 29 January.

Charkham, J. P. (ed.) (1994) *Keeping Good Company: A Study of Corporate Governance in Five Countries*, Oxford: Clarendon Press.

Dimsdale, N. and Prevezer, M. (1994) *Capital Markets and Corporate Governance*, Oxford: Oxford University Press.

Gendai Kigyō Kenkyū Kai (ed.) (1994) *Nippon no Kigyo Kan Kankei* (Intercorporate relations in Japan), Tokyo: Chūō Keizai Sha.

Herman, E. S. (1981) *Corporate Control, Corporate Power*, Cambridge: Cambridge University Press.

Iwanami, F. (1994) 'Kigyōshūdan no jin teki network analysis' (Network analysis on personal relations in a large enterprise group), in G. Sasagawa, T. Inamura, and S. Inoue (eds) *The Basic Problems of Modern Management*, Tokyo: Zeimu Keiri Kyokai.

Kōsei Torihiki Iinkai (1994) *Saishin Nippon no Roku Dai Kigyōshūdan* (The recent realities of six large business combines), Tokyo: Tōyō Keizai Shinposha.

Larner, R. (1970) *Management Control and the Large Corporation*, New York: Dunellen Press.

Maekawa, K. (1993) *Gendai Kigyō Kenkyū no Kiso* (Basic research on modern business enterprises), Tokyo: Moriyama Shoten.

Mizota, S. (1994) *Zōsen Jukikai Sangyō no Kigyō System* (Business enterprise system in Ship-building and heavy industry), Tokyo: Moriyama Shoten.

Ōnishi, K. (1994) *Nippon Handōtai Sangyō Ron* (Semiconductor industry in Japan), Tokyo: Moriyama Shoten.

Prentice, D. P. and Holland, P. R. J. (1993) *Contemporary Issues in Corporate Governance*, Oxford: Oxford University Press.

Sakurai, T. (1994) 'Shihon shijō ni okeru wagakuni kigyō no shikin chōtatsu kōdō' (Financing behaviour of Japanese enterprises in a deregulated market), *Yamaichi Shōken Chōsa Geppō*, April, Tokyo: Yamaichi Securities.

Scott, J. P. (1986) *Capitalist Property and Financial Power: A Comparative Study of Britain, the US and Japan,* Brighton: Wheatsheaf Books.

Scott, J. P. (1991) *Social Network Analysis: A Handbook*, London: Sage Publications.

Scott, J. P., Nakata, M. and Hasegawa, H. (1993) *Kigyō to Kanri no Kokusai Hikaku: Eibei Gata to Nippon Gata* (A comparative study of business and management: Anglo-American type and Japanese type), Tokyo: Chūō Keizai Sha.

Sutton, B. (ed.) (1993) *The Legitimate Corporation: Essential Readings in Business Ethics and Corporate Governance*, Oxford: Basil Blackwell.

Tsūsanshō (1993) *21seiki Gata Keizai System* (The type of economic system in the 21st century), Tokyo: Tsūsan Sangyō Chōsa Kai.

Wasserman, S. and Galaskiewicz, J. (eds) (1994) *Advances in Social Network Analysis,* London: Sage Publications.

Wellman, B. and Berkowitz, S.D. (eds) (1988) *Social Structure: a Network Approach*, Cambridge: Cambridge University Press.

7 Small headquarters and the reorganisation of management

Okubayashi Kōji

The 'bubble economy' has collapsed and in the midst of the recession of the early 1990s Japanese companies are implementing structural reforms in business activities and organisation. Even though the rate of growth has been low since the oil shocks of the 1970s, the Japanese economy had continued to grow steadily until the 1990s. However, during the recent recession the myth of unbroken economic growth has been dispelled; and, as can be seen in the fashionable talk of 'price collapse', deflation has begun to stalk Japan as well as the other industrial economies.

In this situation Japanese companies have been forced to reform fundamentally their management strategies. Some have transferred production bases to other parts of Asia, disposed of unprofitable businesses, and even gone so far as to reorganise inhouse research and development - an area previously considered to be sacrosanct. The corporate management built up during the course of the twentieth century is now searching for new and different management methods for the twenty-first (Yoshida 1993). These radical reforms of corporate management and structural changes are widely dubbed 'restructuring'.

The scope of restructuring extends as far as the structural organisation of the company and personnel management, with rationalisation of personnel now embracing white-collar as well as blue-collar workers. The recession has given birth to a plethora of era names, such as the 'Era of the executive's ordeal', the 'Era of suffering for white-collar workers', and so on. Executive positions are now the object of personnel adjustments, and many white-collar workers have become the target of improvements in productivity, not to mention transfers. In this way, white-collar workers have been the most affected by the 'slimming down' of company headquarters and the restructuring of the company organisation.

In this chapter we wish to introduce the kind of changes now taking place in the organisation of Japanese companies during the 'Age of the white-collar worker's suffering', and seek to explain why these structural reorganisations have become necessary, in what direction such structural reorganisations are heading, and how, in the context of this structural reorganisation, the role of managers is changing.

THE 'SLIMMING DOWN' OF COMPANY HEADQUARTERS

During the 'Heisei recession', one of the most important strategies implemented by large Japanese corporations seeking cost reductions is the 'slimming down' of company headquarters. In addition, corporations have been simplifying the executive structure so as to facilitate quick response to changes in the management environment. These trends can be confirmed from newspaper reports.

Table 7.1 reports on white-collar personnel adjustments found in Japanese financial newspapers over the half-year period from April to October 1993. In one example, at company A, 55 of the 520 personnel at company headquarters, equivalent to around one-tenth of the total staff, have been transferred to new business sections or the sales section. Moreover, in the following three years, company G planned to reduce by 3,000 the number of personnel in administrative sections of the whole company and in the existing divisions of steel manufacturing. Specifically, the plan was to reduce by half the number of white-collar staff at the company headquarters, in sections such as general affairs, accounting and personnel. With regard to personnel reductions at business sections, staff numbers were to be adjusted at the older, but not the newest, sections. At the same time company headquarters are being slimmed down and personnel numbers reduced: indeed, in every business sector a process of 'scrap and build' is taking place. Here lies the reason for dubbing the contemporary era the 'Age of the white-collar worker's suffering'.

Why has the slimming down of company headquarters become necessary? The first reason is that not only in the company headquarters, but also at business establishments in general, the staff ratio has become higher. In our survey (Okubayashi *et al.* 1994: 196), the staff ratio (number of employees in staff sections ÷ number of employees in direct production sections × 100) increased from 39.6 per cent in 1980 to 42.6 per cent in 1985. Furthermore, in the 1993 survey, which targeted companies with more than 1,000 employees, the ratio for manufacturing companies reached 44.9 per cent. In contrast to direct production section employees, or blue-collar workers, the percentage for 'indirect production employees', or white-collar workers, is increasing as a long-term trend.

During the period of low economic growth following the oil crises of the 1970s, every company tried to make the best of limited market opportunities by moving into new business areas, or by working on the development of new products. The acceleration of this type of management diversification and new product development resulted in an increase in the number of personnel required in company headquarters and R&D sections. Even if it is supposed that the increase in the workload of operatives can be dealt with by a switch to more efficient equipment and the introduction of new machinery, and not by an increase in the number of

Table 7.1 Newspaper reports on restructuring white-collar sections

Company A	Among the 520 staff members in company headquarters, 55, or more than 10 per cent of the staff, are transferred to deal with new business sections, and emergency management needs.
Company B	The number of personnel directly involved with management at company headquarters is being reduced by approximately 8 per cent between 1990 and March 1994, by methods such as transfers to the sales section. Under the mid-term management plan finishing in 1994, the number of management staff will be reduced by 700, or around 10 per cent of the total number of 7,500 staff.
Company C	The transfer of staff from management to production sections is being planned in 1994. The plan is to reduce the number of management staff in company headquarters by 10 per cent, and also the number of temporary workers by 10 per cent.
Company D	The number of staff is being slimmed down by approximately 700, or 20 per cent of the total workforce, over a two-year period, between 1994 and 1996. The target is to reduce the numbers of staff in the company headquarters by 500, and the number of staff in branch offices by 200. Staff will be reduced in every section of the company headquarters, including general affairs, accounting and personnel.
Company E	Staff numbers to be reduced by 100 by January 1994. Reductions to be made in all sections, apart from personnel in sales and manufacturing sections. The aim is to reduce the number of staff from the present figure of 4,200 down to 4,100, and these reductions are to be made in sections including general affairs and management.
Company F	A rationalisation plan to reduce staff by 30 per cent over three years, between 1994 and 1997, will be put into effect. At present, the company has 1,400 employees. A reduction of 40 personnel per year will be achieved naturally by the retirement of workers, and an additional 280 workers will be lost by reductions in the management, production, and research and development sections.
Company G	A programme has started to reduce the number of white-collar workers in all sections of management and steel manufacturing sections, from 10,000 to 9,000, over a three-year period. The company has a total of 37,000 employees, and 15,000 of these are white-collar employees. The aim of the programme is to reduce the number of employees in the management and steel manufacturing sections by 10,000. New business sections are not included in these reduction targets. There are just under 2,000 white-collar personnel in management sections, such as general affairs, accounts, and personnel, and the aim is to cut this number in half.

(continued)

Table 7.1 (continued)

Company H	The company has a total of 3,300 employees. By the transfer of approximately 900 employees to production and sales sections, a 12 per cent reduction will be achieved in the number of workers in sections of the company headquarters, such as planning, development, business control, and management. The transfer period is six months, and as a rule workers will return to their original sections after this period is over.
Company I	A reduction of 3,000 personnel in non-manufacturing sections is planned by 1997. The programme of reductions includes white-collar personnel Due to concerns that reductions in the production sections would hamper production, additional reductions are to be made in the sales and management sections.

Source: *Nihon Keizai Shinbun* 1993: April–October

personnel, the enhanced efficiency of staff sections does not proceed smoothly, and the result has been to increase the number of staff required.

The second reason is that, as a response to the 'Heisei recession', companies have reorganised the businesses into which they diversified, and have tried to specialise in those areas in which they are strongest. Table 7.2 shows how the diversification strategy of companies has changed compared to 1985. The diversification of management at the workplace level becomes clear when we ask in what way product markets have become diversified, and to what extent new products utilise new technology and equipment.

According to Table 7.2, the percentage of companies which answered that the product market had become qualitatively different had fallen to 34.8 per cent (19.3 + 10.5 + 5.0) in 1993 for manufacturing companies, whereas in the 1985 survey it had been 52.7 per cent (26.3 + 19.2 + 7.2). In other words, companies did not push forward with the diversification of products in 1993 to the extent that they did in 1985. This can be interpreted to mean that during the 'Heisei recession' management strategies are concentrating on the manufacture of their specialist products and pursuing cost reductions, rather than the diversification of products.

We can examine the compatibility of production technology for new products in the same way. The percentage of companies seeing no compatibility between products in production technology had fallen to 23.4 per cent in 1993 for manufacturing companies, whereas in the 1985 survey it had been 36.0 per cent. During the 'Heisei recession', therefore, a decrease has occurred in the diversification of products which do not share compatibility in production technology. These data show that during the Heisei recession the diversification of management and new product development is no longer being pursued, and white-collar workers active in the old areas now have to be transferred to other areas such as sales and production.

Table 7.2 Changes in corporate diversification strategy

What are the distinctive features of your business corporate environment? On the scale below, please mark the number which best describes your business corporate environment.

A (Manufacturing companies) *To what degree is the product market of your business diversified?*

Extremely homogeneous (unified market, similar customers)	1	2	3	4	5	6	7	Extremely heterogeneous (diverse market and customers)

	1	*2*	*3*	*4*	*5*	*6*	*7*
1985 Survey: N=167	2.4	19.8	12.0	13.2	26.3	19.2	7.2
1993 Survey: N=181 Manufacturing companies	7.7	21.0	15.5	21.0	19.3	10.5	5.0
1993 Survey: N=108 Non-manufacturing companies	7.6	17.1	13.3	10.5	19.0	23.8	8.6

B (Manufacturing companies) *What is the degree of compatibility in the production technology phase (the know-how connected with technicians, plant and equipment and technology) for your business products?*

Extremely compatible	1	2	3	4	5	6	7	Extremely incompatible

	1	*2*	*3*	*4*	*5*	*6*	*7*
1985 Survey: N=167	0.6	13.2	21.0	29.3	21.6	13.2	1.2
1993 Survey: N=181 Manufacturing companies	7.8	19.0	23.5	26.3	17.3	6.1	0.0
1993 Survey: N=108 Non-manufacturing companies	7.8	20.6	18.6	27.5	19.6	5.9	0.0

Source: Okubayashi *et al.* 1994: 179–81
Note: N is the number of sample companies. In the 1985 survey all companies responded to all questions. But in the 1993 survey, there were 2 manufacturing companies that did not respond to question A, and 4 that did not respond to question B. Also in the 1993 survey, 5 non-manufacturing companies did not respond to question A, and 8 did not respond to question B.

The third reason for the slimming down of company headquarters is the sharp increase in the number of employees qualified to hold managerial posts compared to the number of posts available. Figure 7.1 shows the correlation over time between the number of employees qualified for managerial positions, those holding *Sanji* (councillor) status or above, and the number of positions available in a representative food manufacturing

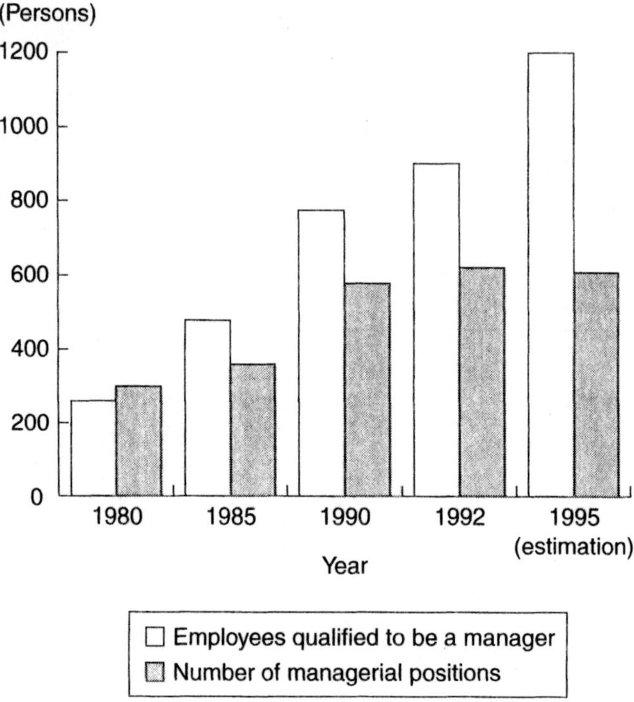

Figure 7.1 Management positions and number of employees qualified to be a manager of X company
Source: Data provided by X company (1996)

company. Under rapid corporate growth, a shortage of qualified staff for managerial positions existed in 1980. However in 1990 the reverse is true, with the number holding *Sanji* status or above exceeding the number of managerial posts. What is known as a 'post-shortage phenomenon' has occurred, and in the latter half of the 1990s this trend is predicted to become further accentuated. Managers who hold *Sanji* status or above have a history of long company service and possess specialised knowledge, with many of them being transferred to the staff sections of the company headquarters and factories. Under the system of seniority-based pay their wages rise ineluctably. Thus in a situation where the number of managerial posts fails to increase, finding ways fully to match the abilities of managers concomitant with their level of pay has become a pressing need for companies. The result is that these managers are moved from staff sections to sales or manufacturing sections, and every company during the process of 'scrap and build' tries to reutilise their abilities.

The 'suffering of the white-collar worker', together with the slimming down of company headquarters, is not simply the product of less diversification of corporate strategy in product markets. We should also note the change in corporate organisational structure with the spread of new technology (micro-electronics and information technology).

'FLATTENING OUT' OF MANAGEMENT ORGANISATION

In what ways has organisational structure changed with the spread of new technology (Mitsubishi Sōgō Kenkyūsho 1992; Imada 1991; Nihon Rōdō Kenkyūkikō 1992; Shi 1992)? This question will first be addressed based upon the results of a survey of changes in management organisation. In September 1993 the author's project team carried out a questionnaire survey of companies with more than one thousand employees, in order to examine technology's influence upon corporate organisational structure. A similar survey also was carried out in November 1985, so we can analyse the long-term changes in organisational structure. Of the companies that participated in the 1993 survey, 183 were manufacturing companies (mainly electrical equipment, transportation equipment, machinery, chemicals, pharmaceuticals and glass), and 110 were non-manufacturing companies (distribution, finance, and service industry centred companies).

Table 7.3A highlights the direction of change made by those companies which have modified their organisational structures over the five years leading up to 1993. If the changes to organisational hierarchy from the top of the establishment (plant) to supervisor level at the workplace are examined first, the table shows that 28.8 per cent of companies answered that organisational hierarchy had shrunk, 16.3 per cent that it had expanded, and 54.9 per cent that it had remained unchanged. Although companies in which the organisational hierarchy remained the same are in the majority, the number in which the hierarchy has shrunk is becoming greater than the number of those in which it is expanding. Therefore, among those companies in which management organisation has changed, the proportion of companies that have adopted a flat organisation is increasing. Also, in the 1985 survey, 25.4 per cent of companies reduced the organisational hierarchy, with a resulting flattening of managerial hierarchies with the spread of information technology.

If decision-making in management is looked at next (Table 7.3A), in the 1993 survey 36.2 per cent of companies answered that it had 'devolved completely to lower management, 23.0 per cent that it was 'concentrated totally among senior management', and 40.8 per cent that it 'remained unchanged'. This clearly suggests decision-making at the management level is being devolved down to lower management, especially in the 1985 survey. When decisions relating to systems and strategy across the company are looked at in sectors such as accounts, personnel and corporate planning, the survey reveals that 28.3 per cent of manufacturing companies answered that decisions were 'concentrated completely at company headquarters', and 31.5 per cent that decisions were 'completely entrusted to the discretion of those in the establishment'(Table 7.3D). In business activities

Table 7.3 Changes in managerial organisational structures

We would like to ask you about how you have implemented improvements to the management organisation of your own establishments over the last five years. Looking at the scale below, please mark the number which you feel is most appropriate.

A Concerning the organisational hierarchy from the top level of management down to shop floor supervisors in your establishments

Greatly expanded 1 2 3 4 5 6 7 Greatly reduced

	1	*2*	*3*	*4*	*5*	*6*	*7*
1985 Survey: N= 130	0.0	2.3	12.3	60.0	19.2	6.2	0.0
1993 Survey: N= 153 Manufacturing companies	0.0	0.0	16.3	54.9	24.8	3.3	0.7
1993 Survey: N= 96 Non-manufacturing companies	1.0	3.1	19.8	54.2	16.7	5.2	0.0

Note: N is the number of sample companies. In the 1985 survey, 37 companies did not respond. In the 1993 survey, 30 manufacturing companies and 14 non-manufacturing companies did not respond.

B Concerning the powers of decision-making in management

Completely concentrated in top management 1 2 3 4 5 6 7 Completely entrusted to lower management

	1	*2*	*3*	*4*	*5*	*6*	*7*
1985 Survey: N= 130	0.8	3.8	11.5	39.2	36.9	6.9	0.8
1993 Survey: N= 153 Manufacturing companies	1.3	6.6	15.1	40.8	34.2	2.0	0.0
1993 Survey: N= 96 Non-manufacturing companies	0.0	9.4	19.8	39.6	31.3	0.0	0.0

Note: N is the number of sample companies. In the 1985 survey, 37 companies did not respond. In the 1993 survey, 31 manufacturing companies and 14 non-manufacturing companies did not respond.

C Concerning the speed of decision-making

Greatly speeded up	1	2	3	4	5	6	7	Greatly slowed down

	1	*2*	*3*	*4*	*5*	*6*	*7*
1985 Survey: N= 130	—	—	—	—	—	—	—
1993 Survey: N= 153 Manufacturing companies	2.0	15.1	46.7	28.3	7.2	0.7	0.0
1993 Survey: N= 96 Non-manufacturing companies	1.0	18.6	50.5	24.7	4.1	1.0	0.0

Note: N is the number of sample companies. In the 1985 survey, this item was not included in the questionnaire. In the 1993 survey, 31 manufacturing companies and 13 non-manufacturing companies did not respond.

D Concerning work duties, such as accounts, personnel and corporate planning

Completely entrusted to the discretion of the business establishment	1	2	3	4	5	6	7	Completely concentrated at the company headquarters level

	1	*2*	*3*	*4*	*5*	*6*	*7*
1985 Survey: N= 130	0.8	0.0	16.2	46.2	23.8	9.2	3.8
1993 Survey: N= 153 Manufacturing companies	0.0	3.9	27.6	40.1	17.8	7.2	3.3
1993 Survey: N= 96 Non-manufacturing companies	1.1	2.1	22.1	35.8	22.1	13.7	3.2

Note: N is the number of sample companies. In the 1985 survey, 37 companies did not respond. In the 1993 survey, 31 manufacturing companies and 15 non-manufacturing companies did not respond.

Source: Okubayashi *et al.* 1994: 197–8

such as accounting, personnel and planning, the move to entrust decision-making to the establishment, and the tendency to concentrate decision-making at company headquarters, are roughly in balance. The trend is, then, for decision-making to be transferred to the lower management, but, depending on the matter at hand, for some decision-making to remain concentrated at company headquarters.

The restructuring of management organisation aims to promote quicker decision-making, with 63.8 per cent of companies claiming to have made changes in order to speed up decision-making, whereas few had acted to slow it down. Only 28.3 per cent of companies had allowed the speed of decision-making to 'remain unchanged', and this was the smallest percentage among the question items in Table 7.3C. In other words, companies which have revamped their managerial structures are carrying out organisational reforms in order to increase the speed of decision-making. The shift in decision-making towards lower managerial staff can also be interpreted as an attempt to implement quick decisions at the point nearest to the workplace. As the scale of corporate organisation grows, the company faces the adverse effects of enlarged bureaucracy, with a reduction in the ability to respond quickly to changing situations. In essence, the reorganisation of management structures is a response to this 'large-scale corporate sickness'.

Information technology (IT) has influenced greatly the speed of decision-making. Not only can more information be dealt with faster, but the range of people able to share that information has burgeoned. Indeed, IT provides more opportunities for the two-way exchange of information between those people. Table 7.4 demonstrates how the frequency of information exchange has changed in areas such as meetings and conferences, as well as in the formation of databases, as a result of IT.

First, insofar as information exchange in the workplace and company headquarters is concerned, manufacturing firms account for 66.1 per cent of those companies which saw information exchange has 'expanded'. Conversely, the number of companies that answered that information exchange had been 'reduced' was an extremely low 5.6 per cent. The number of companies suggesting information exchange had 'remained unchanged' was also low, at 28.8 per cent. Similar trends can be found for non-manufacturing companies. With the development of information technology, information exchange in the workplace and company headquarters is increasing in frequency, and the sharing of information throughout the company is being promoted. Second, 65.3 per cent of manufacturing companies answered that, in the integrated workplace as well, the frequency of information exchange had increased for managers from the level of top management down to the level of shop-floor supervisors. The number of companies saying that information exchange had decreased was 6.3 per cent, and the number saying that it had 'remained unchanged' was 28.4 per cent. These trends are the same for non-manufacturing companies as well. Clearly, shared information is also being promoted within integrated workplaces. Third, at the shop-floor level, the 'section chief' has now become the basic structural unit of the organisation. In addition to the exchange of information up and down the executive hierarchy, the horizontal exchange of information among section chiefs has also become important. Indeed, the number of companies responding that the frequency of exchange between section chiefs had increased was 63.0 per cent, whereas the number of companies seeing a decrease was a very low 5.6 per cent, and the number claiming 'no change' was 31.5 per cent. Hence, in addition to the vertical exchange of information between the executive organisation and the 'shop floor', the exchange of information horizontally at the section chief level has also become commonplace.

Table 7.4 Frequency of information exchange

We would like to ask you about changes in the frequency of information exchange in your establishments over the last five years. Information exchange is defined here as the gathering of information into databases and the ability to access information at any time, in addition to regular conferences and meetings. Looking at the scale below, please mark the number which you feel is most appropriate.

A Concerning the frequency of information exchange between company headquarters and the establishments

Greatly increased	1	2	3	4	5	6	7	Greatly decreased

	1	*2*	*3*	*4*	*5*	*6*	*7*
1993 Survey: N= 177 Manufacturing companies	1.7	20.3	44.1	28.2	5.6	0.0	0.0
1993 Survey: N= 101 Non-manufacturing companies	3.0	27.7	40.6	24.8	4.0	0.0	0.0

Note: N is the number of sample companies. In the 1985 survey, this item was not included in the questionnaire. In the 1993 survey, 6 manufacturing companies and 9 non-manufacturing companies did not respond.

B Concerning the frequency of information exchange between the top levels of management and shop floor supervisors

Greatly increased	1	2	3	4	5	6	7	Greatly decreased

	1	*2*	*3*	*4*	*5*	*6*	*7*
1993 Survey: N=177 Manufacturing companies	0.6	13.6	51.1	28.4	6.3	0.0	0.0
1993 Survey: N=101 Non-manufacturing companies	0.9	18.5	46.3	32.4	1.9	0.0	0.0

Note: N is the number of sample companies. In the 1985 survey, this item was not included in the questionnaire. In the 1993 survey, 7 manufacturing companies and 2 non-manufacturing companies did not respond.

C Concerning the frequency of information exchange between section chiefs

Greatly increased	1	2	3	4	5	6	7	Greatly decreased

	1	*2*	*3*	*4*	*5*	*6*	*7*
1993 Survey N=177 Manufacturing companies	0.6	9.0	53.4	31.5	5.6	0.0	0.0
1993 Survey: N=101 Non-manufacturing companies	0.9	14.8	50.0	30.6	3.7	0.0	0.0

Note: N is the number of sample companies. In the 1985 survey, this item was not included in the questionnaire. In the 1993 survey, 5 manufacturing companies and 2 non-manufacturing companies did not respond.

Source: Okubayashi *et al.* 1994: 198–9

Thus, when structural changes in management organisation are examined, we find the managerial hierarchy becoming flatter, the power of decision-making being devolved to junior managers and the process of managerial decision-making speeding up. What is more, the exchange of information between company headquarters and workplaces, between the top of the company and the shop-floor supervisors, and horizontally between section chiefs, is on the upswing, as is the common sharing of information (Kambayashi 1994). Together with these changes in management organisational structure, the role of the section chief is adapting in response to the demands of the management structure.

CHANGING ROLE OF THE SECTION CHIEF

In Japanese corporate structure the section is the basic unit of business activity and the actions of the section chief, who controls the work duties of the section, as well as the introduction of new technology and changes in management organisation, are especially important. In conjunction with the introduction of new technology, it is argued that the role of this middle management has become redundant.

Table 7.5 is a survey of how the job specifications of the section chief have changed in businesses where information technology has been introduced. First, insofar as diversification in job specifications is concerned, 77.9 per cent of manufacturing companies confirmed an increase in diversification. But only 2.9 per cent of companies noted a reduction in diversification, and only 19.2 per cent answered that it 'remained unchanged'. This trend is particularly strong in non-manufacturing companies.

Second, the 'number of work duties that cannot be specified beforehand' has increased in 63.1 per cent of companies with 6.8 per cent noting an decrease, and 30.1 per cent confirming 'no change'. As a result, the work duties of the section chief have become diversified, and new duties that cannot be specified beforehand have burgeoned.

Third, insofar as the increase in strategic work duties is concerned, such as the planning of new businesses and the development of new products, 69.1 per cent of companies noted an increase. By contrast, the number of companies which answered that their work duties had 'decreased' or 'remained unchanged' was very low, at 2.8 per cent and 28.1 per cent respectively. Hence, along with the flattening out of the executive organisational structure and the devolution of decision-making power to junior managers, the section chief has now come to participate in strategic management duties.

Fourth, insofar as the increase and decrease in management duties for junior staff is concerned, such as the giving of instructions and the checking of results, 63 per cent of manufacturing companies found that recently supervisory duties had 'increased', whereas 9.6 per cent answered that they had decreased, and 27.5 per cent that they remained unchanged. It thus

Table 7.5 Changes in work specifications of section chief

We would like to ask you about changes in the work specifications of the section chief. On the scale below, please mark the number which you feel is most appropriate.

A. Diversity of work specifications

Greatly increased	1	2	3	4	5	6	7	Greatly decreased

1993 Survey	*1*	*2*	*3*	*4*	*5*	*6*	*7*
Manufacturing companies: N=177	1.1	22.6	54.2	19.2	2.3	0.6	0.0
Non-manufacturing companies: N=107	1.9	24.3	57.0	15.9	0.9	0.0	0.0

Note: N is the number of sample companies. In the 1993 survey, 6 manufacturing companies and 3 non-manufacturing companies did not respond.

B Number of unspecified work duties

Greatly increased	1	2	3	4	5	6	7	Greatly decreased

1993 Survey	*1*	*2*	*3*	*4*	*5*	*6*	*7*
Manufacturing companies: N=177	0.0	11.4	51.7	30.1	6.8	0.0	0.0
Non-manufacturing companies: N=107	0.9	9.3	52.3	31.8	5.6	0.0	0.0

Note: N is the number of sample companies. In the 1993 survey, 7 manufacturing companies and 3 non-manufacturing companies did not respond.

C The amount of strategic duties, such as the development of new products and the planning of new businesses

Greatly increased	1	2	3	4	5	6	7	Greatly decreased

1993 Survey	*1*	*2*	*3*	*4*	*5*	*6*	*7*
Manufacturing companies: N=177	1.7	15.2	52.2	28.1	2.2	0.6	0.0
Non-manufacturing companies: N=107	1.0	13.3	56.2	28.6	1.0	0.0	0.0

Note: N is the number of sample companies. In the 1993 survey, 5 manufacturing companies and 5 non-manufacturing companies did not respond.

(continued)

Table 7.5 (continued)

D The amount of managerial duties for overseeing junior staff

Greatly increased	1	2	3	4	5	6	7	Greatly decreased

1993 Survey	*1*	*2*	*3*	*4*	*5*	*6*	*7*
Manufacturing companies: N=177	0.6	13.5	48.9	27.5	9.0	0.6	0.0
Non-manufacturing companies: N=107	1.0	19.0	46.7	28.6	4.8	0.0	0.0

Note: N is the number of sample companies. In the 1993 survey, 7 manufacturing companies and 3 non-manufacturing companies did not respond.

E The amount of organisational duties with other section chiefs

Greatly increased	1	2	3	4	5	6	7	Greatly decreased

1993 Survey	*1*	*2*	*3*	*4*	*5*	*6*	*7*
Manufacturing companies: N=177	1.1	12.9	52.8	30.9	2.2	0.0	0.0
Non-manufacturing companies: N=107	1.9	11.4	51.4	30.5	4.8	0.0	0.0

Note: N is the number of sample companies. In the 1993 survey, 5 manufacturing companies and 5 non-manufacturing companies did not respond.
Source: Okubayashi *et al.* 1994: 201–2

seems that with the spread of information technology the exchange of information with company headquarters has become more frequent, and that management information to be shared by junior staff has become greater. This trend is also the same for non-manufacturing companies. The development of information technology has dictated that the management of junior staff is carried out more carefully.

Fifth, the exchange of information with other sections and the co-ordination of employee duties is examined here as part of the section chief's role. The number of companies which replied that co-ordinating activities with other sections was 'increasing' accounted for 66.8 per cent of the total number of companies, whereas the number of companies noting this co-ordination was 'decreasing' was 2.2 per cent, and even if this figure is combined with the 30.9 per cent of companies stating things 'remained unchanged', the figure is still extremely low. Hence, at the same time as opportunities for the exchange of information between section chiefs are increasing with the spread of information technology, the responsibility of the section chief to co-ordinate these duties is similarly rising.

These changes suggest that, rather than the role of the section chief becoming redundant, new duties are in fact being added to his job description. With the spread of information technology, the former role of the section chief as a transmitter of information has become redundant, but in response to previously unforeseen changes they are taking on strategic duties, strengthening horizontal links with other sections, and indeed taking on a new role. Thus, even assuming the flattening of management organisation, middle-ranking managers will not become totally redundant, but can be expected to take on new roles.[1]

SHIFT TO A 'SOFT' STRUCTURAL ORGANISATION

The introduction of information technology is thus serving to 'flatten' managerial organisation, and the job specifications of the section chief are changing as well. Given these observations, in what direction is the organisational structure of the company, including the managerial organisation, changing?

The organisational structure of companies can be broadly classified into work organisations and managerial organisations. Work organisations are those engaged directly in the production of goods and services, for example, the organisations of supervisors and operatives which are formed around the conveyor belt under the flow operation system. Managerial organisations are those which control the work organisations. They are hierarchical and extend upwards from the section chief to the department manager, and on to the managing directors. These two organisational structures have differed in response to the introduction of micro-electronics technology.

Next, let us examine the trends in those businesses which have already introduced micro-electronics technology (for example, industrial robots and flexible manufacturing systems). Table 7.6 shows how work organisations have changed in those businesses where micro-electronic technology has been introduced. In order to understand work organisations, more clearly the survey asked how work duties were allocated to each operative. The table shows that the most common method of allocating work duties (56.4 per cent) was 'to a certain extent work duties are divided among homogeneous operations, and mutual assistance or job rotation between teams is carried out'. The next most common answer (31.3 per cent) was that 'to a certain extent work duties are divided into homogeneous operations, and are then distributed between every team'.

Answers 1,2 and 3 demonstrate that, even if the specific operation is different, all work duties are allocated by the team unit. This contrasts with answer 4 (7.4 per cent) in which 'the duties of the workplace are allocated to everyone individually and rotation is not carried out'. Answers 1–3 and answer 4 are fundamentally different from each other due to the fact that the former are premised upon the allocation of work duties by team, and the latter is premised upon the allocation of work duties to individuals.

Table 7.6 Work organisation in micro-electronics-based workplace

We would like to ask you about how work duties in your establishments are allocated to each operative. Looking at the four choices given below, please mark the number which you feel is most appropriate.
1) Work duties are evenly allocated to all employees as part of a work team.
2) Work duties are to a certain degree divided into homogenous operations and distributed to every team.
3) Work duties are to a certain degree divided into homogenous operations and mutual assistance between teams and job rotation is carried out.
4) Work duties are allocated to every individual and job rotation is not carried out.

1993 Survey	*1*	*2*	*3*	*4*
Manufacturing companies: N=166	6.7	31.3	54.6	7.4
Non-manufacturing companies: N=102	5.9	27.5	49.0	16.7

Source: Okubayashi *et al.* 1994: 190–1.
Note: N is the number of sample companies. In the 1993 survey, 20 manufacturing companies and 8 non-manufacturing companies did not respond.

Manufacturing companies rarely allocate work duties to individuals, and generally duties are allocated to work team units. This trend is the same for non-manufacturing companies. The choice of whether or not to allocate work duties by the team or individual worker is a functional difference in the make-up of the work organisation. In cases where work duties are divided by team units, the work duties of the individual are undefined, job rotation can be freely carried out within the team, and the operatives can become multi-skilled. The responsibility of accomplishing a task is allocated to the whole team, and the work boundaries and responsibilities of the individual are not subject to demarcation. Thus, mutual assistance within the team is an integral part of the operations.

This type of organisation premised upon the division of work duties by team units may be called an 'organic organisation', as Burns and Stalker (1961) defined 'organic' and 'mechanistic' systems in their research. Conversely, work organisations that divide work duties by individuals could be termed 'mechanistic work organisations'.

The fundamental characteristics of a managerial organisation can be distinguished by whether or not it expands or flattens out the managerial hierarchy. Thus, the companies in the 1993 survey which answered that the managerial hierarchy had expanded or remained the same can be termed the 'hierarchical type', and those companies which answered that they had flattened out the hierarchy can be called 'flat type'. In turn, work organisations can be divided into 'mechanistic' and 'organic' types, and managerial structures into 'hierarchical-type' and 'flat-type' structures, and when grouped together, as in Figure 7.2, four organisational structures can be

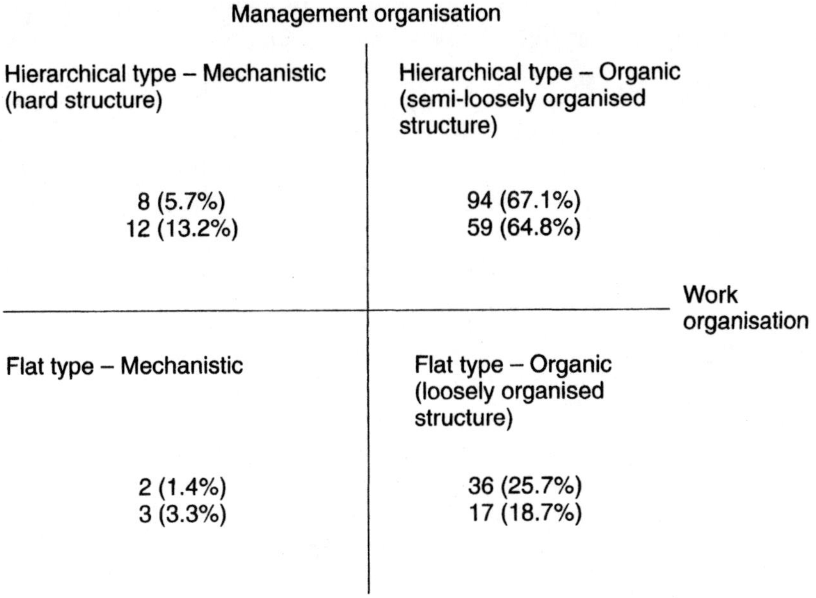

Management organisation

Hierarchical type – Mechanistic (hard structure) 8 (5.7%) 12 (13.2%)	Hierarchical type – Organic (semi-loosely organised structure) 94 (67.1%) 59 (64.8%)	
		Work organisation
Flat type – Mechanistic 2 (1.4%) 3 (3.3%)	Flat type – Organic (loosely organised structure) 36 (25.7%) 17 (18.7%)	

Figure 7.2 Types of organisational structure
Source: Okubayashi *et al.* 1994: 152
Notes:
(a) The number of sample companies for survey was 140 for manufacturing industry and 91 for non-manufactuing industry.
(b) Hierarchical type – companies which answered that management hierarchy had expanded or remained unchanged over the last 5 years; Flat type – companies which answered that they had flattened the managerial hierarchy over the last 5 years; Mechanistic – companies which answered that work duties were allocated to every individual; Organic – companies which answered that work duties were allocated on a team basis.
(c) The top figure in brackets is for manufacturing companies and the bottom figure in brackets is for non-manufacturing companies.

distinguished. The distribution of manufacturing and non-manufacturing into four categories based upon the 1993 survey is shown in Figure 7.2.

Corporate organisational structures in which the managerial organisation is of the hierarchical type, and in which the work organisation is mechanistic, are generally termed 'hard structures'. This contrasts with organisational structures in which managerial organisations are of the flat type, and in which work organisations are of the organic or team work type. These are termed 'loosely structured' organisations. Those organisational structures in between are classified as 'semi-loosely structured'.

Figure 7.2 illustrates that corporate organisational structures are classified into four main types, and the type which occupies the greatest proportion is the hierarchical and semi-loosely structured organisation. Therefore, even under conditions of the spread of micro-electronics technology, and the flattening out of organisation at company headquarters, the most prominent type of corporate organisation is the semi-loosely structured one.

Second, the flat-type, soft structural organisation demonstrates one method of structural reorganisation which is increasing in comparison to the 12.8 per cent in the 1985 survey. In conjunction with the spread of micro-electronics and information technology the percentage of companies adopting loosely structured organisations is increasing. The 1985 survey had as its sample only manufacturing companies, but it is likely that the loosely structured organisations were present among these, and probably accounted for a large percentage of non-manufacturing industries as well.

Third, Figure 7.2 shows that with the spread of micro-electronics technology organisational structures have shifted from 'hard' to 'loose' structures. This shift becomes clear if the distribution across every category in the 1985 and 1993 surveys is compared. Logically, the hard structural organisation is one suited to a limited-product, mass-production system with stable markets. In contrast, the loosely structured organisation is one suited to a multiple-product, medium-sized production system premised upon a changing market. Representative of this is the production of electronic goods such as televisions and videos.

When corporate organisational structures shift from hard structural organisations to loosely structured organisations with changes in the production system and the spread of micro-electronics, a shift also occurs in the managerial organisation, from a hierarchical to a flat type. In addition, a surplus of white-collar workers in the managerial organisations and a change in the role of managers becomes inevitable. It is difficult for managers or white-collar workers whose training has been based upon traditional hard structural organisations to adapt to the new loose structure, and they become the target of personnel adjustments (Hōsei Daigaku Ōhara Shakai Mondai Kenkyūsho 1993; Nomura 1993). When looked at over the long-term, the 'suffering of the white-collar worker' and the 'small company headquarters' are simply phenomena that reflect change in corporate organisational structure. Therefore, the personnel adjustments of white-collar workers, through such means as the introduction of early retirement systems, transfers to allied companies, and the reduction of recruitment of new university graduates, are likely to continue.

CONCLUSION

A shift of organisational structures in Japanese large companies from 'hard' to 'soft' thus can be taken to be influenced by the introduction of micro-electronics and information technology. We may envisage a similar trend in other advanced industrial economies, although they may develop within their own social and cultural contexts. A research project with a similar theme has been carried out in regard to UK business organisation under computer integrated technologies (Bessant 1993), from which evidence has emerged to suggest a trend similar to Japan.

A 'loosely-structured' organisation may not be unique to Japan; rather it may be considered a more universal phenomenon which is emerging as a consequence of the micro-electronics revolution, under which large corporations are required to respond to rapidly changing markets and to introduce a production system suitable for such change. If the case of Japan can be taken as a sign of a general trend, then it is perhaps due to the rapid change of corporate environments as represented by the termination of high growth and globalisation, and the rapid impact of the micro-electronics revolution.

NOTES

1 There is a critical view based upon the research of the British case concerning the theme pursued in this chapter (Marginson *et al.* 1988).

REFERENCES

Bessant, J. (1993) 'Towards factory 2000: designing organization for computer-integrated technologies', in J. Clark (ed.) *Human Resource Management and Technological Change,* London: Sage.

Burns, T. and Stalker, G.M. (1961) *The Management of Innovation*, London: Tavistock Publications.

Hōsei Daigaku Ōhara Shakai Mondai Kenkyūsho (ed.) (1993) *Rōdō no Ningenka no Shintenkai: Hiningenteki Rōdō karano Dakkyaku* (New development of the humanisation of work: getting away from inhumane labour), Tokyo: Sōgō Rōdō Kenkyūsho.

Imada, O. (1991) 'ME Gijutsukakushin to Sagyōsoshiki no Henka' (Microelectronics innovation and changes of work organisation), in H. Hasegawa, T. Watanabe and T. Yasui (eds) *Nyu Tekunoroji to Kigyōrōdō* (New technology and labour in business enterprise), Tokyo: Ōtsuki Shoten.

Kambayashi, N. (1994) 'Kigyōsoshiki kōzō to shokumunaiyō: soshiki sekkeironteki apurochi no yūkōsei (Organisational structure and job content: effectiveness of organizational design approach), *Kokumin Keizai Zasshi*, vol. 170, no. 1: 97–118.

Marginson, P., Edward, P.K., Martin, P., Percell, J. and Sisson, K. (1988) *Beyond the Workplace*, Oxford: Blackwell.

Mitsubishi Sōgō Kenkyūsho (1992) *Jōhōka no Sangyō, Rōdō ni ataeru Eikyō ni kansuru Jittaichōsa* (Report on effects of information technology on industry and work), Tokyo: Mitsubishi Sōgō Kenkyūsho.

Morita, M. (1994) 'Rōdō no Ningenka no Konnichiteki Tenkai' (Recent development of the humanisation of work), in Nihon Keieigakkai (ed.) *Sekai no nakano Nihon Kigyo* (Japanese firms in the world), Tokyo: Chikura Shobo.

Nihon Rōdō Kenkyūkikō (1992) 'Gijutsukakushin no shinten ni tomonau ginōhenka ni kansuru chōsa kenkyū' (Report on skill changes caused by technological innovation, manufacturing industry), *Chōsa Kenkyū Hokokushō*, no. 35, November.

Nomura, M. (1993) *Toyotizumu: Nihongata Seisan Shisutemu no Seijuku to Henbō* (Toyotism: maturation and changes of Japanese-style production system), Kyoto: Mineruva Shobo.

Okubayashi, K., Shomura, H., Takebayashi, H. Morita, M. and Kanbayashi, N. (1994) *Jūkōzōsoshiki Paradaimu Jōsetsu* (An introduction to a paradigm of flexible structure in organisation), Tokyo: Bunshindo.

Shi, S. (1992) *Kigyō no Genbasoshiki to Gijutsu* (Shop floor organisation of business enterprise), Tokyo: Chūō Keizaisha.

Yoshida, K. (1993) *Nihongata Keieishisutemu no Kōzai* (Pros and cons of Japanese-style management), Tokyo: Tōyōkeizai Shinpōsha.

8 The rise of flexible and individual ability-oriented management

Watanabe Takashi

This chapter examines the new trends in employment management arising from changes in the employment environment taking place in recent years in Japan. From the late 1980s to the mid-1990s environmental changes have affected jobs in both quality and quantity through a whole range of different factors: the introduction of revolutionary micro-electronics technology, the 'greying' of society, the decrease in youth labour, the increase in higher educated women in employment, the mobility of the labour market, the diversification in occupational consciousness and sense of values, the explosion in the variety of work and life styles, and the implementation of new life-and-labour-related laws for workers, e.g. the Equal Opportunities Law, Labour Standards Law Amendment, and Child-care Leave Law.

In such situations major businesses are now drastically changing their mid- and long-term employment strategy from a uniform single-line type of employment management, based on a collective philosophy, to a mixed, flexible and individualistic multi-line type. One recent example of the above changes is the introduction of the career course selection system. This chapter is based upon the author's research findings during 1992–4 on the career course selection system and its impacts upon the employment of women (Watanabe 1995b).

DEVELOPMENT OF A PLURALISTIC APPROACH IN EMPLOYMENT MANAGEMENT

Let us first turn to the recent trend towards diversity in employment management. We can identify a new trend now emerging in which different human resources are employed and dealt with differently. This has become widespread, particularly in major companies and banks, and indicates the direction of employment strategy from a mid- to long-term point of view. In this approach, people with differing capabilities are employed in a way meant to tap individual enthusiasm and ability, and employees are treated more as individuals who are progressing via various career courses to retirement. Such a system is totally different from the previous single-line mode of employment management, which itself had retained elements of the past system of lifetime employment and seniority ranking.

Therefore, 'diversity in employment management' involves the following points:

- diversification in the human resources being employed;
- diversification in recruitment;
- diversification in working styles, times and places;
- diversification in career courses.

In regard to the first point, in order to prepare for expected labour shortage in the future, a wide range of people of different age groups, gender, experience and nationality is now required. The use of older people with rich knowledge and experience is particularly needed as youth labour is likely to become scarce. In line with the international and domestic trend towards equal opportunities, the use of a female workforce, including returning employees as well as new graduates, will be a strong demand at certain levels. The employment of immigrant workers, which is actually in operation in some areas, is moving forward not only at blue-collar level in factories, but also in white-collar positions in offices in line with the increasing internationalization of the Japanese economy.

Second, the mode of recruitment is taking on new forms. Most importantly, while in conventional permanent employment regular workers are hired as stock, flexible means of employment are now widely used, with non-regular workers hired as temporary (direct or via an agency), part-time, casual, assigned, or subcontracted workers. The growing mobility in the labour market has witnessed the growth of head-hunting, mid-career recruitment and secondary 'new' graduate recruitment. In general, such flexible modes of recruitment aim to avert a mismatch in the supply and demand of labour, both in quantity and quality.

Third, time and location factors are also diversifying. Other than the situation where all workers have to keep to regular working times, flexible and staggered working hours and a part-time system have been developed according to specific requirements. A similar trend applies to workplace, i.e. satellite office, home-based work, and limited area employment arrangements.

Finally, various career path modes have been created in connection with the above conditions. For example, the career course selection system, career path selection system, and internal open recruitment system have become widespread as multi-line types of employment systems, and employees are encouraged to select for themselves a career course in line with their individual preference. On the other hand, the flexible age-limit system, childcare leave programme, homecare leave programme and the redeployment of female employees are examples where employees are allowed to take a break from their career of their own volition.

In this way, employment management has become more eclectic in a number of respects, including human resources, types of recruitment, working time/place and career courses, and the career course selection system.

DIVERSITY IN EMPLOYMENT MANAGEMENT

The following points suggest why employment management has recently become multifaceted, and the new method of career course selection system has been introduced.

In the first place, due to the recent development of micro-electronics technology and office automation, job conditions have been changing in both quantity and quality, and this has required a demand for various multi-line types of employment management. Quantitatively, by minimizing operations a large amount of redundancies was brought about. This has been intensified by workforce reductions following the onset of recession after the so-called 'bubble economy' of the 1980s. In terms of quality, planning, decision-making, managing and similar tasks increasingly centre on a small number of people, while routine and subsidiary jobs like administration and sales are performed by a relatively large proportion of the workforce. This has resulted in greater centralization of authority at headquarters, and much of the relevance of middle management's job role has disappeared, leaving managerial organization much flatter. This has led to a need for traditional, uniform management to be reorganized in order to carry out rationalization in accordance with new changes in job conditions.

Second, the problem of middle-aged male workers, a relatively important part of the workforce structure, needs to be resolved. The aforesaid trends, like the polarization of labour and flat organization due to the development of micro-electronics technology and office automation, is actually incompatible with the fact that middle-aged male workers now make up a relatively large part of the workforce. Most of these workers were employed en masse during the high economic growth period, when mass production and mass consumption were the order of the day. Now, acute personnel problems have arisen in the process of streamlining organizations through office automation and the growth of routine jobs (i.e. difficulty of rewarding seniority by ranking, shortage of management positions, etc.). Such workers thus have been the target of mass redundancies by means of transfer to other workplaces, often affiliate companies, but a long-term solution is needed which takes account of the changes in overall job conditions. Any such solution would have to accord with employee management and be reinforced on the basis of individual ability, not seniority as in the past. The prior qualification system based upon competence influenced by seniority considerations such as age and length of services has had to be fundamentally reviewed, and a multi-line type of individual management – the so-called career course selection system – has been proposed as a new alternative for employment management. As Keizai Dōyūkai has stated:

> When the requirement of the efficient use of personnel and the utilization of workers' specialities and creativity is considered, the existing hierarchical ranking system dominated by line management positions will harm the running of the organization. In order to utilize people more effectively in terms of individual preference, ability and aptitude, multiline management positions should be introduced, such as line management and specialist management, and specially assigned management positions should coexist.
>
> (Keizai Dōyūkai 1992)

Thus the employment management system has been under pressure to become multifarious and diverse so as to achieve an ability-oriented, individual-based management as indicated in the above concept.

Third, measures are needed to boost female rates of participation in employment and the prolongation of their employment period. Recently, more and more women are joining the workforce, aided by the Equal Opportunities Law and their rising educational standards. Nevertheless, employers' attitudes towards women workers remain ambivalent: on the one hand, very few women are encouraged to climb the hierarchy; on the other, the proportion of women working for a short period has been allowed to rise, thereby carefully avoiding offences under Equal Opportunities Law. This is a way for companies to maintain and continue the low-wage structure throughout the system. On this point Sakurai Minoru, a business consultant, reflects the view of management:

> What the Equal Opportunities Law will influence most is that women workers who tend to stay with their job will continue to rarely leave their jobs [but] unfortunately, personnel management at banks has a two-sided approach. Management systems, like wages, have been based on the assumption that women workers tend to resign their jobs at certain ages, so that if they stay longer, the system will be under strain. It has survived so far because women workers do normally leave at around 25 or 26 years old, but if they do not resign at such young ages in the future, problems are unavoidable unless the system is redesigned . . . hence career course selection.
>
> (Sakurai 1985: 7–10)

That is why the minor career course has been initiated, in which advancement of ranking, promotion in position and pay increments are restrained, so that 'women workers will probably still leave their jobs at certain ages'. Thus the rising participation of women in employment has exerted some impact on employment management.

Fourth, we should also be aware of the response to the increasing demand for new types of human resources in line with changes in job content created by restructuring and the growth of internationalization. Some enterprises have moved into other tangential areas of business, thereby complicating competition among companies in the affected areas. Individual companies see this in terms of wider business opportunities, which can change the existing profit structure. Particularly in the large-scale development of the information network system, there is greater possibility of developing and supplying new products and services in line with the enlargement of business, and this is one of the new areas for competition among companies. Under such a situation there is an urgent need to train and keep staff who can develop new systems and software. Whether such human resources are available and how to use them – i.e. human resources management strategies – are crucial factors in successful competition. On the other hand, if time is limited, head-hunting or mid-career recruitment will be the order of the day.

Insofar as the internationalization and globalization of company management is concerned, many major companies have recently launched businesses overseas, thereby becoming multinational in seeking profit opportunities worldwide. A new type of employee, able to adjust to the international business world, is thus needed. Such people must be able to adapt to different cultural conditions and ways of thinking, should have a language facility adequate for communication and be familiar with international business. It is important to train and keep such staff. In order to achieve an international strategy, overseas business trips or a lengthy overseas postings 'without their consent' are often required (Watanabe 1987).

Thus, the process of restructuring, changing business content and internationalization has created the urgent need for the education and development of new types of human resources as well as developing business opportunities. This calls for a system adapted to the fluctuating demand and supply of human resources, relating also to the reduction of redundant middle-age male employees, and consequently will influence the reorganization of employment management systems.

Fifth, employees' work and life styles have been changing as their sense of values (working morale, life plan, etc.) diversify. Many surveys have shown that more employees now want to enjoy their social and family life, rather than being just a company worker. Occupational awareness among women workers has also been changing as their educational backgrounds have risen, the Equal Opportunities Law has been implemented and public campaigns on women's issues have shot up. 'Fewer and fewer women now leave employment at marriage and even those who do leave their jobs often intend to resume employment after a certain stage of their child care' (Sōrifu 1994). Therefore, the introduction of new employment management systems in accordance with the diversification of values and life styles is essential.

Sixth, the labour market has lately become highly mobile. With the development of micro-electronics technology and information network systems throughout society, industrial structure and the labour process of individual enterprises have been drastically reorganized and the complex social relationships and human networks have been greatly reorganized. This has caused labour demand and supply to change rapidly in quality and quantity and has encouraged considerable mobility in the labour market to cope with the effect of redundancy schemes. Although a small number of core employees in business organizations is still in lifetime employment, the majority of peripheral workers is used flexibly so that the required number of people with the required skill levels is utilized as need arises and any mismatch in the balance of labour demand and supply can be avoided. This new trend in the labour market has influenced diversification in employment management.

Seventh, we should note that such diversification was encouraged and assured by a series of legal measures in the late 1980s, namely the implementation and amendment of workers' life-related laws like the Equal Opportunities Law (July 1986), Worker Despatch Law (July 1986), Law of Stable Employment for the Aged (1986, amended 1990), Labour Standard Law Amendment (April 1988), Childcare Leave Law (April 1992) and Homecare Leave Law (1995). Such legal arrangements still leave some limits, but generally aim to allow jobs to fit into various individual life styles. Thus they are based on the diversity of employment management and promote and assure the development of further changes.

Finally, theoretical considerations such as 'plural approaches to employment management', based on organizational behaviour theory, should be noted. More prescriptive theories like the 'Multi-line type of employment management' (Masaru Hagiwara, Kantō Keieisha Kyōkai), 'In-firm career path selection system', 'Multi-mode personnel management system' (Takizawa Saori), and 'Selective career development' (Yamada Makiko) have been presented in connection with the recent changes in the employment environment. Their main theme is how to integrate the individual into the logic of the organization as a whole, boosting individual morale by satisfying the desire for self-actualization based on personal values and respecting personal autonomy, self-enlightenment and individual ability. Therefore, it can be said that these theories are at the root of the diversification in employment management and provide a theoretical framework for the various approaches (Watanabe 1995a). Recent employment management in Japan thus has become multifaceted, especially since in the wake of the 'bubble economy' all industries in difficult economic circumstances have promoted management rationalization, demanded by cost considerations and the severe competition among companies. Such action first led to the reduction of sales and total labour costs, and then calls for wage restraint, redundancy and even longer intensive work. Still, employers must adjust to meet such demands for rationalization.

A new employment management system has been sought in order to meet various changes, both within and without companies, related to employment, such as changes in labour process due to the development of micro-electronics technology, in job quality and quantity, in industrial structure, in the labour market, in occupational awareness and value systems, in working styles, the rising proportion of women entering employment and the requirements of the new laws mentioned above.

Freed from the constraints of uniform management based on past forms of collectivism, by seeking various possibilities of employment in terms of human resources, recruitment, working conditions and career selection, intensified individualistic management has been demanded. The above are the socio-economic factors for the introduction of the course selection employment system (an individual-oriented personnel management) and its widespread use by large-scale companies.

CAREER COURSE SELECTION SYSTEM

The career course selection system is not always uniform and is difficult to specify. The Ministry of Labour defines it as 'determining the course of several different job types, such as planning or routine work, and with the presence/absence of transfer, including domestic relocation, and including allocation, promotion, education and training for employees, which are performed per course' (Rōdōshō 1991). As this definition indicates, the career course selection system is in general based totally on the assumption of institutional classification and determination of career course. The following is a typical course classification:

In the major career course or path A, the employees are engaged in essential jobs which have no limitation in content and may be transferred to remote areas inland or overseas where their consent is not always necessary. In the minor career course or path B, the employees do routine and subsidiary jobs under the inclusive instructions of management, but will not be transferred to a distant workplace requiring domestic relocation. In the special career course/path C, employees are engaged in specialist work in very specific fields, but will not be transferred outside the area of work normally performed. According to my interview survey in 1992 of the Daiichi Kangyō Bank Ltd, the following three courses were set up. The major career course is for employees who engage in core administrative jobs in business, administration, planning/research and other important jobs. Employees in this category will be sent to any place in Japan or abroad regardless of the kind of job. The minor career course is for those who engage in mainly standard and regular jobs in business and administration. Employees in this category are not expected to move from their original place of employment. The special career course is for those who engage in jobs which require special knowledge and skills in specific fields. Employees in this category are not allocated work other than in the original specialist area.

Apart from these cases, new courses, like the so-called 'area major career course' or the 'new major career course' (where job conditions are the same as in the major career course, but involve no distant transfers), have been set up recently, and included some institutional adjustments. In my interview in 1993, for example, the major career course has been divided into two groups in the Bank of Tokyo Ltd. The 'new major career course' will not require a change of living place. Similarly, in the Long-term Credit Bank of Japan the major career course introduced in April 1985 does not call for transfer. Finally, in the Sumitomo Bank Ltd, in the new major career course introduced in July 1990, the employees will engage at first in marketing for individual customers, but in accordance with their performance they will be promoted to the position of deputy head of a branch, which requires some decision-making function.

Various systems ranking competence by job group type or personnel grading systems combine with these career courses, assigning appropriate advancement in ranking, promotion and pay incrementation. Thus, the previous single-ranking system, evaluating competence by type of job group can be broken down into two or three constituents, connected with each career course. Normally, in minor career courses, the upper limit of advancement in rank, position and pay is pre-set at a low level and implies no promotion to management rank. For similar working conditions as applied in the past, one must opt for a major career course. In most cases it is possible to switch courses midway, but in practice it is easier to move from major to minor courses than vice versa, because of various conditions and stipulations. Moreover, the deployment of female employees is established as a subsystem. Although women's occupational awareness has increased and fewer women are leaving work at marriage, many still prefer temporarily to interrupt their employment to raise children. For such women, a deployment arrangement system is preferable.

PROBLEMS WITH CAREER COURSE SELECTION

If career course selection is examined from the viewpoints of employee education, ability development and working conditions, the following problems can be noted.

Predefined and arbitrary course setting and ability development

The career course selection system was designed to appeal to individual values and desires for personal growth, and is in these senses innovative. On the other hand, employees are asked to choose between two or three alternatives which have been defined by a third party and contain certain stipulations like the obligation or absence of distant transfer. The choice is therefore rather narrow and not entirely conducive to personal growth.

In assigning career course, job content is basically categorized into 'essential' or 'subsidiary' work; yet it is 'impossible to classify jobs in such a dualistic way, i.e. as essential or non-essential' (judgment handed down by the Tokyo District Court, 4 December 1986, on the *Tekkō Renmei* (Japan Iron and Steel Federation) case. Normally, 'essential' job content is unspecified and unlimited, while 'subsidiary' jobs are those considered to assist the 'essential' jobs, which are themselves lacking in specification and limitation in context – hence the classification becomes totally meaningless. Nonetheless, jobs are sorted into 'major' or 'minor' career courses, and employee competence is assessed by respective grading structures, which determine personnel treatment. The mechanism of the system can be seen to generate its own stresses. In addition, the allocation of only routine and subsidiary jobs to minor course employees, who happen to be mostly women, imposes institutional restrictions upon their personal aspirations, so that advancement of position or the development of occupational ability is curtailed. As Japanese business in general regard highly on-the-job training and job rotation, establishing a career course involving only subsidiary work is dysfunctional for the system, especially in terms of improving positions, educating staff and developing occupational ability; it is also against the spirit of the Equal Opportunities Law.

Differences in working conditions per career course

Contrary to its proclaimed aim, the career course selection system does not assure the freedom of the individual. Most of the major companies adopting the system recruit per career course, which means that course selection is made at the time of application. Therefore, the candidate's scope for selecting a course is restricted by the company's personnel authority; applicants considered to be choosing an inappropriate course may not be employed at all. It is particularly the case that women, who are at a disadvantage owing to the balance of labour demand and supply, have to accept what the company chooses to offer them. It is well known that when women state their preference for a major career course, companies will try to dissuade them, drawing their attention to extreme circumstances such as overseas transfer or promotion problems. Women are therefore treated very differently from men, and as a result the majority enter the minor career course in which improvements in rank, position and pay are curtailed beforehand.

In the Daiichi Kangyō Bank Ltd, for example, only a very few number of employees are recruited to the major career course A, as shown in Table 8.1. Indeed, the number was only 4 out of 849 new female recruits in 1990, 8 out of 846 in 1991, and 20 out of 850 in 1992. The majority of new female recruits were thus in the minor career course B in each respective year. On the other hand, 572 male employees were recruited in 1990, 473 in 1991 and 475 in 1992 and all these male employees were in the major career course A.

The major career course is combined with the condition of distant transfer 'without the employee's consent', and such an unreasonable con-

Table 8.1 Employment trend at the Daiichi Kangyō Bank Ltd

1 Course

	Course A (Sōgō-shoku)		*Course B (Ippan-shoku)*	*Course C (Tokutei-shoku)*	
	Male	*Female*			*Total*
4/1990	572	4	832	13	1,421
4/1991	473	8	820	18	1,319
4/1992	475	20	790	40	1,325

2 Gender

	Male	*Female*	*Total*
4/1990	572	849	1,421
4/1991	473	846	1,319
4/1992	475	850	1,325

3 Schooling

	University		*Junior college*	*High School*	
	Male	*Female*			*Total*
4/1990	572	62	735	52	1,421
4/1991	473	112	695	39	1,319
4/1992	475	155	660	35	1,325

Sources: Ginko Shinpōsha, 1991, April, no. 1731; 1992, April, no. 1781

dition of employment must surely be criticized. Without questioning whether such a condition is necessary for the particular job, employers coerce candidates by making the acceptance of this condition, which implies domestic relocation, a crucial factor in their application. Whether candidates should accept such a condition depends considerably on their family circumstances, such as housing, childcare, children's schooling and parental care, which are irrelevant to their occupational ability. Nevertheless, the decision is forced upon candidates while they are still in their final year at university and far from clear about their future family life. Unfairness therefore exists.

Even if transfer is an area over which employers reserve rights, they are not legally permitted to force their employees to go to a distant location or to move house at the firm's convenience, as several court cases have indicated. The 'inclusive consent of employees' to transfer may be said to exist, but the stipulation to accept distant transfer without the employee's consent as a precondition of employment, adopted to avoid the risk of allegations of misuse of authority over personnel, is totally unreasonable and serves to discourage male as well as especially female candidates at the recruitment stage.

It should also be observed that each career course corresponds to a different ranking system, so that selecting any one involves differences in promotion, rank, position and wage incrementation, in addition to the presence or absence of transfer. Thus, at recruitment, would-be employees are supposed to select a course where the specified working conditions are part of the job offer on a 'take it or leave it' basis. In other words, before starting employment they must condone and accept discriminatory treatment offered as part of a set plan; this is obvious in the case of the minor course, where the ceiling of rank, etc, is preset at lower levels. However, as noted above, the ability to switch course, though present, is easier from the major to minor level. The other way round is limited by various stipulations, hence placing institutional limitations on an individual's desire for personal growth, hindering staff education and development of occupational ability and tending to keep minor course employees at low wage levels.

Voluntary selection as direct and indirect discrimination

Officially, the career course selection system is designed to 'be fair and respect employees' voluntary decisions' and 'not to discriminate against women'. Employers claim that 'the fact that some women are selected for major career courses shows that sexual discrimination does not exist', and the following circumstances allow them to feel justified in this claim.

First of all, the course range is tiny, with only two or three courses from which to choose. If distant transfer with domestic relocation is a problem, many women may feel restricted in going for another – or the other – course, simply because they are uncertain whether, in a society that is still male dominated, they will be able in the future to move house for the sake of their job. The pressure is thus upon women to opt for a minor career course, which, although free from transfer preconditions, restricts their pay and potential advancement. This means that course selection effectively functions as indirect discrimination, while its basis as the 'free voluntary decision' of the applicant allows the theoretical claim that sexual discrimination does not exist.

Disadvantages or differences in working conditions, promotions and rewards are then specified to be internal issues of the recruitment/employment category, via course selection. It is declared that 'such differences naturally occur due to the difference between the courses', and that responsibility ultimately lies with the individuals who select the course. The outcome is that if only women are employed for the minor career course, any disadvantageous treatment they receive is not sexual discrimination and does not contravene the Equal Opportunities Law, 'as there will be no male employees in that group with whom comparison may be made'.

Eliminating sexual discrimination and developing women's position, as well as educating staff and improving occupational ability, is a social issue for both the public and private sectors (in addition to being a worldwide historical issue), but is here trivialized or sublimated into a matter of recruitment and employment practices in individual companies, i.e. an internal problem of course selection.

Recently, some city banks have been treating female employees on minor career courses according to their contract specifications, but have been putting them to work normally reserved for their major career courses, such as public relations (*Nihon Keizai Shinbun* 1992: 20 Sept.). Other companies have adopted conditions for the minor career course in regard to job allocation, promotion and education and training for women on their major career courses. These are obvious indications that the idealism of career selection has collapsed, and that female employees are still regarded as cheap labour among whom temporary and part-time employment is promoted. Again, this is not accepted to be sexual discrimination, but an internal problem of classification of the major and minor career courses.

CONCLUSION: THE FORMATION OF INDIVIDUALISTIC MANAGEMENT

As regards the reinforcement of ability-oriented management, the career course selection system, which was recently introduced to and has become widespread among major companies, has brought unacceptable levels of discrimination upon employees as well as a degree of selection, differentiation and division, under the guise of employing a wider range of human resources in a wider range of contexts. In fact, this may result in intensifying competition and weakening of workers' unions. On this point, it would seem inevitable and even natural for workers throughout society to criticize this system, either directly or indirectly (Watanabe 1990).

Yet, looking at the system in general, it aims to deal with employees according to their desire for personal growth. Individuals are not asked, as previously, to change themselves to fit into the organization, but rather the organization seeks flexible employment patterns that will allow the treatment of workers as individuals and satisfy their inclinations, independence, needs, aspirations, occupational consciousness and value systems (see Table 8.2). We may say therefore that the system acknowledges that people are different individuals and attempts to foster a wide range of independent individuals within it.

The *Keizai Dōyūkai* (Japan Committee for Economic Development) has the following to say:

> In the past, people sometimes tended to sacrifice even their own lives for the sake of hard work, but now a different kind of occupational enthusiasm is required. As independent individuals, workers are asked to maintain a balance between their work (occupational life) and leisure (family life and local community), to improve their abilities and activate their creativity and personal autonomy in order to acquire a sense of

Table 8.2 Model of a new employment system proposed by Japan Federation of Employers Association

	Employment form	*Category of employee*	*Wages*	*Bonus*	*Retirement lumpsum pension*	*Promotion*	*Welfare*
Accumulated ability group	Contract without definite terms	Managerial post holder, major career employees, key technicians	Monthly or annual salary system Pay for job ability Promotion system	Regular wage rise and bonus for performance	Point system	Promotion to managerial positions Promotion of job qualification	All-round welfare measures
Specialized ability group	Contract for definite terms	Special fields (planning, business, R&D)	Annual salary system No pay rise No payment by performance	Distribution by results	None	Evaluation of achievements	Livelihood protection measures
Flexible employment group	Contract for definite terms	Minor career employees Skilled employees Sales employees	Hourly wage system Payment by job No pay rise	Regular wage rise	None	Change to upper rank jobs	Livelihood protection measures

Source: Nihon Keieisha Dantai Renmei. 1995

> accomplishment and job satisfaction through their work, and to aim for self-realization.
>
> (Keizai Dōyūkai 1992)

This image of the 'independent individual' is not one that can be expected to be fostered by company education, but may be generated objectively in the modern corporate system itself. In this system today, the comprehensive information networks and new media have aided the socialization of production and labour worldwide, and as a result a complex and large-scale social interrelationship has been established of individual co-operation and endeavour, i.e. a human network has been established.

Company organization cannot now survive without such complex social relations, nor can general activities in the production and distribution of goods take place. In order to maintain such wide complex relations, organizations must be established that are rationally and systematically structured and individuals must be fully independent and responsible enough to accomplish personal goals. This is the kind of human model proposed in McGregor's Theory Y (McGregor 1960)[1] and under this model individuals are thought to grow not through the company ethic but by the objective developing process of the corporate system. In other words, general activities of production and distribution based on co-operative social relations have reached the stage where they will only survive if the individuals within them are autonomous and responsible. Moreover, as social relations become broader and more complex, individuals will be required to continue developing autonomously, with independence and conscious responsibility vis-à-vis their self-development and self-realization. This is not the only reason why people in organizations are expected to be 'independent individuals', in the interests of enterprise management and the enhancement of general activities of production and distribution, but also the basis on which theorists of organizational behaviour like McGregor promote the human model of 'independent individuals'.

From this kind of individual's point of view, on the other hand, employees would prefer to be a member of the social community and family unit rather than a company employee driven by the competition principle. No longer trapped in the restricted relationships of collectivism and a paternalistic company structure, value may be obtained in everyday life and satisfaction in family relationships through the action of a broad social human network consisting of individuals with a liberal and broadminded perspective. People are increasingly turning towards such a life style, perhaps in a desire for the elements of social belonging – love, social respect, and personal development within the social framework. Many surveys have indicated the recent growth of awareness of home and social issues in personal life. According to Akaoka, this implies the enrichment of the 'three Ls' – work life, social life and family life (Akaoka 1993).

It is therefore necessary for employers to change their style of management from one centred on the company, as has been the case to date, to one where the three factors of society, company and individual are well balanced and individuals are highly esteemed as 'good members of society, local community and family' (Keizai Dōyūkai 1992). Whether such a concept is intended to improve the morale of individuals or to function as a model of unifying individuals towards an organizational goal, it clearly reflects a new tendency, a new human model generated by a modern company system as outlined above.

As this discussion has shown, the recent development of the career course selection system is based on 'independent individuals' and also further promotes the increase of such individuals. If these individuals then go on to raise their own social consciousness and combine it with a democratic awareness through a social network, a very strong basis is assured for the total development of individuals within today's major company systems, despite employers' intentions and attitudes.

Assuming this, the career course selection system does indeed create a new type of independent individual, although simultaneously imposing on employees discrimination, categorization, differential and division and a new kind of work pressure. As a result, there can be no doubt that the uniform, collectivistic management, known until now as 'Japanese-style management', will sooner or later be replaced by a flexible, pluralistic and individualistic approach, as hinted at recently by the introduction of the annual salary system (see Figure 8.1).

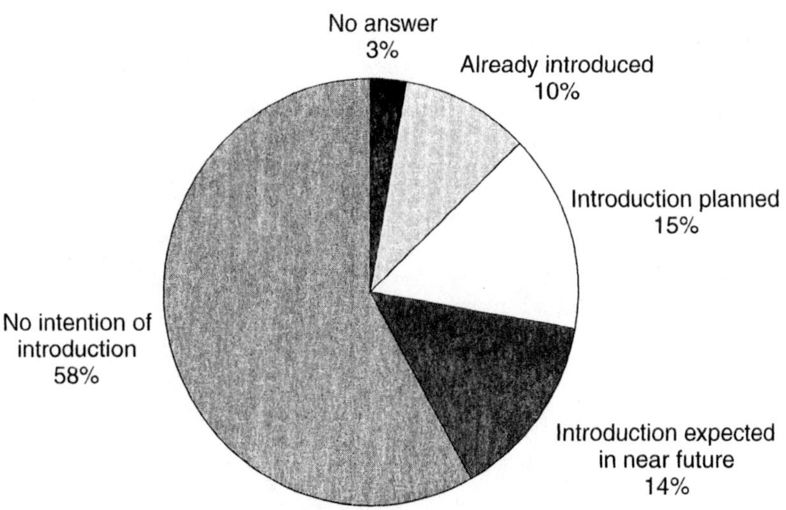

Figure 8.1 Moves for introduction of annual salary system
Source: Nihon Seisansei Honbu 1992

NOTE

1 McGregor, D. identified two patterns of management behaviour – Theory X and Theory Y. The former assumes that human beings do not like work, so have to be coerced, supervised and ordered in order to have them work adequately; namely it is an authoritarian management, wheras Theory Y assumes that human beings do like to work and are able to realize their personal goals in work and contribute to organizational goals as an independent individual (McGregor 1960).

REFERENCES

Akaoka, I. (1993), *Ereganto Kanpani* (Elegant company), Tokyo: Yūhikaku.

Keizai Dōyūkai (1992) *2010 nen ni Mukete Kore kara no Rōdō no Arikata* (Vision of work for 2010), Tokyo: Keizai Dōyūkai.

Ginko Shinpōsha (1991) *Ginko Shinpō*, April, no. 1731.

Ginko Shinpōsha (1992) *Ginko Shinpō*, April, no. 1781.

McGregor, D. (1960) *The Human Side of Enterprise*, New York: McGraw-Hill.

Nihon Keieisha Dantai Renmei (1995) *Shinjidai no Nipponteki Keiei* (Japanese-style management in new era), Tokyo: Nihon Keieisha Dantai Renmei.

Nihon Seisansei Honbu (1992) *Nenpōsei ni Kansuru Chōsa* (Survey on annual salary system), Tokyo: Nihon Seisansei Honbu.

Nippon Keizai Shinbun (1992) 20 September.

Rōdōshō (1991) *Kōsubetsu Kanri no Nozomashii Arikata* (Ideal operation of career course selection system), Tokyo: Rōdōshō.

Sakurai, M. (1985) 'Henkani chokumen suru kinyūkikan no jinji rōmu kanri' (Employment management in financial services facing changes), *Sōgō-Ginkō*, October: 18–19.

Sōrifu (1994) *Josei no Genjo to Shisaku* (Current situations and measures for women – 1993 edition), Tokyo: Sōrifu.

Watanabe, T. (1987) *Gendai no Ginko Rōdō* (Labour in contemporary banking), Tokyo: Ōtsuki shoten.

Watanabe, T. (1990) 'New office technology and the labour process in contemporary Japanese banking', *New Technology, Work and Employment*, vol. 5, no.1: 61–4.

Watanabe, T. (1995a) *Kigyō Soshiki no Rōdō to Kanri* (Labour in business organization and management), Tokyo: Chūō Keizaisha.

Watanabe, T. (1995b) *Kōsubetsu Koyō Kanri to Jyosei Rōdō* (Career course selection system and employment of women), Tokyo: Chūō Keizaisha.

Part III

Restructuring in labour

9 The end of the 'mass production system' and changes in work practices

Munakata Masayuki

The past two decades have witnessed a lively debate in business, academic and media circles on the unique characteristics of the Japanese production system: the 'secrets' of international competitiveness, the universality and specificity of its operation, the feasibility of its overseas transfer, and the results of those transfers, have captured headlines worldwide. This debate has emerged in response to the problems faced by European and US industry, the corresponding growth in the competitive power of Japanese manufacturing industries, and the profound influence which Japanese transplants have exerted under conditions of increasing globalization, market unification, and intensified international competition. Following on from this, and based upon comparative research of production systems, discussion emerged on the rationalism, effectiveness and applicability of a universal model of production, as represented by the 'lean production' systems used in the Japanese automobile industry. At the same time, the various types of production systems that have resulted from the diverse historical and social context of each country now are being reconsidered. The subsequent debate over the future shape of production systems has become the focus of attention.

In the 1990s, Japanese manufacturing industry entered a phase of low growth. This has been partly brought about by increased competition resulting from rationalization and structural reform in the manufacturing industries of other countries, increased American competitiveness in the wake of the yen's appreciation, and severe competition from developing countries, especially in Asia. This has resulted in a review of 'Japanese-style management', the need for 'restructuring' and 're-engineering', and the search for 'post-lean' production methods.

In this chapter we seek to examine, within the framework of the debate on production systems, the future development of Japanese management. To do this, the debate on production systems will be divided broadly into two parts:

1 A compilation of the concepts associated with the current discussion on the specificity of the Japanese production system, and an explanation of my own position.
2 A discussion of the direction of reform in the manufacturing industry.

By examining the significance of the key words 'mass production' and 'flexibility' as connected with the current debate on production systems, the basic specificity of the Japanese production system will be first briefly outlined. Next, having set out the concepts central to the debate, the changes in the production systems of Japanese manufacturing and work practices will be identified, and their significance examined in relation to international trends in the development of production systems.

THE DEBATE ON MASS PRODUCTION AND FLEXIBILITY

One of the main trends in the development of the current international debate on production systems is the emergence of a view that can be described as follows:

1 An emphasis on 'beyond mass production', based upon a recognition of 'the crisis of mass production' (Aglietta 1979) in relation to the debate on 'post-Fordism' and 'post-Taylorism'.
2 An emphasis on the key element in transforming the production systems as the increasing flexibility of the system, in response to changes in the management environment.

These two points can be found not only among those who posit the effectiveness of a universal model of production, such as theories of 'flexible specialization' (Piore and Sabel 1984), 'lean production' (Womack *et al.* 1990) and 'innovation-mediated production' (Kenney and Florida 1993), but also among those who doubt the effectiveness of such a universal model of production, and present other possibilities (Appelbaum and Batt 1994; Schumann *et al.* 1994). This can be seen, particularly, in relation to the 'lean production system'. The above viewpoint is common to discussions which assume some sort of new production model, predicated upon the production practices of so-called 'excellent companies' and the existence of a paradigm shift from the 'mass production' or 'Fordist' system (Badham and Matthews 1989).

Nevertheless, such a viewpoint does not adequately account for present conditions or predict future development in Japanese production systems in the international arena. There is a number of reasons for this. In the first place, leaving aside the recent criticisms of 'lean production' (Wood 1991; Williams *et al.* 1992; Berggren 1991, 1992; IAT/IGM/IAO/HBS 1992; Elger and Smith 1994), the main Japanese industries to develop significantly after World War II and reach a position of strong international competitiveness are mass production industries in the broadest sense of the term, ranging from automobiles, electronics and semiconductors right through to piano manufacturing. More than other industries in other countries, these manufacturers have benefited from the specific process advantages associated with mass production to establish the basic conditions for improvements in international competitiveness. Second, as is well known, the original elements of mass production techniques were learned faithfully and introduced from the USA. In essence, the aim was to realize a 'flow line production' based on the principles of division of labour and the '3 Ss' (standardization, specialization, simplification), as established by Taylor and Ford. Typical of this approach – 'learn from Ford' – is Ōno (Ōno 1978: Chap. 5) who developed the Toyota production methods.

Third, the flexibility issue, which is often discussed with reference to deficiencies in the mass production system, deserves further scrutiny. The reason is straightforward: the characteristics of the 'Japanese model', as found in terms such as the 'flexible firm' (Atkinson 1985), are regarded frequently as 'unique' or 'specific'. The ambiguity embedded in these terms can be seen in the following usages. For instance, the MIT Sloan School of Management group uses 'flexible mass production' – which was already employed by Henry Ford as early as 1930 as a 'legitimate' form of mass production representative of 'his' system (Ford 1930) – as a special feature of today's Japanese auto production compared to that of America (MIT Commission 1989). But this context is lost in the discussion of 'lean production' and the distinction between 'mass production' and 'craft production' and an aspect of 'pardigm shift' are emphasized – thus, an ambiguity in the meaning of 'lean production' in terms of 'mass production' exists. In other word, the group distinguishes flexible 'lean production' from rigid 'mass production', and regards this lack of distinction as one of the causes of ambiguity in 'lean production'. As suggested by the concept of 'flexible rigidities' (Dore 1986), the exact meanings of 'flexibility' and 'rigidity' vary greatly, depending upon what is meant to be targeted and designated. It follows that a clear definition of this comparatively vague and multivocal term is required on the technological, sociological and economic levels.

The basic specificity of the 'Japanese model', and the associated theoretical problems, can be summarized as follows:

Mass production system

At least two conceptualizations of mass production need to be distinguished; first, the abstract, general concept of mass production based on economic and technological rationalities. This signifies the principles of a high-speed flow line production passed on a division of labour and standardization for mass production and mass sales of standardized goods (Wild 1972); second, the specifically historical concept, in which is reflected the social context of each country as well as the differences in the stage of sophistication and development of mass production. Within the context of this dual understanding, at the very least a distinction must be made between the original system devised by Henry Ford, the variant developed in the USA and Europe from the 1930s onwards and particularly after World War II, and the variant developed in Japan and represented by the Toyota system. In short, we must understand specific cases within the general framework of the mass production system, based upon the specific characteristics and the development stages of each.

Flexibility and inflexibility

The concept of 'flexibility' needs to be understood in the context of its generally inseparable relationship to 'inflexibility' or 'rigidity' in the given setting. Following on from this, and even when considering the significance of the concept in terms of the system's adaptability to the changing environment, we still need to distinguish between instances indicating a degree of freedom in functional change within a unified basic structure ('functional flexibility'), and instances indicating a degree of rigidity and freedom in change in the basic framework and structure itself ('structural flexibility').

To take the argument one step further. This formal classification also has to be considered taking into account the distinction between the technological and economic flexibility (or elasticity) of the utilization of production factors, as exists in classical market economics and machine model analysis, and societal flexibility, as found in the possibility for change in the context of a nation's social order. The problems of 'flexible rigidity' in the 'Japan model' are concerned with the latter level. Finally, this implies the need to understand and recognize that, because of the existence of differences in the social order between Japan and western countries, different issues and contexts of rigidity and flexibility exist in each country.

Japanese model

The significance of the 'Japanese-style production system' (Japanese model) is that, in terms of basic technological and economic characteristics, it is a mass production system. However, it is more sophisticated than the 'American model' in realizing improvements in cost, quality and elasticity (functional flexibility). The basis for this improved 'trade-off' relationship between cost, product quality and flexibility is to be found in the socially distinctive organizational characteristic of the 'Japanese model'.

Mechanistic/organic principle

In theoretical terms, this distinction arises from the ability to accommodate and unify into a single system what was considered previously in the western world to be a choice or 'trade-off' relationship between 'mechanistic' and 'organic' types of organization. It goes without saying that organizational design theory in western systems has been premised upon such a trade-off (Burns and Stalker 1961). The 'Japanese model' attempts to maximize an employee's abilities both qualitatively and quantitatively in an 'organic system', while at the same time trying to maintain the order and certainty of operations to be found in a 'mechanistic system'. In the western context, some limitations tend to be placed on the mobilization of an employee's abilities in order to maintain systemic order, as in the case of Taylorism, which relies on the principles of 'mechanistic' organization. On the other hand, to achieve the benefits of 'organic organization', as in the 'socio-technical systems approach', the level of 'hierarchical' control tends to be reduced in order to enhance worker autonomy or empowerment. Both approaches have limitations in trying to improve economic performance (built-in results limitations). To a certain extent, the Japanese model aims to overcome these limits, and seeks to ease the problem of the 'trade-off' relationship found in previous western conceptions of organization. This point may help to explain the basis of the correlation between the high performance and organizational characteristics of the 'Japanese model' (Munakata 1989, 1993, 1995a), as often discussed in relation to the limitations of western-style 'Fordism' or 'mass production' in the context of 'lean production' or the 'theory of Japanization' (Oliver and Wilkinson 1988).

'Human' vs 'inhuman' model

The 'mechanistic' characteristics of an organization found in the 'Japanese model' are part of the technologically and economically rational planning and control of production, based on standardization and scientific management as well as the hierarchical order supporting the system. The 'organic' characteristics of organization are realized in this framework of planned control and hierarchical order in such a way that the framework is not seen as static and fixed, related or tied to specific societal or individual relationships, but as dynamic, furthering limitless human resource utilization and development; that is, as a 'high density labour system' (Tona 1993) for system maintenance, adaptation and improvement.

The evaluation of the relationship between the potential for the development of human resources and their limitless utilization is central to the controversy over whether the 'Japanese model' is 'human' or 'inhuman', as in the recent *karōshi* (death from overwork) debate.

'Class' order difference

Underlying the specific way of unifying the 'mechanistic principles' and 'organic principles' in the 'Japanese model' is a 'class order' difference from that in the west. In Japan social class does exist functionally, or as a 'function'. However, as 'substance', as a way to divide or differentiate individual lives, class as the basis for order is not as fixed as in the west.

What permits this type of fluidity within the class structure may be the historically prescribed social stability of Japan as a 'nation state' since ancient times, in contrast to Western Europe, where a relatively set class order can be found in relation to a certain instability in social order and the artificial forces involved in the process of modern 'nation-state' formation.

Homogeneity

The traditional stability of the Japanese 'nation' or 'nation-state', in turn, has brought about a strong sense of self-identity, homogeneity, and 'closedness' in Japanese society – without denying the existence of minority groups (e.g. Korean minorities). From the onset of modern industrialization, this homogeneity and the closed nature of society have enabled firms to become not only basic units of production, but also foundations for this specific mode of social organization, which restricts the free movement of labour between firms and the members' freedom of behaviour in this micro-system.

Thus, social context lies at the root of the rigidity of the 'Japanese model'. The functional elasticity or flexibility, which is regarded as a distinctive characteristic of the 'Japanese model', is only another side of this structural rigidity, and the two are inseparable.

REFORM OF THE PRODUCTION SYSTEM AND CHANGES IN WORK PRACTICES

From the 1980s onwards, industry in the USA and Europe has looked to the 'Japanese model' and 'lean production' as the way to restore international competitiveness. They have been seen as the basis upon which to plan reforms and move forward with the rationalization of their own production systems. These policies have sought to lessen the technical and economic rigidity in US and European mass production systems, and to completely rationalize the system. In these circumstances, the initial strategy aims to strengthen competitiveness against Japanese manufacturing through technology; that is, a strategy implicitly aimed at taking on Japanese shop-floor organization in a positive way. In the automobile industry, as typically seen in GM and Volkswagen, 'flexible automation' was introduced, which relied as far as possible on new technology in the workplace. The results of this strategy nevertheless fell short of expectations. There is a number of reasons for this, including the overestimation of the flexibility of new technology, on the one hand, and the underestimation of the importance of technological, social, and economic uncertainties in a complex automated system, on the other (Bushnell 1994; Schumann *et al.* 1994).

As a result, an awareness grew of the importance of 'social reform' in realizing the potential of new technology. Allied with the concentration of resources into product development strategies, the partial introduction of elements of the Japanese model (just-in-time, quality control, team or group organization, parts supply systems), 'Japanization', and a move to 'lean production' were planned. This was an attempt to remove the partial rationalization inherent in the production system in relation to the above-mentioned static structure of western-type class society, by means of the full deployment of human resources within the system, and especially the full development of the shop-floor workforce.

In this way, western companies, particularly US companies, paid serious attention to the 'Japanese model' and sought to restore competitive power by means of the introduction and further rationalization of this model. In contrast, Japanese industries, from the 1980s onwards, and especially in the 1990s, saw a comparative reduction in international competitiveness, limits to their growth, and a reduction in profitability. This led them to move towards restructuring existing production systems under circumstances of fierce price and cost competition. The main trend, expressed as 'super lean production' (Kojima 1994), 'lean on balance system' (Fujimoto and Takeishi 1994), 'new Toyota production system' (*Kōjō Kanri* 1994a) are recognized as follows (Munakata 1995b).

First there has been a review of the over-application of diversification strategies. In the 'lean production' model, the ability of Japanese-style production to achieve productivity and flexibility (multi-product manufacture and rapid development of new products) or compatibility between 'scope and scale' is evaluated highly. The basis of this compatibility is sought in a flexible organization. But as already stated, the 'Japanese model' embodies characteristics of a mass production system, so that there is a limit to the compatibility of the two prerequisites, i.e. productivity and flexibility. In the case of the automobile industry for instance, the development of Japanese industry from the 1980s onwards was based upon a response to the diminishing possibilities of enlarged market scale. The result was a high value added strategy, with a move towards luxury products, the expansion of product lines, and quicker product development. This strategy contained the same basic logic as the 'Sloan marketing policy' ('selling more car per car') (Rothschild 1973), which was previously adopted by the US car industry after reaching maturity. The strategy brought economic gain to the Japanese auto industry as far as was possible, given the purchasing power of the market. However, it made the production system more complex, reduced rationality in production – a key feature which had been maintained due to a limited 'full-line policy' centred on a relatively small range of car models – and gave rise to various wastage problems.

Production development activities became diversified, and produced many duplications. In general, such burdens brought on by increased flexibility were absorbed into the Japanese model by the innate organic nature of its structure, but only to a certain extent: these problems led to cost rises, and together with limits to growth, brought profits down. There is an irony in this: whereas the US automobile industry, confronted with the Japanese challenge, turned away from the past Sloan Policy to concentrate energy on new strategic products and the restoration of competitiveness through the absorption of the rationalism inherent in the Japanese systems, the Japanese automobile industry adapted past US strategy, thereby creating new problems. The MIT concept distinguishing 'lean production' from 'mass production' is theoretically based on this review of production practices by the Japanese automobile industry. It was carried out beyond the boundaries of the technological and economic rationality of mass production, and is quintessentially no more than a simplistic attempt to combine the 'scale' and 'scope' factors in the production system. The result of this inexact conceptualization may be found in the recent development from 'lean production' to 'lean enterprises', where the emphasis is now upon the effectiveness of 'value streams' within a product line, and not on 'scope' factors (Womack *et al.* 1994).

Along with this course of development, the trend of present Japanese production systems is a return to a basic view of cost as the vital factor in competition and the renewed pursuit of economy-of-scale benefits. As a product strategy, this consists of the reduction and integration of over-diversified product lines. In the midst of this process, as can be seen at Toyota, the concept of a new 'world car' has emerged.

With regard to product development, this means a movement towards a 'multi-product' strategy which eliminates duplication and reduces the rationalism caused by the previous 'single-project' strategy. It attempts, overall, to raise efficiency (Nobeoka and Cusumano 1994). In the area of parts development, this means to co-ordinate a diverse range of parts and promote parts compatibility.

Second, in the area of technological production processes, we find an attempt is now underway to review actively the method of mechanization and automation, and modes of floor line are being reconsidered. The basic aim is to lessen the rigidities of production, and reintegrate improvements in productivity and flexibility by constructively exploiting the adaptability of individuals. In Japan during the 1980s, various methods of 'flexible automation', such as FMS (Flexible Manufacturing System), IR (Industrial Robot), DNC (Direct Numerical Control) and CIM (Computer Integrated Manufacturing) were introduced into manufacturing and assembly. But, as in the USA and Europe, examples abound of flexible automation being pushed to the point where it exceeds the technological and economic rationality of the new technology (e.g. Nissan's Zama plant, Toyota's Tahara plant). The effects of increased flexibility from new technology are limited in that we continue to rely upon the concept of mechanical technology (Munakata 1989). The utilization of new technology beyond this limit actually lessens the system's adaptability to fluctuations in demand, and also its technological and economic flexibility in production. In addition, excessive automation can hamper the opportunity for the full employment of human flexibility in the workplace. It reduces the significance of workers' initiatives on the shop-floor, and at the same time causes an increase in the indirect workforce needed to maintain complicated large-scale plant and production processes.

The new design principles, which aim to correct the over-emphasis upon flexible automation, as in the case of the 'new' Toyota production methods, are sometimes viewed as a production line in which humans and machinery co-exist. The idea is said to be the break-down and reorganization of large-scale machine production lines to seek the optimum division of functions between the plastic abilities of humans and those which can only be carried out by machines (Ogawa 1994; *Kōjō Kanri* 1994a).

With regard to the organization of the production line itself, the effects of long line formations are under review. Previously, in accordance with the product and parts specification, and without considering the functional characteristics of the unit operation, stages of manufacture and assembly lines tended to be formed by connecting the elementary operation as closely as possible to make long lines. These former organizational principles contributed to the creation of the shortest lead-time production by means of the curtailment of stock inventory in process and the elimination of slack (Ōno 1978). However, these methods maintained the essential characteristic of production labour as being monotonous repetitive work under strict time control, known as 'Fordist mass production'. The 'Japanese model', in contrast, which was designed to eliminate slack in production, had the effect of increasing the strain upon the human element ('stress' under 'high-density labour'). Due to their nature as additional devices to the basic structures of work organization under mass production, steps such as multi-skilling, job rotation and quality circles have not been able to alleviate sufficiently deficiencies in worker performance. Furthermore, they have not satisfactorily answered the demands of management to instil further flexibility in the production structures and the more efficient use of human resources that have become more expensive with the appreciation of the yen; nor have they answered the demands of labour, which seeks a more attractive and comfortable workplace.

In this situation, the trend in production-line composition is to subdivide previous long continuous lines formed by a mechanistic linking of operation elements, thereby creating shorter 'self-finished' operation lines related to the unity of products, components and operation functions. In between these lines, a larger 'slack' inventory is inserted. By means of the relaxation of integration, an increase in structural flexibility of production, clearer and unified tasks at every workplace, and a more effective use of the initiative of individual workers can be expected. For example, at Toyota's Motomachi plant, the previous 1,000-metre assembly line has been subdivided into five 100- to 200-metre lines according to the unified production 'function'. At Toyota's Miyata plant in Kyūshū the line has been subdivided into eleven shorter ones. By the introduction of such systems, the functional and complete unity of the operations of every line, and their significance within the overall operation, have been made clearer. In addition, by the adoption of small-scale automated machinery in such work units, a reduction in workloads is expected (*Kōjō Kanri* 1994a; Ogawa 1994).

A similar trend can be found in other industries. For example, at NEC's Nagano plant, due to their 'production revolution movement', even 'one man–one unit assembly' has resulted in the strengthening of multi-processing, and the experimental abolition of conveyor lines is under way in accordance with rationalization, particularly the shortening of the production line in parallel with the strengthening of JIT (just-in-time) principles in the assembling operation (*Kōjō Kanri* 1994b, 1995).

Third, the orientation towards strengthening cost competitiveness has led to the extension of alliances and the growth of transactions across the previous boundaries of the *keiretsu* system. A former characteristic of the 'Japanese model' was the way leading companies within an industry formed their own respective corporate *keiretsu* from allied companies, which extended vertically from the top to the bottom of production. Within this stabilized framework, activities ranging from product development and sales were carried out flexibly. However, with the intensification of international competition resulting from the high yen, the scope for co-existence of *keiretsu* organizations, and their ability to cope with competition by means of rationalization within the former *keiretsu* framework, is being lost gradually. As a result, and in order to pursue larger economies of scale, joint product development and production of common main parts beyond the boundaries of individual *keiretsu* is moving ahead (Maruyama 1994). This trend is particularly strong in overseas production where there is comparatively little resistance to change, and can be seen to be spreading in home production. As a typical case the supply of common engine parts between Toyota, Nissan, and Isuzu can be cited. Furthermore, inside the *keiretsu* organization, secondary and tertiary parts suppliers are being selected; those which refuse to rationalize are being discarded; and the purchase of parts and raw materials across different *keiretsu* organizations and from overseas companies is increasing. At the same time, small parts suppliers that had been dependent upon parent companies are strengthening their own product development abilities, trying to increase their autonomy, sometimes forming horizontal networks with other companies, diversifying their client base, and moving towards reducing their reliance upon the *keiretsu* (Yoshida 1994). Along with the enforced rationalization inside the pyramid-like structure of *keiretsu* organizations, rationalization by means of 'market elasticity' through the externalization of markets is becoming apparent in Japan in contrast to the trend in Europe and the USA, where the systematization and organization of parts suppliers is moving forward.

CONCLUSION

Outlined above are recent trends in the development of the production systems of leading Japanese manufacturers in relation to the characteristics of the 'Japanese model'. With respect to the significance of these changes to the mass production system and work practices in general, the following conclusions can be drawn.

In the first place, the mass production system, with its low costs and high-speed production as a result of flow-line production and potential economies of scale, remains the world's principal and basic production system. In the 1990s, even in the attempts to correct the 1980s over-emphasis on diversification, Japanese industries have returned to basic production principles, albeit at a more sophisticated level. This is a kind of historical 'refrain' from the actions of the US automobile industry in the 1980s to correct their former Sloan marketing strategies, rationalize production and restore competitiveness, founded upon strategic product formation. The continuity of the mass production system at this level is, in principle, conditioned by the limitations of the flexibility of new technology and the buying power of the general public in the world market.

Second, changes can nevertheless be seen within the basic framework of the mass production system. In relation to the existing Japanese working practices, the changes can be seen as attempts to introduce into the production system alterations in work specifications so as to make more positive use of individual potential as well as group ability. Alterations in work practice include a move away from the simple, monotonous and repetitive work tasks of American-style mass production. These had also been viewed functionally in the 'Japanese model' – that is, as additional and supplementary devices for the mobilization of a worker's creative abilities – in spite of the model's orientation towards multi-skilling, job rotation and quality circle activities. The further change in the concept of line formation which is seen as a change from technological integration to that of division, with allowances for slack between lines, namely to the creation of 'self-contained lines' and 'one man–one unit workplaces', will go beyond supplementing the monotonous nature of the work in conventional mass production by the direct utilization of workers' initiative and creative abilities. This is significant because the previous mass production system expected average ability from an average worker, with the 'Japanese model' limiting itself to expecting only 'average creative ability of grouped workers'. Thus, in the past restrictions were placed upon the utilization of the potentially diverse abilities of individual workers in their direct execution of task. Under conditions of steeply rising labour costs, the present process of reform aims at incorporating directly the deployment of these diverse or 'marginal' abilities and potentials of the individual worker by means of changes in designing work organization towards a more sophisticated integration of the effects from mass production and maintenance of flexibility. In this sense, the new trend may be thought of as one that presages an end to those principles of working practice typical of traditional American-style mass production.

With regard to the principle of work organization, these changes might be seen as related to the so-called 'Volvo method' or the 'Swedish model'. However, these orientations are not to be confused, because the 'Swedish model' is premised upon traditional 'quantity production' based upon parallel settings of plural 'autonomous' work sites as its technological principle of work organization (Wild 1972), and also assumes the 'political autonomy' of the workshop (Berggren 1991, 1992; Appelbaum and Batt 1994).

Finally in regard to the background of new trends in Japanese production practices under the conditions of increasingly intense global competition, we have been able to clarify the limits of the 'functional flexibility' of Japanese management in its effectiveness for further development in the system and its ability to strengthen competitive power. Functional flexibility has been kept in relation to the organic nature of the organization within the confines of Japanese social relations, companies and Japanese society; however, a situation has now arisen where the structural rigidity arising from these confines has become an obstacle to the further rationalization of management. Under these conditions, the Japanese production system is likely to undergo a qualitative change from a closed national system to an open one, with higher structural flexibility. This trend is also significant for the mode of utilization of labour resources, as it signifies a shift from the former collective utilization to a mode which relies more on the creativity and unique characteristics of individual workers.

The characteristics of any mass production system are prescribed by the social context of each nation and the institutional framework as well as the development of technology. This point often arises when discussing the 'end of mass production'. If we take into consideration, even if only as a contributory aspect, such social factors, we find that they imply the removal of economically irrational elements in each country's system. This is promoted by economic forces inspired by economic competition under conditions of internationalization in industry and the integration of the world market.

REFERENCES

Aglietta, M. (1979) *A Theory of Capitalist Regulation*, London: NLB.

Appelbaum, E. and Batt R. (1994) *The New American Workplace: Transforming Work Systems in the United States*, New York: ILR Press.

Atkinson, J. (1985) 'Flexibility: planning for an uncertain future', *Manpower Policy and Practice, the IMS Review*, vol. 1: 26–9.

Badham, R. and Matthews, J. (1989) 'The new production system debate', *Labour and Industry*, vol. 2, no. 2: 194–246.

Berggren, C. (1991) *Von Ford zu Volvo: Automobilherstellung in Schweden*, Berlin/Heidelberg: Springer-Verlag.
Berggren, C. (1992) *The Volvo Experience: Alternatives to Lean Production*, New York: ILR Press.
Burns, T. and Stalker, G. M. (1961) *The Management of Innovation*, London: Tavistock Publications Ltd.
Bushnell, P. T. (1994) *Transformation of the American Manufacturing Paradigm*, New York/London: Garland Publishing.
Dore, R. (1986) *Flexible Rigidities: Industrial Policy and Structural Adjustment in the Japanese Economy 1970–80*, London: Athlone Press.
Elger, T. and Smith, C. (1994) *Global Japanization?: The Transformation of the Labour Process*, London: Routledge.
Ford, H. (1930) *Moving Forward*, New York: Doubleday, Doran & Company.
Fujimoto, T. and Takeishi, A. (1994) *Jidōsha Sangyō 21 Seiki e no Shinario* (Automobile industry: scenario for 21st century), Tokyo: Shakai Keizai Seisansei Honbu.
IAT (Institut für Arbeit und Technik), IGM (IG Metall), IAO (Fraunhofer-Institut für Arbeitswirtschaft und Organisation), HBS (Hans-Bocker-Stiftung) (eds) (1992) *Lean Production/Schlanke Production: Neues Produktionskonzept humanerer Arbeit?*, Düsseldorf: Hans-Bocker-Stiftung.
Kenney, M. and Florida, R. (1993) *Beyond Mass Production: The Japanese System and its Transfer to the US*, New York: Oxford University Press.
Kojima, T. (1994) *Chō rin kakumei: ' monozukuri ishin' ga hajimatta* (Super-lean revolution: 'renovation of manufacturing' has begun), Tokyo: Nihon Keizai Shinbunsha.
Kōjō Kanri (Industrial management) (1994a) 'Kore ga "shin" Toyota seisan shisutemu da' (This is the 'new' Toyota production system), vol. 40, no. 11: 17–79.
Kōjō Kanri (Industrial management) (1994b) 'Ō-ru NEC no seisan kakushin undō' (Production innovation movement of all NEC), vol. 40, no. 14: 17–67.
Kōjō Kanri (Industrial management) (1995) 'Kore ga uwasa no "hitori seisan" rain da' (This is the one-man production line), vol. 41, no. 8: 17–50.
Maruyama, Y. (1994) 'Nihon seisan shisutemu no sukeiru to sukōpu' (Scale and scope of the Japanese production system), *Rikkyō Keizaigaku Kenkyū*, vol. 48, no. 2: 1–27.
MIT Commission on Industrial Productivity (1989) *The Working Papers*, vol. 1: 1–51.
Munakata, M. (1989) *Gijutsu no Riron: Gendai Kōgyō Keizai Mondai e no Gijutsuronteki Sekkin*, (Theory of technology: a technological approach to contemporary industrial management) Tokyo: Dōbunkan.
Munakata, M. (1993) 'Social innovation as a condition for technological progress', in H. J. Pleitner (ed.) *Small and Medium-sized Enterprises on their Way into the Next Century*, St. Gallen: Schweizerisches Institut für gewerbliche Wirtschaft an der Hochschule St. Gallen Wirtschafts-, Rechts- und Sozialwissenschaften.
Munakata, M. (1995a) 'Das japanische Produktionssystem im Kontext des internationalen Vergleichs', *The Annals of the School of Business Administration* (Kobe University), vol. 39: 151–67.
Munakata, M. (1995b) 'Seisan shisutemu hatten no kokusaiteki dōkō o megutte' (On international trends of development in production systems), *Kokumin Keizai Zasshi*, vol. 171, no. 3: 23–56.
Nobeoka, K. and Cusumano, M. (1994) 'Multi-project strategy, design transfer and project performance: a survey of automobile development projects in the US and Japan', *MIT Sloan School of Management*, Working Paper 3687: 1–29.

Ogawa, E. (ed.) (1994) *Toyota Seisan Hōshiki no Kenkyū* (A study of the Toyota production system), Tokyo: Nihon Keizai Shinbunsha.

Ōno, T. (1978) *Toyota Production System: Beyond Large-scale Production*, Cambridge: Productivity Press.

Oliver, N. and Wilkinson, B. (1988) *The Japanization of British Industry*, Oxford: Blackwell.

Piore, M. and Sabel, C. F. (1984) *The Second Industrial Divide: Possibilities for Prosperity*, New York: Basic Books.

Rothschild, E. (1973) *Paradise Lost: The Decline of the Auto-Industrial Age*, New York: Random House.

Schumann, M., Baethge-Kinsky, V., Kuhlmann, M., Kurz, C. and Neuman, U. (1994) *Trendreport Rationalisierung: Automobile Industrie Werkzeugmaschinenbau Chemische Industrie*, Berlin: Sigma.

Tona, Naoki (1993) *Nihongata Furekishibilichi no Kōzō: Kigyo Shakai to Komitsudo Rōdō Shisutemu* (Structure of Japanese-style flexibility: corporate society and highly intensive labour system), Kyoto: Horitsu Bunkasha.

Wild, R. (1972) *Mass-production Management: The Design and Operation of Production Flowline Systems*, London New York: John Wiley & Sons.

Williams, K., Haslam, C., Williams, J., Cutler, T. with Adcroft, A. and Johal, S. (1992) 'Against lean production', *Economy and Society*, vol. 21, no. 3: 321–54.

Womack, J. P., Jones, D. T. and Roos, D. (1990) *The Machine that Changed the World*, New York: Lawson Associates.

Womack, J. P. and Jones, D. T. (1994) 'From lean production to the lean enterprise', *HBR*, vol. 72, no. 2: 93–103.

Wood, S. J. (1991) 'Japanization and/or Toyotaism?', *Work, Employment & Society*, vol. 5, no. 4: 567–600.

Yoshida, K. (1994) 'Nihongata seisan shisutemu no saikōchiku to chūshō kigyō no sonritsu mondai' (Restructuring of Japanese-style production systems and the issue of survival of small and medium enterprises), *Tōyō Daigaku Keizai Ronshū*, vol. 19, no. 2: 1–20.

10 Japanese-style industrial relations in historical perspective

Nishinarita Yutaka

This chapter reconsiders 'Japanese-style' industrial relations from an historical perspective, critically analysing the popular cultural approach, and the approach which emphasizes the 'universality' of Japanese industrial relations. Japanese industrial relations are composed of 'seniority-based wages', 'lifetime employment' and 'enterprise unions'. In this context, the wages of both blue-collar and white-collar employees are examined at critical stages in the post-war period, especially in terms of the influence of management and union leaders. The first stage of the post-war period began with the formation of proto-type unions (1950s), followed by the development and establishment of unionism (1960–73, 1974–90), and then by dramatic changes to unions with the advent of the recession of the early 1990s. The first two elements of Japanese industrial relations noted above have already been modified considerably, while 'co-operative' enterprise unions will continue to survive. These unions are the product of a business organization into which the company can thoroughly integrate its employees.

THE DEBATE ON JAPANESE INDUSTRIAL RELATIONS

The origins of the industrial relations model which exists today can be found in the past. Still, historical investigations which regard history as merely the process of growth of this model, ignore the individual structure and characteristics of each stage of history, and as a result contain serious flaws. In addition to recognizing these flaws, we must also examine the specific factors in the formation and growth of Japanese industrial relations over as long a time span as possible (Nishinarita 1988). This is done in order critically to evaluate the cultural approach which explains Japanese industrial relations and management in terms of traditional and cultural characteristics, and the approach, often found in advanced nations, which emphasizes the worldwide 'universality' of Japanese industrial relations. But before this is attempted let us first briefly outline some of the definitions attached to Japanese industrial relations, and some of the debates connected thereto.

What are the basic elements of Japanese industrial relations? The popular view is that Japanese industrial relations are composed of the *sanshu no jingi*, or the 'three sacred treasures' of seniority-based wages, lifetime employment, and enterprise unions. This view of Japanese industrial relations was confirmed by the 1973 OECD report on Japan's manpower policy, which accepted the three elements above as the 'pure model' of the Japanese employment system (OECD 1973).

However, further discussion is needed in order to fully explain and understand the exact characteristics of the *sanshu no jingi*.

Seniority-based wages

Two influential theories have been put forward to explain why the wages of both white- and blue-collar Japanese employees rise by following an uneven age-based curve. The first theory is the hypothesis of livelihood guarantees. This points out that at the time when employees leave full-time education and enter the company, they are young and single, have low living costs and, therefore, receive low wages. But as the living costs of the employees increase, brought on by the commitments of marriage, family, education of children, and house purchase, wages also begin to rise. As will be discussed later, the age-based curve reaches its peak when the employee is 50 to 55 years old, but then falls sharply as living costs decrease when the employee's children marry and leave home. The reason given to explain why the wages of women employees do not follow the age-based curve is that the main burden of household expenses is usually borne by the man.

The second theory is the hypothesis of specific skills in an enterprise (Koike 1977, 1981, 1991). A distinctive feature that accompanies the attainment of advanced industrialization and monopolies by corporations is the accumulation of fixed capital and plant, and technical expertise, the reorganization of labour and, in turn, the formation of an internal labour market within the corporation. In this situation, work tasks are divided by degree of difficulty, and new employees begin by supervising simple tasks, and then move on to more difficult tasks. Under the system of internal advancement, as workers become older, they accumulate specific skills within the enterprise, and their wages move in line with the age-based curve. Seniority based wages decided by the level of specific skills have come about as a result of the move to advanced industrialization, but they are not unique to Japan, and can also be seen among white-collar workers in EU nations. In the case of Japan, though, the wages of blue-collar workers also follow the age-based curve, suggesting that this marks the 'white collarization' of blue-collar workers. This trend reflects the formation of an advanced industrial society, and demonstrates the highly advanced nature of Japan in this respect.

Lifetime employment

As can be seen from the personnel nationalization which took place with the Dodge Line[1] in 1949, and with the oil crisis of 1973, Japanese employment practices cannot strictly be said to guarantee lifetime employment. The report on Japan's manpower policy (OECD 1973) was published before the oil shocks, and, as will be explained later, rarely considered the employment system found in the Occupation period. Therefore, its description of lifetime employment as the 'pure model' of Japanese employment, refers mainly to the system which existed during the periods of high growth, and in particular the 1960s. More accurately, the distinctive characteristic of Japanese employment practices is 'long-term stable employment within an enterprise', rather than lifetime employment.

Enterprise unions

One of the aspects of the 'pure model' of Japanese employment practices to which the report on Japan's manpower policy paid particular attention was the existence of co-operative enterprise unions that did not criticize management policies (including shop-floor management). The report stated that:

> Looking at the merits of the Japanese employment system from the point of view of employers, these found it advantageous that the enterprise unions – in return for job and income security – leave management the responsibility to manage, in what may be said to be a vicarious form of 'productivity bargaining' . . . the workers want their enterprise to be as efficient and profitable as possible, but do not apparently challenge management responsibilities.
>
> (OECD 1973: 102).

The formation of co-operative attitudes of enterprise unions took place from the 1960s onwards, but before this, and especially in the Occupation period, the influence and regulatory power of enterprise unions in the workplace and management was very strong.

It is fair to say that the distinctive characteristic of labour unions under the Japanese employment system is that they exist as co-operative enterprise unions, while at the same time their organizational form is separate from that of the company. Looked at in more detail, specific types of labour organization can be found within enterprises, and that the situation which produced collaborative relations (or the integrated relations of labour and capital) being not specific to the high growth period that followed World War II. Indeed, it is a phenomenon that occurred in the pre-war period, too, and is thus significant for an historical investigation of Japanese industrial relations.

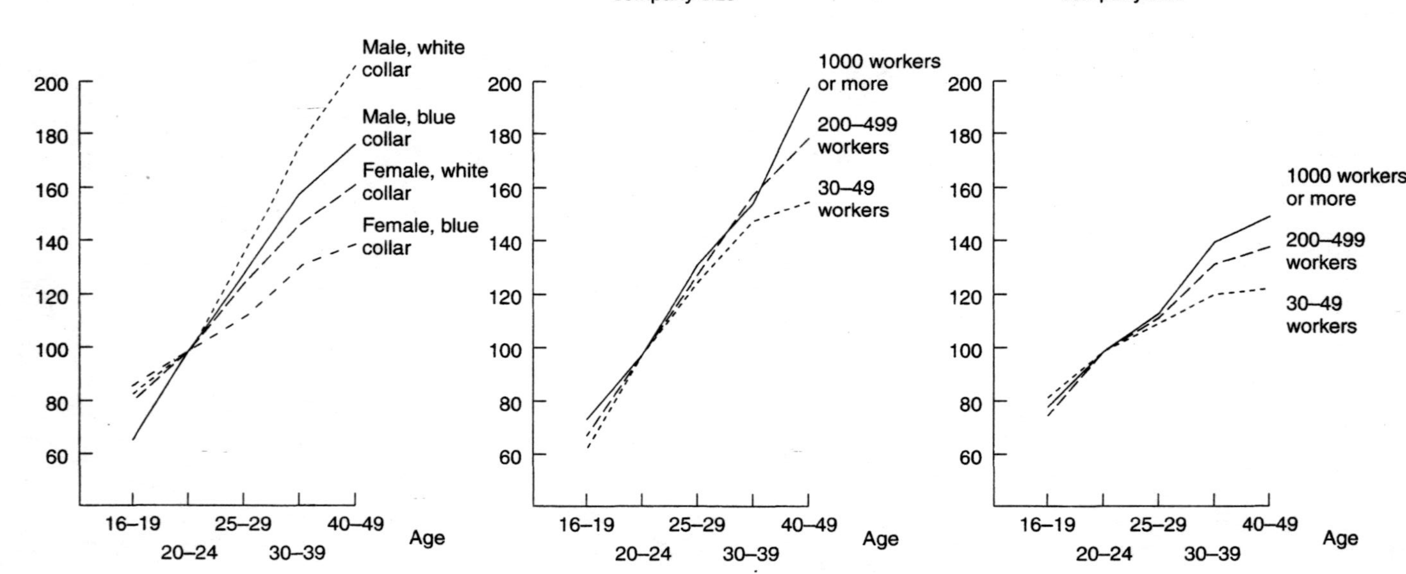

Figure 10.1 Wages by employee age, 1946 (100 = 20–24 age group)
Source: Chūō Rōdō Gakuen 1946
Note: Survey conducted for 233,971 industrial employees, workers of 50 or older excluded.

Next, let us turn to consider the historical stages in the development of Japanese industrial relations.

INDUSTRIAL RELATIONS IN OCCUPIED JAPAN, 1945–9

Figure 10.1 shows wage structures of workers during the Occupation period. 'The survey report on wages – the report of temporary workers' wage' by the Ministry of Welfare (Chūō Rōdō Gakuen, June 1946) was the first post-war wage survey showing the seniority factor in wage. Although the correlation between age and wage is clear, the survey gives no information on length of service. The seniority wage curves for male workers, white-collar staff and workers in large enterprises rise more steeply than for females, blue-collar workers and employees of small and medium-sized enterprises. Nonetheless, it does show that even among these workers a seniority factor existed.

The survey was carried out against a background of post-war deterioration in facilities and equipment and demoralization and disruption in workplaces; this situation could hardly be considered an advanced level of industrialization. Yet the fact that the seniority wage factor even at this period extended to women and workers in smaller enterprises demonstrates that wages were not assessed purely on the basis of skills required by the company, but on the notion of guaranteeing a worker's livelihood.

Four months after this survey, in October 1946, the Japan Electric Industry Union took action to support their demands for a minimum wage related to the cost of living, as well as 'the protection of existing rights' and 'the acquisition of the right to live' (Rōdōshō 1960: 292–6). This dispute led to the creation of the so-called 'electric industry wage system', which established as fundamental principles both a guaranteed minimum living wage and a minimum age-related increment.

As we can see, the seniority wage system in the Occupation period is adequately explained by the adoption of a guaranteed living wage, and on this point there was continuity throughout the war and during the Occupation period.

After the passage of the Labour Union Law in December 1945, a number of labour unions were formed across the country, and by the end of December 1947 28,000 unions with a total membership of 6,268,000 had sprung up. It is estimated that 45 per cent of the workforce was unionized (Nimura 1994: 42, 67). The unions were enterprise based and unique in that membership comprised both blue- and white-collar workers. As the wartime *Tan i Sanpō* (Unit Industrial Report Organization) was similarly comprised of clerical and manual workers, it seems likely that the new unions must have succeeded the form of these previous organizations, but I do not have any evidence that the post-war enterprise unions emerged simply out of *Tan i Sanpō*, as some have argued.

The crucial factors differentiating the post-war enterprise unions from the pre-war and wartime in-firm associations is that the later organizations developed a very powerful workers' movement in opposition to managerial authority. In the year after the enactment of the Labour Union Law, many of the enterprise unions negotiated with their employers agreements of a unique character. Although space does not permit a full description of their provisions here, they included the following points:

1 Consent to be obtained with the union in matters related to personnel employment, dismissal, transfer, promotion, rewards and disciplinary measures.
2 Consent to be obtained concerning changes in wages and working conditions.
3 Consent to be obtained on workplace regulations and organization and job titles and descriptions.
4 Requirement of employers to support union affairs, including the freedom of union representatives and members to participate in union activities during working hours, acceptance of union-related business trips as legitimate work-related time, facilitation of the activities and management of the union and payment of salaries by the company to full-time union staff (this last item was not stated clearly in work agreements, but was generally present in most unions of the time).
5 Establishment of a management consultation to discuss wages, management policy and personnel affairs.

It can be seen that the workers' movement at this time managed to create clear pro-worker unions, with a measure of control over management sufficient to impose constraints upon their authority. In other words, the workers were the more powerful partner in the labour–management relationship (Nishinarita 1992, 1994), which constitutes a crucial difference from the earlier in-firm labour organizations. However, this powerful position was destroyed by the Labour Union Law Amendment of June 1949, which led to the revision of the agreements negotiated under the previous conditions, although it did not yet imply the defeat of the proactive workers movement and the establishment of management friendly 'co-operative' enterprise unions.

An important background to the Amendment was the vital role played by the Dodge Line in restoring Japanese economic independence. It brought serious uncertainty into financial circles in a kind of 'birth pang' of Japanese economic independence, but pressured companies into personnel reduction and other rationalization measures. Indeed, between February 1949 and June 1950 jobs lost in the private sector totalled 152,000 in the machinery industry, 64,000 in chemicals, 42,000 in metals, 37,000 in coal mining, and 32,000 in textiles; in all, including other businesses, 400,000 people lost their jobs as 10,375 companies imposed redundancy policies. The government, meanwhile, carried out an administrative readjustment among public service workers under a strictly balanced budget, reducing national and local government staffing levels by 285,000 and 134,000 respectively (Nishinarita 1990). If this is considered along with the factory closures and enterprise scale-downs that followed defeat in war, secure long-term employment certainly did not exist in the Occupation period.[2]

Thus, Japanese industrial relations, as established before and during the war, were during this period continuous in some respects, but showed a clear cut-off in others.

EMERGENCE OF JAPANESE INDUSTRIAL RELATIONS, 1950–59

As mentioned above, the government's wage surveys stressed the correlation between an employee's wage and age, by which a seniority based wage system can be deduced. However, in the 1950s, specifically from November 1949, government surveys published by Ministry of Labour (Rōdōshō) also highlighted the correlation between wages and length of service, as in 'The report on the wage survey of individuals' (1949–50), 'The report on the wage survey by occupation' (1952–3), 'Survey on wages by occupation; report on wage survey by individual' (1954), and 'Report on wage survey by occupation' (1955–April 1957). Thus from the end of 1949 into the 1950s, as part of the process of restoring and developing the national economy, the government's growing attention to statistical assessment covered the correlation between wages and length of service. This seems to indicate the formation of pools of skill and experience, or the establishment of particular skills in a firm, taking place within the enterprises surveyed. We must ask which factor, age (i.e. assurance of livelihood) or length of service (i.e. specific company-related skill), was active in determining the seniority based wage: only the 1954 Rōdōshō survey showed the correlation among all three factors of age, length of service and wage level; the other cited surveys indicate wages separately by age or by length of service and thus show no correlation of the three.

Looking at examples of typical job types, a female spinning mill worker and male turner from the 1954 survey, Figure 10.2 shows their seniority wage. The (female) spinning worker's wages do not apparently correlate with age but do so strongly with length of service. The turner's wage, on the other hand, clearly relates to both age and length of service (or experience). It should be borne in mind that experience and length of service are not necessarily the same, but nevertheless it may be said that the determinant factor in the mill worker's seniority wage was the special skill related to her company, while the turner's wage reflected both skill level and the guarantee of livelihood.

During the rebuilding of the Japanese economy, both 'permanent'

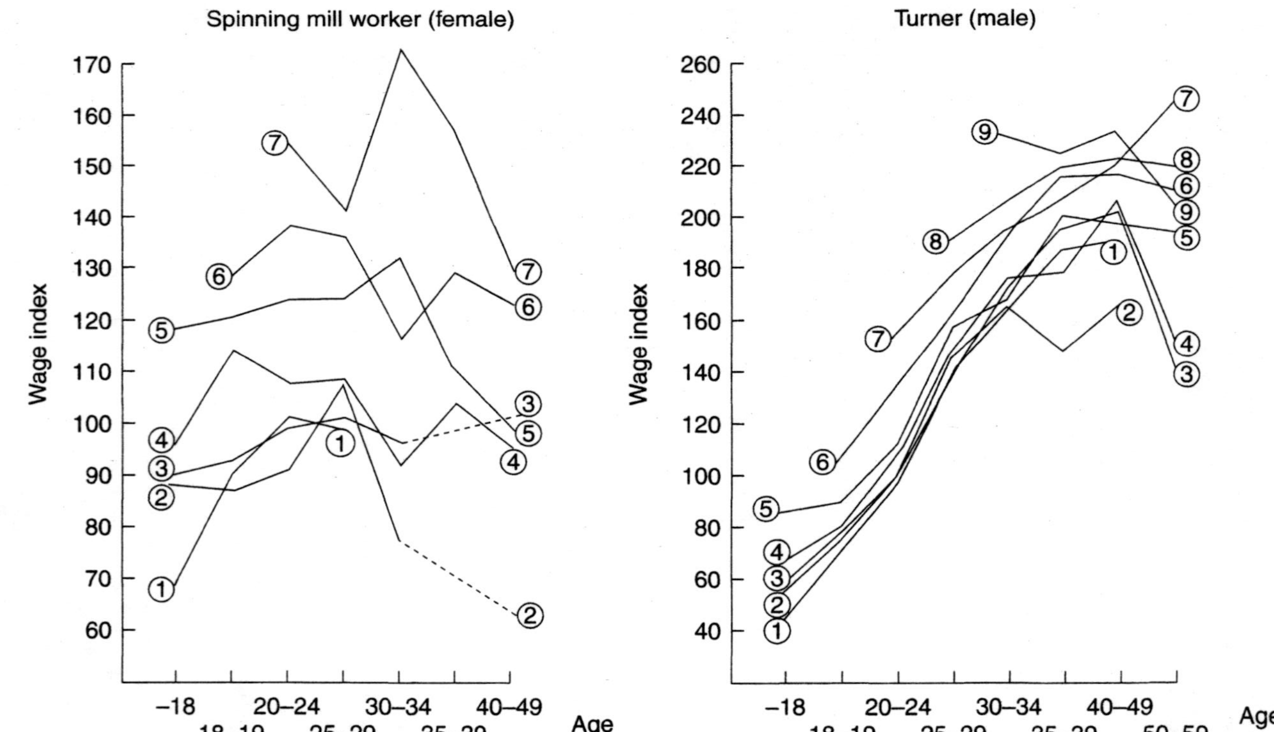

Figure 10.2 Wages by age and length of service, 1954

Source: Compiled from Rōdōshō 1954

Notes: Length of service or experience: (1) less than six months; (2) more than six months and less than one year; (3) more than one year, less than two years; (4) more than two years, less than three years; (5) more than three years, less than five years; (6) more than five years, less than ten years; (7) more than ten years, less than fifteen years; (8) more than fifteen years, less than twenty years; (9) more than twenty years, less than thirty years.

Index 100 = wages of employees of 20–24 years old with between one and two years' length of service/experience.

workers subject to the kind of seniority wage system described above and temporary workers were employed; the latter provided a buffer of temporary employees for economic fluctuations, just as had occurred between the two world wars. Such temporary workers increased with the rapid expansion of markets after the Korean War broke out in June 1950. In Hokkaido, their percentage in the workforce gradually increased: 8.2 per cent in 1950 to 11.6 per cent in 1951 and 12.9 per cent in 1952 (Hokkaidōritsu Rōdō Kagaku Kenkyūsho 1955: 39). In Osaka, the same figure rose from 8.5 per cent before the war to 18.4 per cent in 1952 (Itozono 1978: 8). Employment of these contracted workers was possible under amendments to the regulations of the *Shokugyō Anteihō* (Employment Security Act), and the practice subsequently spread to every enterprise. Subcontract workers jumped from 11.6 per cent of the workforce in April 1952 to 40.6 per cent in 1957 and 52.6 per cent in March 1960 in Yawata Iron and Steel Ltd (Meiji Daigaku Shakai Kagaku Kenkyūsho 1961: 230).

Despite this 'permanent–temporary subcontract' system, companies continued to cut staff, even among their permanent workers. The boom period of special procurement orders came to an end with the July 1953 settlement of the Korean War. This led directly to labour protests against the loss of employment, as at Nikkō-Muroran (July 1954), Mitsubishi Nihon Jūkō Shimomaruko (January 1956) and Sagami Kōgyō (May 1956). In each of these cases, the management was victorious. This period also saw the shift of energy production from coal to oil, a radical change that brought about workforce cuts at all major collieries. Mitsui acted first in January 1959, followed by Meiji in February, and then Mitsubishi, Sumitomo, Furukawa and Yūbetsu together on 6 May; in all, at both major and minor collieries 28,000 people lost their jobs. One such case resulted in the Mitsui-Miike dispute in August of that year, which escalated into a major confrontation that lasted until 1960 and became characterized as 'the struggle between all capital and all labour'.

In retrospect, therefore, employment conditions were extremely insecure during this decade; the principle of in-firm, long-term secure employment – so-called 'Japanese life-time employment' – had not yet been established.

The 1950s were a time of significant labour disputes in major enterprises and the enterprise union system began to emerge in companies affected by the disputes. Those at Nissan (August 1953), Nikkō Muroran, Sagami Kōgyō, Ōji Seishi (1958), Tawara Seisaku-sho (April 1959) and Miike (1959–60) have an important event in common – in the middle of the dispute, alternative workers' organizations were founded representing more the management point of view, which implied a challenge to the logic of the labour unions.[3] Serious splits and conflicts arose in the latter, and thus the birth of the co-operative enterprise union in place of the previous conflictual enterprise organizations is a major feature of the 1950s.

This decade can be identified as the origin of various aspects of modern Japanese relations between capital and labour. The term 'modern' refers to two points – the change in the determining factors of seniority wages and the birth of 'co-operative' enterprise unions on the basis that the workers' basic right to organize was assured.

HIGH ECONOMIC GROWTH AND FORMATION OF INDUSTRIAL RELATIONS, 1960–73

Figures 10.3 and 10.4 show the correlation between workers' age/length of service and wages as of 1965. Male blue-collar wages rose in a clear correlation with both age and length of service, while male white-collar salaries demonstrate a very steep seniority curve in relation to age but a weaker association between salary and length of service – only 30 per cent difference between new recruits' salaries and those of workers with 20 to 29 years' service. By contrast, the wage curve of females, both blue and white collar, is rather flat with regard to age, indicating that it is not age which activated seniority wage increments so much as length of service, which shows a steep curve; this is more marked for blue-collar than white-collar workers. Such characteristics among employed men and women are

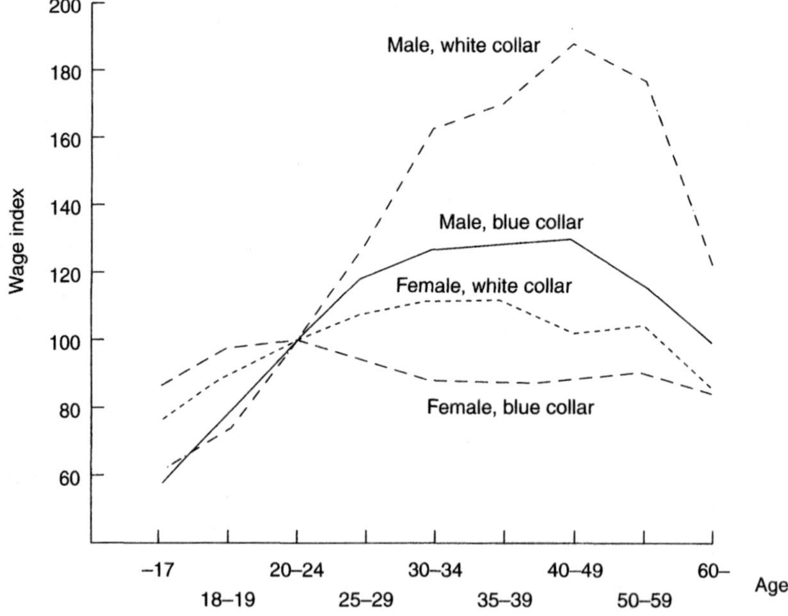

Figure 10.3 Correlation between age and wage, 1965 (manufacturing industry, length of service less than one year)
Source: Compiled from Rōdōshō, Employment Statistics Dept, 1965
Note: Index 100 = 24–25 age group.

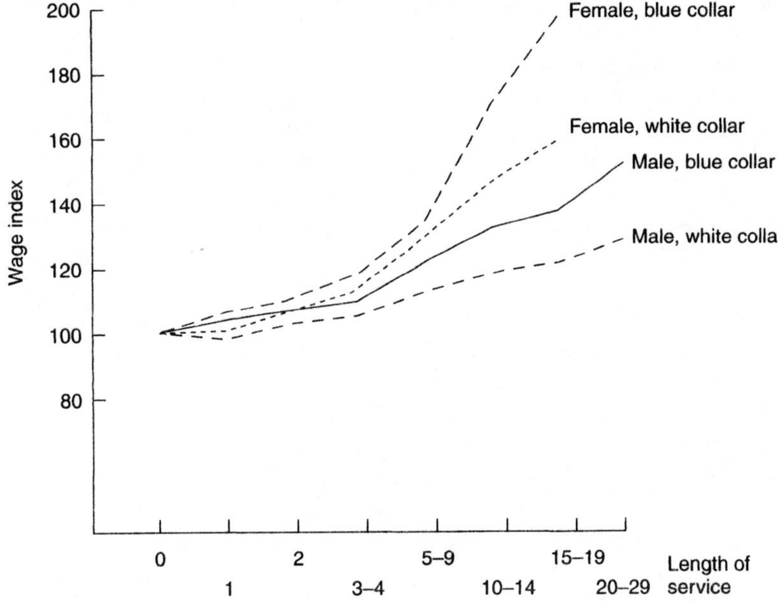

Figure 10.4 Correlation between length of service and wage, 1965 (manufacturing industry, 30–34 year-old group)
Source: Compiled from Rōdōshō, Employment Statistics Dept, 1965
Note: Index 100 = less than one year's service.

noticeable in enterprises of all sizes from less than one hundred to more than one thousand employees, although space does not allow full figures here.

We can therefore conclude that the principal determining factors of wages in each employee group were age and length of service for blue-collar males, mainly age for white-collar males, and length of service for both blue- and white-collar females.

As noted earlier, the factor of age represents a guarantee of a living wage, while length of service represents a firm's gratuity to its own special skills pool; this implies that white-collar male wages are best understood as based upon a livelihood guarantee policy, while blue-collar workers' wages are predicated upon livelihood guarantee plus enterprise-related skills. Females, on the other hand, benefit only from their developed skills. This skills reward factor supports theories about Japan's expertise and highly developed industrial society, but leaving these aside we should note that this factor is most marked among female occupations, which are generally the most peripheral jobs in Japan's economy. This accords well with the 1950s analysis of the female spinning mill workers and male turners. In addition, it is in the middle of the reconstruction and high-growth period of the economy, following the 1950s, that the wages of blue- and white-collar females lose their age-related seniority basis, while in the

Occupation period the guaranteed livelihood principle, reflected in the strong correlation between age and wage, was a strong factor in women's wages as well as men's.

Although gender and job type (blue or white collar) affect the determination of seniority wages, and management in this period keenly sought to introduce a wage system based on job evaluation, the seniority wage system widely survived, largely for two reasons.

First, under the seniority wage system wages did not strictly correspond with job evaluation, so that a flexible work organization was adopted; a professional/businesslike attitude was thus fostered among workers, relieving them of anxiety about the job evaluation. This made it easier to introduce new technology appropriate to the high economic growth.

Second, the demand for workers rapidly expanded owing to the favourable economic growth, and the seniority wage system actually served to restrain the total wage bill as the relative proportion of lower paid young workers increased. The conditions conducive to high growth in general, i.e. flexible work organization (flexible job allocation, etc.) and the growing demand for labour, created long-term secure employment in companies during this period.

At the same time, co-operative unions were established. The following three factors were key points in this trend.

First, the defeat of the labour movement in the Miike dispute of 1959–60 was pivotal. The late 1950s saw conflict and confrontation between unions and management over policies; while the unions were engaged in struggles for the effective control of the workplace, the management aim was 'rationalization'. As Miike mine was the focus of the 'workplace struggle', its defeat entailed the loss of union control in workplaces and the establishment of co-operative labour unions within enterprises. From that point on, labour disputes in the essential heavy industries effectively disappeared. Second, as if to accept this situation, the Sōhyō's (General Council of Trade Unions of Japan) proposal on organization policy in 1962 made it clear that workplace struggles were to be subordinate to the union's 'unifying function'. This decision was a great setback for a movement that was supposed to enhance workers' control. Finally, federations of co-operative enterprise unions – IMF, JC (International Metalworker's Federation, Japan Council) and Dōmei (Japanese Confederation of Labour) – were founded in 1964. 'Co-operation' for these organizations meant a co-operative working relationship between labour and management at company level, whereas co-operatism in industrial relations in the West refers to agreements at national level where the economy in general is concerned, or at industry level where a common industrial interest is involved. We may identify the Japanese experience therefore as 'enterprise co-operativism', meaning that its implication for worker unification by the state is small.

The formation of co-operative enterprise unions and 'enterprise co-operativism' rendered collective negotiation meaningless. As shown in

Table 10.1, the prevalence of management–labour consultation reached 50–60 per cent during this period. In large companies with a thousand or more employees, this figure increased rapidly from 60 per cent in 1962 to 90 per cent in 1972. As the system became more widespread, the issues which would previously have been discussed in collective negotiations decreased and became limited in scope; what happened was that collective negotiation was transformed into the management–labour consultation exercise. This trend weakened the rights and obligations inherent between labour and management, which was a significant development allowing a sense of enterprise 'community' to emerge. Before the 1950s, community relationships in Japan were largely focused upon neighbourhoods and villages, but the industrial demands of the high growth period tended to break these down; however, companies came to absorb and re-establish such community relationships. Still, in arguing that an enterprise community was formed under particular descriptive and historical conditions in the high economic growth of the 1960s, this is not to suggest that Japanese cultural characteristics such as *ie* (house), *mura* (village) and paternalism, represent a general trait of Japanese labour management (Fujii and Maruyama 1991; Mito 1994).[4]

Looking back, we could consider this period to be the formative stage of modern Japanese industrial relations and characteristics. However, the developments were yet limited to large companies in the private sector, and the co-operative trend represented by IMF, JC and Dōmei was still unable to assume control over the labour movement, owing to the Sōhyō-related public sector unions movement such as Kokurō (National Railway Workers' Union) Nikkyōso (Japan Teachers' Union) and Jichirō (All Japan Prefectural and Municipal Workers' Union) and numerous disputes in small and medium-sized enterprises. All in all, it is apparent that modern industrial relations were not in operation throughout the economy.

Table 10.1 Prevalence of labour–management council by company size

Company size (employees)	*1962* %	*1972* %	*1977* %	*1984* %	*1989* %
Over 5,000	59.8 (Over 5,000 and 1,000–4,999)	90.0 (Over 5,000 and 1,000–4,999)	92.6	94.2	83.2
1,000–4,999			85.7	83.6	76.1
500–999	53.7	80.6	73.0 (500–999 and 300–499)	74.4 (500–999 and 300–499)	75.2 (500–999 and 300–499)
300–499	51.0	78.9			
100–299	51.1	56.4	54.7	57.6	57.2
50–99	42.5	—	—	—	50.5
Total	49.5	62.8	70.8	72.0	69.4

Source: 1) Rōdōshō Rōsei Kyoku 1964: 154; 2) Rōdōshō 1972, 77, 84, 89.
Note: Company sizes for 1962 are different from those indicated: 300–499 → 200–499; 100–299 → 100–199; 50–99 → 30–39.

LOW ECONOMIC GROWTH AND ESTABLISHMENT OF UNIONISM, 1973–90

In this period, the correlation between employees' age and length of service and wage, including differences due to gender and job classification, remained as in the previous period. However, after the first oil crisis in 1973, management based upon individual ability began to operate in practical terms (Nikkeiren had already announced its principle of 'ability-based management' in 1969) and remuneration according to an employee's ability came to be emphasized. This system finely divided wage increments along the seniority wage curve by performing personnel assessment which mainly concerned a worker's ability, achievement and attitude (e.g. obedience to rules, dynamism, co-operativeness and responsibility) and aimed to motivate all workers towards constant improvement of 'work efficiency'.[5] Thus, the seniority wages of this period in theory had the multi-line system shown in Figure 10.5. One point in common between the principles of a guaranteed living wage and reward of enterprise specific skills was that although they were dealing with wage structures after the 1970s they did not refer to the personal assessment factor which was introduced into the seniority wage system in this period.

After the first oil crisis, which brought the high growth period to an end, what the enterprises were pursuing – apart from realizing ability-based labour management – was thorough slim-line management. This adjustment came in two stages: the first from 1973 to 1978, beginning with the first oil crisis, and the second from 1978 to 1983, marked by the second oil shock (Kansai Daigaku Keizai-Seiji Kenkyūsho 1989). In the prior

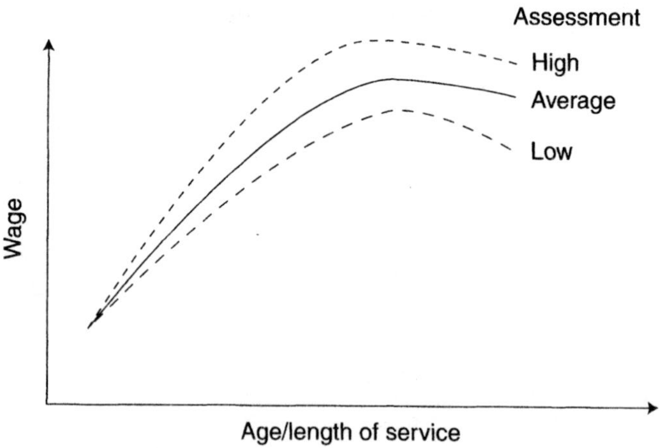

Figure 10.5 Correlation model of age, length of service and wage
Source: Nomura 1994
Note: Diagram has been slightly changed from the original.

stage, readjustment commenced with immediate measures, such as dismissing temporary workers or offering temporary leave, natural wastage (leaving vacancies unfilled on resignation, etc.), encouraging voluntary redundancy, and the development of job displacement and temporary or permanent job transfer. These were particularly applied in the shipbuilding and textile industries, where immediate measures like voluntary redundancy were the primary feature of 1973–8. As Table 10.2 shows, in enterprises of 500 or more employees, the total workforce decreased during this period from 9,170,000 to 8,720,000, a drop of 450,000. The process continued in 1978–83, with new procedures taking shape, such as readjustment involving a wider range of industries and the emergence of new relationships facilitating transfer arrangements between industrial conglomerates. In addition, new companies were established as a solution to the problem of surplus workers. Direct personnel reduction, however, decreased. Table 10.2 shows that after 1979 larger enterprises even began to get bigger.

In the context of in-firm, long-term secure employment, temporary transfer has a significant role: employees so transferred still keep their link with their original company, thus maintaining the customary Japanese employment pattern, and hence temporary transfer and job displacement are the preferred measures. Thus, although secure long-term employment was disrupted in the direct personnel reduction activity of the mid-1970s, it was subsequently re-established.

If we look at Japanese employment behaviour in this period, it is important to notice that 'unstable' employees – those without security of employment, such as part-time, casual and temporary workers – increased. Table 10.3 shows how these classes of employee, defined as employed for

Table 10.2 Number of employees of large companies (500+ employees) among non-agricultural industries (unit: 10,000 persons, percentage)

Year	*Number of employees of large companies*	*Proportion of the whole employees*	*Year*	*Number of employees of large companies*	*Proportion of the whole employees*
1973	917	29.3	1983	1,002	27.3
1974	926	30.6	1984	1,026	27.5
1975	902	28.8	1985	1,017	27.0
1976	902	28.0	1986	1,020	26.6
1977	892	27.3	1987	1,039	26.7
1978	872	26.5	1988	1,065	26.7
1979	888	26.4	1989	1,103	26.7
1980	916	26.6	1990	1,148	26.8
1981	932	26.6	1991	1,200	27.0
1982	961	26.9	1992	1,254	27.5

Sources: Sōrifu (Somu-cho), Tōkei Kyoku: Annual Surveys

Table 10.3 Number of short-time employees in non-agricultural industries (unit: 10,000 people, percentage)

Year	*Males and Females*			*Males*			*Females*		
	Total (A)	*Employees working under 34hrs/wk (B)*	*Ratio (B)/(A)*	*Total (A)*	*Employees working under 34hrs/wk (B)*	*Ratio (B)/(A)*	*Total (A)*	*Employees working under 34hrs/wk (B)*	*Ratio (B)/(A)*
1973	3,585	279	7.8	2,406	109	4.5	1,180	170	14.4
1974	3,607	303	8.4	2,444	119	4.9	1,164	184	15.8
1975	3,617	353	9.8	2,458	154	6.3	1,159	198	17.1
1976	3,682	314	8.5	2,487	122	4.9	1,195	192	16.1
1977	3,738	321	8.6	2,495	119	4.8	1,242	203	16.3
1978	3,770	330	8.8	2,498	115	4.6	1,271	215	16.9
1979	3,846	366	9.5	2,546	130	5.1	1,300	236	18.2
1980	3,941	390	9.9	2,597	134	5.2	1,345	259	19.3
1981	4,008	395	9.9	2,626	128	4.9	1,382	266	19.2
1982	4,068	416	10.2	2,660	132	5.0	1,408	284	20.2
1983	4,176	433	10.4	2,701	128	4.7	1,475	306	20.7
1984	4,236	464	11.0	2,728	136	5.0	1,508	328	21.8
1985	4,285	471	11.0	2,745	138	5.0	1,539	333	21.6
1986	4,350	503	11.6	2,776	151	5.4	1,574	352	22.4
1987	4,399	506	11.5	2,795	141	5.0	1,604	365	22.8
1988	4,507	533	11.8	2,848	148	5.2	1,660	386	23.3
1989	4,648	602	13.0	2,910	169	5.8	1,738	432	24.9
1990	4,806	722	15.0	2,984	221	7.4	1,823	501	27.5
1991	4,972	802	16.1	3,065	252	8.2	1,907	550	28.8
1992	5,086	868	17.1	3,125	276	8.8	1,962	592	30.2

Sources: Sōrifū (Sōmu-chō), Tōkei Kyoku: Annual Surveys

34 hours or less per week, rose annually to comprise over 10 per cent of all employees in non-agricultural industries after 1982. The basic reason for this was the micro-electronics (ME) revolution. The extensive introduction of ME equipment expanded the number of jobs requiring only simple monitoring. Moreover, the costs of its introduction were high, as technological progress quickly rendered such equipment obsolete. With such depreciation, in order to make the best use of ME equipment, systems of shift work or irregular working hours needed to be adopted. With such obsolescence, management realized that occupational training for permanent employees was becoming more and more inefficient and wasteful. On top of this, the rapid technological turnover meant that the main sales basis of ME equipment was by rental, under which the vendors assumed responsibility for the maintenance and control of their products (Miyoshi 1988: 122–3). These reasons indicate why the introduction of micro-electronics caused a growth in an unstable, readily adjustable workforce, a trend which, as can be seen in Table 10.3, particularly affected women – among the male workforce, unstable employees only registered 5 per cent even in the 1980s. Thus, it may be wrong to say that the introduction of a temporary workforce induced a small and selected core group of male permanent employees who were themselves protected by the customary modes of Japanese employment.

The increased recruitment of non-permanent workers, particularly of women, also reduced union organization rates in this period; yet at the same time, the co-operative union movement grew to be the dominant force in the labour movement. First, Tekkō Rōren (Japanese Federation of Iron and Steel Workers' Unions), at their spring 1975 congress, stated: 'we must aim at the substantial improvement of wages in line with economic growth' and proposed a Japanese incomes policy (social contract) emphasizing linkage with prevailing economic trends. During the high growth period, even under conditions of co-operation between union and management, the attitude was one of 'co-operation in production, but opposition in distribution'; now, however, the unions had to drop their opposition to distribution. Second, the defeat of Kōrōkyō (Public Enterprise Union Confederation) in November 1975 over the restoration of public employees' right to strike led to a change in their strategy to one of co-operative industrial relations in the public sector. A third point of note was that in contrast to the high strike rate, particularly among small and medium-sized companies, in the booming economy of 1960 to 1973, in this period the number of strikes fell dramatically, and even where trade unions existed, including among the smaller companies, co-operative enterprise unions were formed. Fourth, the formation in October 1976 of the policy promoting Rōso-Kaigi (Labour Union Conference), which emphasized co-operation with political parties, led to the creation of Zenmin Rōkyō (All Private Enterprise Union Confederation) in July 1982 and Rengō (Japanese Trade Union Confederation) in February 1989, representing an enormous tide of co-operative tendencies within workers' organizations. As well as the spread of social acceptance of co-operative unionism, this period also saw the rapid increase of QC circles (see Figure 10.6).

As mentioned earlier, an important precondition for the development of 'co-operative' enterprise unions was the workers' loss of control over the workplace. In that sense, there was a risk that the expansion of co-operative enterprise unions might induce alienation among workers at work and a loss of morale in the workplace. It was imperative to avoid this at a time when international competition was intensifying after the oil shocks, and what was required was a scheme to encourage workers' voluntary participation (Suzuki 1994: Ch.5) at the workplace (co-operative unions had ignored this) and to generate identity with their own labour. Hence, via the twin factors of management 'compulsion' and workers' 'voluntary' association, participatory workplace control was to be established. This is the background to the increase of Quality Control circles, and thus the social acceptance of co-operative enterprise unions and the rapid rise of QC are two sides of the same coin.

As can be readily seen, it is during this period that the contemporary Japanese industrial relations were instituted as a paradigm for organizing Japanese society. It can be argued that the reason why Japanese industrial relations drew so much international attention at that time is because the notion of workers organized by enterprise rather than by, say, the state, held particularly significant implications for multinational corporations or globalized capital, which was the emerging trend of world history.

CONCLUSION: RESTRUCTURING OF INDUSTRIAL RELATIONS IN THE HEISEI RECESSION

The historical development of Japanese industrial relations reviewed here has focused upon seniority wages, in-firm, long-term secure employment and co-operative enterprise unions. In conclusion, let us review the latest developments in these areas in the light of the so-called Heisei recession of the 1990s, particularly concerning the trend of employer awareness.

In 1993 the *Nihon Keizai Shinbun* circulated a questionnaire to the top executives of 450 companies in the first rank of the Tokyo Stock Exchange, asking them what, in their opinion, were the three most important things that should be preserved or abolished in Japanese management practices. The most important things to be kept up were enterprise unions (51.3 per cent), QC (50.7 per cent) and lifetime employment (39.1 per cent), while the practices that should be abandoned were the seniority ranking system (79.8 per cent) and, again, lifetime employment (24.9 per cent) (*Nikkei Sangyō Shinbun* 1993).

In August 1993, Tokai Sōgō Kenkyusho circulated a questionnaire to 284 companies whose turnover exceeded 100 billion yen. Responses were ascribed a value based on subtracting the proportion answering 'no' from

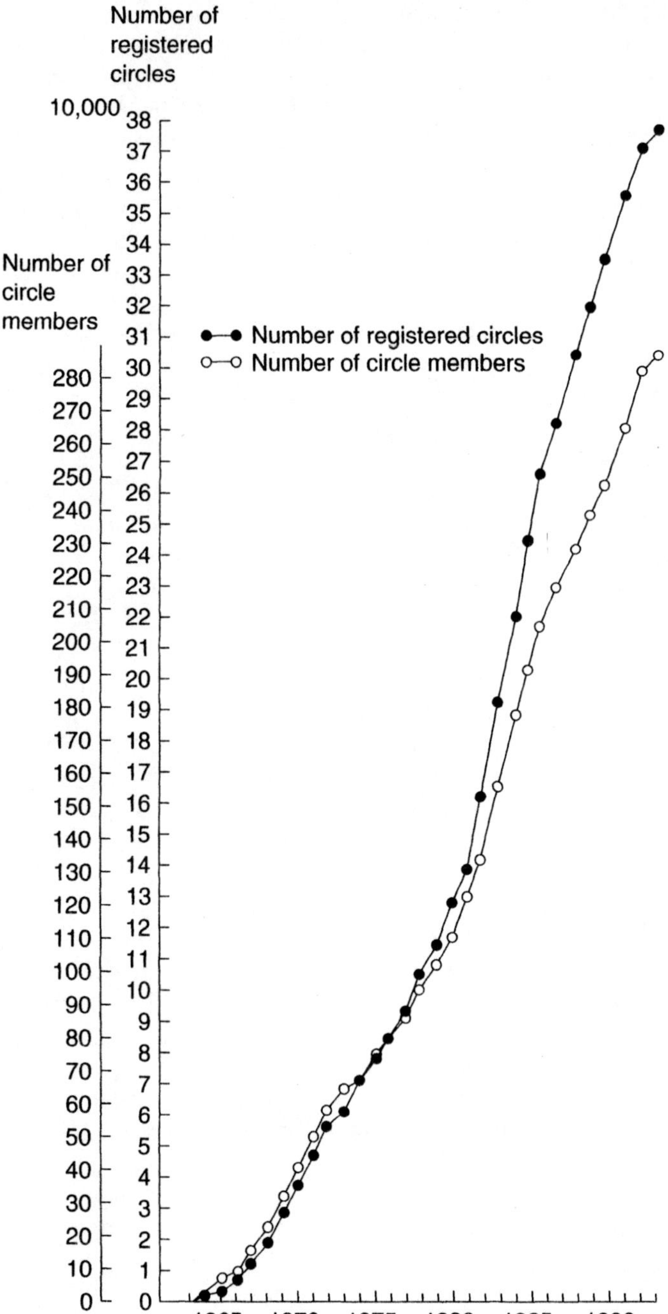

Figure 10.6 Change in the number of QC circle registrations, 28 February 1994
Source: Material supplied by Japan Science & Technology Association

those answering in the affirmative. Questions relating to seniority wages were 'is your company still operating the system?' and 'is the system still in general operation in society?', to which the answers came to –23.3 and –20.7 respectively. Questions on whether respondents' companies still offered lifetime employment and whether they thought the system was still in general use received +65.9 and +42.3 respectively (*Asahi Shinbun* 1994: 14 Jan).

Another survey was carried out between May and June 1993 by Nihon Seisansei Honbu (Japan Productivity Centre), and again indicated that management in general still prefers lifetime employment. The most common response from personnel managers of 308 top-ranking companies to the question of employment of staff was 'employees are kept on until retirement age except in special circumstances' (56 per cent). Answers like 'there is no need to keep employees until their retirement' or 'the role of lifetime employment is declining' received favour from less than 10 per cent of the companies surveyed (*Asahi Shinbun* 1994: 22 Jan.).

The above surveys seem to demonstrate that the major enterprises of the 1990s, despite the recession, are trying to preserve in-firm, long-term secure employment, co-operative enterprise unions and QC circles, while disassembling or reorganizing the seniority wage system by pushing forward with ability-based management.

But this is not to suggest that no adjustment in employment under the Heisei current recession took place. For example, the number of those designated as surplus employees in 1993–4 amounted to 22,749 in Hitachi. But this was composed of 16,779 (73.8 per cent) employees of Shukkō (dispatch), 3,931 (17.3 per cent) employees of Tenkin (transfer), 1,240 (5.5 per cent) employees of Ōen (assistance) and Tenseki (change of company) which suggests direct redundancies amounted to only 799 (3.5 per cent) (interview with the Labour Union of Hitachi 1995).

Japanese employers know well that direct and large-scale sackings might invite instability, which could lead to political change. We may say that they are seeking various ways to make readjustments within the framework of stable long-term employment. On the other hand, reorganization or termination of the seniority-based wage system has already begun to be replaced by an individual ability-based annual salary system. When the Japanese employers and management forced the workers to choose between 'employment' or 'wage', the answer was already in their hands. The Japanese-style industrial relations will continue as a modified Japanese-style system which involves a momentum to implement assessment of individual ability.

NOTES

1 This is an economic policy enacted in January 1949 by an economic adviser to the US occupation army. It included nine principles, a single exchange rate of

one dollar = 360 yen, a termination of post-war inflation and a new tax system, which as a whole aimed to revive and redevelop Japan in view of the progress of communism in China.

2 See Ōno (1989) and An (1982) for a discussion on how the seniority-wage system can be established, even in a fluctuating and highly mobile labour market.

3 See the analysis by Kurita (1994).

4 See Mito (1994: Ch. 1).

5 See Suzuki Ryōji (1994: Ch. 4); to the best of my knowledge, this is the most convincing and in-depth study of the Japanese production and management system.

REFERENCES

An Shunjōku (1982) *Shushin Koyōsei no Nikkan Hikaku* (Comparison of life-time employment between Japan and Korea), Tokyo: Ronsōsha.

Asahi Shinbun (1994) 14 January, 22 January.

Chūō Rōdō Gakuen (1946) *Chingin Chōsa Hōkoku* (Report of wage survey), Tokyo: Chūō Rōdō Gakuen.

Fujii, M. and Maruyama, Y. (1991) *Gendai Nippon Keiei Shi* (Business history of contemporary Japan), Kyoto: Mineruva Shobo.

Hokkaidoritsu Rōdō Kagaku Kenkyusho (1955) *Rinji Ko – zenpen* (Temporary workers – part one), Tokyo: Nippon Hyoron Shinsha.

Itozono, T. (1978) *Nippon no Shagaikō Seido* (System of subcontracting workers in Japan), Kyoto: Mineruva Shobo.

Kansai Daigaku Keizai Seiji Kenkyūsho (1989) *Wagakuni Kyodai Kigyō no Koyo Chōsei Katei – Jigyōsho Tan i no Koyō Hendō, 1973–1983* (Employment adjustment process of large-scale enterprises in Japan – change in employment by establishments, 1973–1983), Osaka: Kansai Daigaku.

Koike, K. (1977) *Shokuba no Rōdō Kumiai to Sanka – Rōshi Kankei no Nichibei Hikaku* (Labour union at workplace and participation – a comparison of industrial relations in Japan and the US), Tokyo: Tōyōkeizai Shinpōsha.

Koike, K. (1981) *Nippon no Jukuren* (Skills of Japan), Tokyo: Yūhikaku.

Koike, K. (1991) *Shigoto no Keizaigaku* (Economics of work), Tokyo: Tōyōkeizai Shinpōsha.

Kurita, K. (1994) *Nippon no Rōdō Shakai* (World of labour in Japan), Tokyo: Tokyo University Press.

Meiji Daigaku Shakai Kagaku Kenkyūsho (ed.) (1961) *Tekkōgyō no Gōrika to Rōdō* (Rationalization of iron and steel industry and labour), Tokyo: Hakutō Shobo.

Mito, K. (1994) *Ie to shite no Nippon Shakai* (Japanese society as home), Tokyo: Yuhikaku.

Nikkei Sangyo Shinbun (1993) 17 May.

Miyoshi, M. (ed.) (1988) *Gendai Nippon no Rōdō Seisaku* (Labour policy of contemporary Japan), Tokyo: Aoki Shoten.

Nimura, K. (1994) 'Sengo Shakai no Kiten ni okeru Rōdō Kumiai Undō' (Labour union movement as a starting point of the post war society), in J. Banno (ed.) *Nippon Kin Gendaishi* (Modern and Contemporary History of Japan, vol. 4), Tokyo: Iwanami Shoten.

Nishinarita, Y. (1988) *Kindai Nippon Rōshi Kankeishi no Kenkyū* (A study of industrial relations history in modern Japan), Tokyo: Tokyo University Press.

Nishinarita, Y. (1990) 'Senryō seisaku no tenkan to Nippon keizai' (Change of occupation policy and Japanese economy), in Rekishigaku Kenkyūkai (ed.)

Nippon Dōjidaishi 2 (Contemporaneous history of Japan, vol. 2), Tokyo: Aoki Shoten.

Nishinarita, Y. (1992) 'Senryōki Nippon no rōshi kankei – kōsōku sareta keieiken no mondai o chūshin ni' (Industrial relations in the period of occupied Japan with particular reference to constrained managerial prerogatives), in M. Nakamura (ed.) *Nippon no Kindai to Shihonshugi* (Modern period in Japan and capitalism), Tokyo: Tokyo University Press.

Nishinarita, Y. (1994) 'Sengo kiki to shihonshugi saiken katei no rōshi kankei – Nippon to Nishidoitsu no hikaku' (Post-war crisis and industrial relations in the reconstruction process of capitalism – a comparison of Japan and West Germany), in T. Yui, M. Nakamura and N. Toyoshita (eds) *Senryō Kaikaku no Kokusai Hikaku* (International comparison of reforms by occupation), Tokyo: Sanseidō.

Nomura, M. (1994) *Shushin Koyō* (Lifetime employment), Tokyo: Iwanami Shoten.

OECD (1973) *Manpower Policy in Japan*, Paris: OECD.

Ōno, A. (1989) *Nippon teki Koyō Kankō to Rōdō Shijō* (Japanese-style employment practices labour market), Tokyo: Tōyō Keizai Shinpōsha.

Rōdōshō (1946) *Shiryō Rōdō Undōshi Shōwa 20–21* (Material history of labour movement, 1945–6), Tokyo: Rōdōshō.

Rōdōshō (1954) *Shokushubetsu to Chingin Jittai Chōsa: Konjinbetsu Chingin Chōsa Kekka Hōkokusho* (Survey of wages by occupations: report on individual wages' survey results, vols 2 and 4), Tokyo: Rōdōshō.

Rōdōshō (1960) Shiryo Rōdō Undōshi (Data on history of labour movement: 1945–6), Tokyo, Rōdōshō.

Rōdōshō (1961) *Rōdō Gyoseishi 1* (History of labour administration, vol. 1), Tokyo: Rōdōshō.

Rōdōshō (1965) *Chingin Kōzō Kihon Tōkei Chōsa Hōkoku* (Basic statistical survey report on wage structure), Tokyo: Rōdōshō.

Rōdōshō (1972, 1977, 1984, 1989) *Rōshi Komyunikeishon* (Communication between employers and employees), Tokyo: Rōdōshō.

Rōdōshō Rōsei Kyoku (1964) *Rōdō Kyoyaku to Rōshi Kankei* (Labour agreement and industrial relations), Tokyo: Rōdōshō.

Showa Dōjin Kai (1960) *Wagakuni Chingin Kōzo no Shiteki Kōsatsu* (Historical consideration of Japan's wage structure), Tokyo: Shiseidō.

Sōrifu Tōkei Kyoku (Annual Report) *Rōdoryoku Chōsa Nenpō* (Annual report of workforce), Tokyo: Sōrifu.

Suzuki, R. (1994) *Nipponteki Seisan Shisutemu to Kigyō Shakai* (Japanese-style production systems and corporate society), Hokkaidō: Hokkaido Univeristy Press.

11 New trends in enterprise unions and the labour movement

Ōhki Kazunori

This chapter examines two issues connected with enterprise unions and the labour movement. First, in what ways have Japanese labour unions, and in particular enterprise unions, changed in the fifty-year period since World War II? Second, what kind of changes and new trends are Japanese labour unions experiencing, now that the industrial production system and the high growth of Japanese corporations, which supported them until today, are facing serious difficulties?

THE CURRENT SITUATION

Analytical approaches to enterprise unions

The term 'enterprise union' was coined in order to describe the dominant characteristic of Japanese labour unions in the post-war period.[1] These characteristics are:

1 Labour unions based not on individual membership of unions organized by industry or profession, but based on unions organized at the level of individual companies or businesses.
2 Both white- and blue-collar employees are members of the same union.
3 Permanent employees are recruited collectively into the union, whereas temporary employees are excluded from union membership.
4 The unions of those companies with factories and businesses across the country form councils and federations which are often more influential than industrial federations.

A labour movement based upon enterprise unions is weak in several respects.[2] For example:

- union activities are confined within the company, and tend to be dominated by company values;
- employees' consciousness of themselves as union members is weak;
- conflicts of interest between union members are common, and splits in their organization easily occur;

- the structure of personnel control and union control often seem to be indivisible;
- unions ignore the problems of temporary employees and the unemployed, and instead concentrate on activities exclusively to the benefit of permanent employees.

These weak points often result from the distinctive characteristics of enterprise unions. In order to rationalize the reasons behind the decline of Japan's labour unions, a range of scholars has stressed that, due to the unique features of the labour market, the *Dekasegi*-type of labourers (migrant wage labour) working away from their homes in rural areas – a specific characteristic of Japanese capitalism – would inevitably mean that labour unions would become enterprise unions.[3]

There is no doubt that the theory of the enterprise union stated above has some utility in explaining the characteristics of the labour unions and labour movement in Japan since the war. However, when viewed from a present-day perspective, fifty years after the war, limitations are apparent in such an explanation of the unions' characteristics, and a number of important problems present themselves.

First, this debate and theory fails to explain the historical and important presence of various qualitatively different types of labour unions alongside and among enterprise unions. Second, the theory of *Dekasegi*-type of wage labour does not sufficiently explain why enterprise unions have survived over the long term, even though the various structural and socio-economic conditions of Japanese capitalism in the post-war period have changed dramatically. Third, the globalization of Japanese corporations has led to doubts over whether or not the enterprise union can be unique to Japan.

Interpretations of the enterprise union often place too much emphasis upon the distinctive characteristics of its organizational form. But the significance of labour unions is more than their specific organizational form and has to take into account certain characteristics of union movements, including the beliefs of union members, culture, behavioural models, and union activities. Indeed, from the viewpoint that organizations represent the constant form of movements, then the characteristics of union movements are the most important thing to consider.[4] The theory of enterprise unions devoid of this viewpoint has led to disregard of the course of the labour movement, and to the deterministic view that the decline of Japan's labour movement is inevitable. What is more, such a view overlooks the fact that the distinctive characteristics of Japanese unions have been produced and defined historically by confrontational relations between labour and capital, and class struggles as a whole, and does not acknowledge the dynamic impact of history. Finally, the theory of the enterprise union pays far too little attention to subjective factors in history, and tries to explain the significance of labour movements from objective economic conditions and organizational characteristics. But such an approach is bound to be divorced from the reality of the development of the labour movement, which is full of contradictions.

When dealing with the problems associated with the enterprise union it is thus important to keep these points in mind.

HISTORICAL DEVELOPMENT OF THE ENTERPRISE UNION

The development of Japanese enterprise unions can be said to have undergone the following changes over the fifty-year period since the war.

Jigyoshobetsu Kumiai (unions at business establishment) in occupied Japan

Following the defeat of Japan, and in the period in which a militant labour movement developed centred upon the Congress of Industrial Unions (*Sanbetsu*), the first enterprise union to emerge took the form of a union organized at the level of the business establishment. At this time, literally all employees, including shop-floor and office workers were organized into one labour union at this level. These types of unions promoted struggles which forged links beyond the boundaries of individual companies, in defence of workers' lives at the industrial and local levels, and which promoted the class-conscious concentration of workers into local trade union centres and industrial federations. At the national level, moreover, the development of the mass labour movement led to the creation of a national and united organization – National Liaison Council of Labour Unions (*Zenrōren*), including the anti-Communist and class-collaborationist Japanese Federation of Labour (*Sōdōmei*). The organizations formed nationally and around individual industries were confederations with member unions of equal status. Enterprise unions organized at the level of the business establishment decided their own policies on the labour movement, and they all exercised independently the three rights of labour: the right to organize, the right to collective bargaining, and the right to strike.

However, in this period the labour unions had only limited experience in running a labour movement, and among workers and the unions, the prewar and wartime feudal and anti-communist sentiments remained strong. In the immediate post-war period, the ruling class supported those pre-war union leaders who had co-operated with pre-war militarism, and sought to create unions that were collaborationist and anti-communist, with *Sōdōmei* at their centre. Since then, the mass labour movement has been split and forced into decline by various other factors, such as the development of social instability, the activities of unions in support of particular political parties, the Occupation authorities' shift to a policy of suppressing labour movements, and the implementation of the 'Red Purge'.[5]

Enterprise unions in high economic growth

The second stage is characterized by enterprise unions organizing only permanent employees, which occurred in the era of high economic growth. Along with repression and intervention by the US occupation forces (the ban and dissolution of *Zenrōren*, the split in *Sanbetsu*, the 'Red Purge', and the formation of *Sōhyō*), labour unions organized at the level of the business establishment went into decline, and instead '*honkō kumiai*' (unions organized around permanent employees), came to the forefront with high corporate growth and began to spread rapidly. This process first began with major changes in the framework of labour unions organized at the level of the business establishment due to a shift to reactionary labour policies. The factors which accounted for this shift included moves to protect the powers of corporate management by political power; amendments to the labour laws and administrative guidance which eased restrictions on the labour supply business, and which allowed the introduction of temporary workers and workers from outside the company; and the acceptance of the Red Purge by the labour unions under the revised Labour Union Law in 1949. In addition, the basic conditions for the existence and growth of enterprise unions greatly changed as the financial circles and the conservative political establishment strengthened their labour policies, including the spread of a system of discriminatory and hierarchical employment; the reconstruction of systems of status within corporations; the adoption of the job-ranking system; the promotion of policies to establish and spread co-operative labour–management system; and the strengthening of company–employee education.

As a result of these policies, together with the rise in unstable employment brought about by high economic growth, the move towards *keiretsu*-type relations with subcontracting and allied companies, and the huge growth of non-unionized labour centred on small and medium-sized companies, enterprise unions came to be premised upon a discriminatory and hierarchical structure of labour. In turn, labour–capital 'collaborationism' based on big enterprise unions became the mainstay of the labour movement, a large number of enterprise unions included in their membership only permanent employees, and those with unstable employment were effectively excluded from the union organization. Another result of these changes was that, rather than being a strengthening of collective industry and regional-based movement that went beyond the boundaries of the company, instead union activities tended to be concentrated in individual companies and company groups, and among permanent employees only. Finally, within the corporations themselves, because most everyday demands and matters were entrusted to labour–management councils, ordinary shop-floor workers tended to participate in union activities in name only.

However, during this period of development in the activities of enterprise unions, the tradition of struggle derived from the *Sanbetsu* still survived, and even though it was known as the *honkō kumiai* (union of permanent employees), it was nevertheless a union which worked for the achievement of the workers' demands as a whole. Later, from the end of the 1960s until the mid-1970s, a mass labour movement centred on the people's 'Spring Offensive' (Shuntō) developed,[6] and as the influence of a class-conscious labour movement strengthened among union members, the *honkō kumiai* also sought to break the 'structure of low wages', began to recognize the need to deal with the problems of workers in unstable employment, the unemployed, and the poor. In this context, moving beyond enterprise unions became an issue for the labour movement. The company union was to appear as another model of the enterprise union designed thoroughly to prevent the possibility of progressive changes in the enterprise unions.

Company unions

Third, the most dominant form of the enterprise union today is the company union, which took root in large corporations following the 1970s 'oil crises'. In this case, the functions of union officials and the structure of labour–management began to overlap, unions began to co-operate in the company's policies of 'rationalization' and wage restraint, and acquiesced if not actively supported the company in the transfer, relocation and dismissal of union members. This strengthened the tendency for labour unions to act as another layer in the structure of labour management. The enterprise union functioning as a company union only represents the interests of permanent employees and, rather than protecting the interests of workers as a whole, tends to represent the interests of the company.[7] Thus, these unions are now criticized for representing solidarity between labour and capital. As the company union lacks the basis for mass support, it has strengthened organizational controls on union members and employees.

The change in enterprise unions in the period of high economic growth resulted from the following circumstances:

1 Only during the latter half of the 1970s, due to large-scale rationalization plans for the 'streamlining of management', more than a quarter of employees experienced personnel reshuffles, and a large number of labour movement activists became the target of transfers and dismissals.
2 At the same time as various kinds of unstable employment were introduced into the production process of big enterprises (dispatched workers, re-transferred workers, subcontracted workers and part-time employees) a 'corporate reserve army' of transfer, support, and '*madogiwa zoku*' (middle-aged and older employees who have been demoted and no longer have a useful function) employees were created among permanent employees who had not yet reached retirement age, and a new discriminatory organization of labour was put in place.

3 Officials and activists from the previous enterprise unions, even those who co-operated with the company, had increased within the labour movement, but the core officials and activists of the company unions were selected and trained by the company's labour management sections in order to make them the dominant force in the unions.
4 Company unions were not only dominated by officials dispatched by the company, but were also overseen and controlled by various types of informal bodies organized by the company and managerial bodies (for example, various supervisors' organizations in the company and anti-communist groups outside the enterprises).
5 The democratic rules at the heart of trade union activities were trampled upon by various practices such as the detrimental changes in election systems, limits to the rights of union members, and enforcement of union member support for a specific political party and candidates.

In this way, the company unions emerged as an aggressive enterprise union supportive of capital. Presently, the majority of enterprise unions which make up the Japanese Trade Union Confederation (*Rengō*, formed in 1989) are company unions.[8] In this organization the officials representing a small number of large unions enjoy the overwhelming influence, and the top levels of the organization have the power to dominate the personnel and finance of the levels lower down. The members of the executive dispatched from companies have not only taken advantage of the system of control, and have worked for the creation of company unions among companies as well as at the levels of the same companies and individual industries, but have also dissolved existing union centres and established a new national organization, pushing forward with the systematic creation of company unions that cover all industries.

Changing enterprise unions

Fourth, nevertheless, what should not be overlooked in relation to these facts is the existence of a class-conscious workers' and trade union movement, which has carried on the militant traditions of the *Sanbetsu* and the *Zenrōren*, and was formed in opposition to the corporate based and collaborationist line of the enterprise unions of the high growth era. Included among these types of unions are the class-conscious industrial federations in the areas of local government, education and medicine; unions suffering from splits and the existence of minority group unions in large private companies; general unions of workers in small and medium-sized companies which go beyond the boundaries of the individual company; and regional unions organizing workers in unstable employment. These collaborate closely with the movements of workers critical of the company that exist inside enterprise unions, and the activities of strikers, consisting of workers in employment as well as dismissed workers. Many of these unions are seeking to break away from enterprise unions and are developing organizations and movements that go beyond the concept of the enterprise union. They are aiming to adopt methods of unionizing individual workers of unions not limited to one company; they are expanding the qualifications of union membership to embrace more than the permanent employees, thereby organizing temporary employees; they are conducting activities of plural unions in the same company or business establishment; they are promoting united struggles at the industrial and regional levels beyond the boundaries of a single enterprise; and they are pursuing various forms of solidarity and joint action with non-unionized workers. It can be said that this is a movement to change enterprise unions and make them qualitatively different from before. The movement developed from the end of the 1960s through contacts between workers and unions, but it is now showing new signs of development as a national labour movement centred on the National Confederation of Trade Unions (*Zenrōren*, formed in 1989).[9]

Although they have been generally called 'enterprise unions', Japanese trade union organizations have greatly changed their characteristics over the last fifty years. In turn, it is possible to see that today, as the structural contradictions of post-war capitalism deepen, Japanese unions have now reached a major turning point. This issue, along with the nature of the production system and the high earnings structure of large corporations, will be examined next in detail.

JAPANESE-STYLE PRODUCTION SYSTEM AND COMPANY UNIONS

The enterprise union has served as one of the most important mainstays of the high growth of Japanese corporations in the post-war era. Its role has not just been to ensure stable corporative operations and the speedy introduction of new technology through labour–management collaboration. During the period of high growth it also contributed by promoting the expansion of domestic markets, resolving the demands and dissatisfactions of union members, promoting specific socio-economic reforms, and strengthening the integration of workers and citizens into corporations and the state. Now, the company union is more directly indispensable for the high profits of large corporations.

Labour under the Japanese-style production system

The Japanese-style production system, which is represented by Toyota production methods, has achieved thorough cost reductions by a variety of means. Included among these are the elimination of waste and the denial of even 'allowance rates' for operations; quality control carried out simultaneously in every operational stage; the 'just-in-time' system, which flexibly adjusts parts and employee numbers in response to production targets, ensures the multi-skilling of excess workers so as to make them employable in other areas of the production process, overcomes 'bottle necks' in production, utilizes 'stress control', and seeks the unlimited employment of labour; and, finally, group working, which fully employs the knowledge and abilities of workers.

In order to discover what kind of impact these methods have upon the situation of labour in the workplace, let us examine labour operations on the Toyota production line, as carried out by the Aichi Labour Research Institute (1994). Table 11.1 is instructive.

1 For most workers, the cycle time is extremely short, and the number of actions required in each cycle time is enormous. The time allocated for one action is less than one second (this estimate deducts walking time). For the process of fitting tyres, which requires the handling of heavy components, 213 actions are demanded within a 7.5 minute cycle time, and the time allotted for each action is less than 2 seconds. Shop-floor workers regard these working processes as ones which 'leave no time even for one to wipe the sweat from one's brow', and which 'require a brainless and robot-like movement'.
2 The same processes require the repetition of the same tasks a great many times in one day. The frequent repetition of short-time opera-

Table 11.1 Work on Toyota production line, May 1993

Example of operation	*Cycle time (secs)*	*Number of actions*	*Walking distance for each action (metres)*	*Time taken for each process (secs)*	*Number of times process is repeated in one day*	*Distance walked in one day (metres)*	*Remarks*
Radiator fitting	60	49	25	0.77	450	11,250	1.5 hours overtime
Preparation for waxing	47	47	30	0.47	500	15,000	1.0 hours overtime
Shaft process (a)	44	50	27	0.5	700	18,900	
Tyre fitting	450	213	120 (approx)	1.64	70	8,400	(b)

Source: Aichi Labour Research Institute, 1994: 127.
Note: (a) This process is for the handle main shaft.
(b) This operation involves the fitting of tyres in 70 cars per day, and calls for the physical handling of heavy load in an uncomfortable position. The operative fits 350 tyres per day, and also fits small components 2,660 times per day.

tions over a long period of time places too great a burden on specific parts of the body, robs the worker of the power to think, and increases health risk.

3 The operational tasks on the production line change frequently, and workers have to be able to respond quickly to this. Included specifically among operation processes is the need to evaluate and respond quickly to operational tasks and procedures after looking at the *Kanban* (notices signalling the need for new components), signs and computer terminals, processes for estimating, positioning and inspecting under quality control methods, and the need for fast responses to accidents on the line. Workers not only carry out physical labour, but are also subject to a high degree of mental stress.

4 Nominally, all workers who fail to keep up with operations can always stop the line, but in practice they are fearful of personnel evaluations and inspections; even in the event of accidents, the tendency is to deal with the situation without stopping the line.

In this way, workers on the shop floor have now reached a situation where their level of impersonal or robotic-like labour is far greater than that of any existing robot. The problem is compounded by the fact that this kind of intense labour is carried out continuously, over a long period of time. Even though the work is intensive, the number of actual and set working hours is the same as for other industries, and, in addition, two hours of overtime are included in the production plan. Excluding lunch breaks, each rest time in the morning and afternoon is only ten minutes, which means that intense and continuous operational time extends to two hours. On top of this, because the line is in operation when the worker begins his shift, he has to spend extra time in making preparation for his own shift. In other words, he is forced to work with no compensation outside his normal working hours. What is more, these working conditions are exactly the same for both the day and night shifts.

A shift system is in operation at the majority of work sites, with shift hours changing every other week. This results in a considerable number of workers being unable to secure a stable life style: they suffer from lack of sleep, eating disorders, mental anxiety, and are unable to control their emotions over even small matters. Indeed, many cannot lead a normal family and social life. As the company's production plan decides the days on which paid holiday can be taken, it is striking how large a number of holidays are taken due to poor health.

Under the Japanese-style production system, which emphasizes workplace production practices, the kinds of problems experienced by shop-floor workers also affect other workers, in areas such as administration and research and development. In essence, therefore, the root reasons for the low costs and high profits of Japan's giant corporations are the burdens and sacrifices of their workers.[10]

Labour management and industrial relations

The organization and maintenance over the long-term of the above-mentioned 'lean production' system, and the accompanying intensive labour system, were not easy to achieve. Even though the introduction of new technology, such as micro-electronics, made it feasible, this was not the decisive factor in its realization. Quintessentially, Japanese-style production methods aim to maximize the efficiency of existing plant, equipment and materials through improving operations in order to raise earnings and profits. For this purpose, emphasis is placed more upon the intensive physical and mental efforts of the workers than upon the introduction of leading-edge technology; in fact, the introduction of the newest technology is limited.

These kinds of production methods have become possible for the first time with the company's total and complete control of the workers. That is to say, Japanese-style production methods cannot be established without the following conditions:

- the organization of competition between workers by personnel evaluations and inspections, and the creation of workplace groups dominated by the management and disciplined like an army;
- the existence of labour unions which accept labour–capital collaboration and take no action to restrict intensive working, working outside normal hours, and changes to the production system;
- the nurturing of workers who are willing to work intensively for the benefit of the company through education and intra-company human relations;
- the suppression of workers' dissatisfaction and opposition by means of institutionalizing corporate–labour management methods for individuals and groups of workers (including unions).

These conditions were created and guaranteed by Japanese-style labour and personnel management systems, and the company union which is inextricably tied to them. The labour and personnel management systems maintain the long-term employment of key workers. By chiefly utilizing the discriminatory system of rises in rank, promotion and wages, these systems:

- divide workers from each other and encourage competition between them, thereby destroying worker solidarity;
- seek to control employment, working hours, labour intensity, wages and training of employees;
- attempt to integrate workers into the company on an organizational and mental level. This is achieved by mobilizing various informal organizations that are separate from work duties but connected with the company, and the organization of group activities, such as Quality Control Circles, the suggestion system and activities to promote human relations.

Table 11.2 demonstrates the surprising depth of informal organizations and

Table 11.2 Examples of 'independent' activities at Toyota, February 1992

Activity type		*Activity frequency*
Improvement suggestion activities		More than 2 suggestions per month for each worker.
QC activities		1 theme every 3 months for each group/ announcement in rotation; twice a month.
Kaizen activities		1 theme every 3–4 months for each group.
Proposals for accident prevention	Workplace accident prevention	More than 2 proposals per month for each worker.
	Traffic accident prevention	More than 2 proposals per month for each worker.
Workplace safety activities	Section safety checks	5 checks carried out by each worker, with workers in groups of 7 to 10.
	Safety month	Twice a year (activities to examine hazardous places, etc.).
	Safety designated workplace	Practice for countermeasures against workplace accidents, every two months.
Traffic safety activities	Reconsideration of traffic safety on commuting routes	Once a year.
	Traffic safety chorus	Every day.
	Traffic safety groups	Carried out in groups for around a one-week period prior to the spring, summer and end of year holidays.
	Traffic safety month	As above, for a one-month period.
	Accident information	Carried out when accidents occur (held at morning meetings, etc.).
	Traffic safety designated workplace	Designate accident spots, and carry out activities until these areas are declared safe.
PT (Personal Touch) consultations		Once a month in groups (presentation of reports on consultations).

Source: Aichi Labour Research Institute. 1994: 150

activities. Even when shop-floor workers are away from work, 'on holiday', they seem just as busy in friendship societies of working teams and sections, organizations of team, group and section leaders, event organizations, associations of people from the same prefectures, class reunion societies, traffic safety groups, residents' associations, and so on.[11]

The role of company unions in 'lean production'

The company union co-operates in the development of the above-mentioned methods of labour and personnel management, and organizes and mobilizes its members so that all can contribute to the company's high growth. There follows a number of examples of union activities:

1 Through means such as labour–management joint declarations, praising the benefits of labour–capital collaboration (mutual trust between employees and employer, the stability of workers' lives resulting from prosperity and growth).
2 Rejection of 'outdated' union movements which struggle against and oppose exploitation and controls on workers, replacing them with a movement which reforms the consciousness of union members by leading them to find their life worth living in their work.
3 Incorporation into labour agreements connected with the basic rights of workers and unions items which are generally thought to be disadvantageous to the workers. Specifically, these include:

- Detailed provision of regulations concerning union activities, the settlement of grievances, and strike action.
- Working conditions are not set out in detail, and are entrusted to the work regulations set down by the company, and in general are at the discretion of the company (for example, there are no rules set down between the company and union concerning working cycle time and line speed, so the company decides and alters these at will).
- Collective bargaining is limited to the individual company and the relevant enterprise union, and collective bargaining with unions organized at the level of individual industries is not accepted.
- All union–company negotiations relating to working conditions are carried out in labour–management councils, at which the obligation is to make every effort for the independent and peaceful settlement of problems. This results in the effective 'hollowing out' of the union's rights of collective bargaining.
- The provision of a 'peace keeping' clause which sets down careful regulations on a system of preventing strikes, and actually makes strike action impossible.
- The trade union and political activities of workers on the company's premises, and even during the workers' break time is restricted and

prohibited by labour agreements, and the freedom of union activities is also restricted.

- In order to prevent members from breaking away from the union, the union shop system, which force employees to join the union under the threat of dismissal from the company, has been introduced. As a result of this, today's company unions are acquiring the character of being a type of organization with compulsory membership, rather than being a free association of labour.

4 Company unions accept the shop regulations which require the loyalty of the employees towards the company. Under shop regulations, along with provisions imposing the moral improvement of employees, others seek to prevent 'whistle blowing' likely to harm the interests of the company, rules to stop anything emerging which may damage the honour and credibility of the company or individuals belonging to it, and regulations to prevent political and religious activities inside the company that take place without permission. In addition, under the labour agreements, rules are laid down to ensure that unions and members, even when carrying out union activities, respect shop regulations.

5 In elections for union officials, the election of candidates supportive of the company must be ensured by an overwhelming majority, and opposition candidates should be excluded. This issue is extremely important among the company union's activities. In order to achieve these aims, the following methods are employed:

- Various restrictions are placed on the candidature for union officials, for example, only allowing candidates to stand who have been recommended by the signatures of more than 50 union members.
- Limiting the election activities of candidates.
- Permitting tacitly that the organization of supervisory staff supports and promotes the candidates supportive of the company's candidates.
- The pro-company candidates are able to monopolize the elections for union officials by exploiting such voting methods as the plural ballot system.
- The secrecy of balloting and the openness of its results are not sufficiently guaranteed. The company candidate is decided by consultation between the enterprise union and the labour management section of the company, and the results of the balloting mean that most union official positions are filled by the supervisory staff such as group and team leaders.

6 Activities dealing with the improvement of working conditions, such as wages and working hours, and responses to the rationalization and restructuring policies of the company have various distinctive features. These include efforts to communicate in detail the company's proposals, and to demonstrate the union's understanding of the fact that policies

which hurt the interests of union members in regard to wage restraint and personnel downsizing are necessary for the long term well-being of the company. In addition, in cases where there are differences of opinion, the union and the company reach agreement easily through deliberations in the labour–management councils, and the union quickly accepts the company's proposal in the first round of bargaining. Once the union has agreed to the rationalization policies of the company it actively co-operates in cost-cutting activities, downsizing in shop-floor personnel, the everyday transfer and relocation of workers, and personnel cuts. The union also shows restraint in its wage demands when the company's results are down.

7 Education and propaganda critical of communism and socialism is repeatedly carried out among ordinary union members and officials. The aims of this type of education are not based on ideology, but are designed more to exclude from the company the activities of workers and unions critical of the company. In instances where this proves difficult, the emphasis is placed upon isolating ordinary shop-floor workers and union members from the influence of such critical activities.

Problems of company unions

The inevitable result of company unions engaging in the type of activities which can be regarded as the integration of labour and capital, is that they invite strong criticism from union members and employees. Even though they cannot openly make statements which would attract the attention of the personnel sections of the company, an increasing number of workers is even more critical of the unions than of the company. Voices critical of the unions have recently appeared even among supervisory staff and junior union officials, and the union is no longer able to secure mass support from shop-floor workers.

The decline and 'hollowing out' of the enterprise union now is becoming salient. Shop stewards are unable to explain satisfactorily the policies of the union, and because they cannot answer the queries of shop-floor workers, union meetings have been abandoned; even when shop-floor union meetings are convened, only the policies of the union executive are explained, leaving no time for questions and answers. In addition, the real state of union activities is being increasingly concealed from ordinary union members by means of restrictions on viewing the meeting of senior officials, abolition of union newsletters, and restrictions upon the distribution of union literature.

Moreover, even stricter controls have been placed upon union activities organized by rank and file members independently of the guidelines of top officials. In order to compensate for the decline and 'hollowing out' of union activities, enterprise unions have strengthened their activities in support of particular political parties, and have made capital out of their activities for social and economic policy objectives. However, recently they have become involved in the coalition politics of the conservative parties, and the incompatibility of interests between the unions and their members has become even clearer in the 1990s. Incidents have also occurred in which company unions that supported corrupt Diet members and those who lied about their backgrounds have been severely criticized by union members and the members' electoral districts.

Another serious problem for the company union is the separation of workers from unions.[12] As the mobility of labour between companies and business establishments becomes commonplace (dispatch, transfer, change of employment, etc.), and as the range of this mobility exceeds the boundaries of individual *keiretsu* and corporate groups, company unions are now unable even to organize permanent employees. Added to this, new employees and those of a younger age are drifting away from the union. This creates various difficulties in mobilizing union personnel, finance, and finding union officials, and results in moves to solve these problems by amalgamating unions and industrial federations.

The number of shop-floor workers who now take a stance critical of the company union is increasing. Co-operation with activists critical of the company union is increasing, the newspapers and leaflets they distribute receive a good response, and support for activist candidates critical of the company in union elections is on the upswing. If the company union can still gain a certain level of support from shop-floor workers, the reason might be the expectation among workers that the union is still able to maintain continuous employment and decent wages for permanent employees. However, recent shifts in the management strategy of large Japanese corporations are undermining these expectations.

NEW CONTROLS ON WORKERS AND THE LABOUR MOVEMENT

Large Japanese corporations globalized rapidly during the boom of the 'bubble economy', and despite the difficulties brought about by the bursting of the 'bubble', they are working hard to maintain their position. In order to do so, large-scale depreciation of debt and excess plant and equipment are being pushed forward, mergers between the large corporations and integration of allied companies are being implemented, and new large monopolies are being created. Even in international business relations (especially between the USA and Japan), which had previously been based on intense competition, co-operative enterprises, mergers and investments are now being organized between large overseas companies, and new international consortiums can be seen to be developing. It is notable that many of Japan's large corporations, which in the past had built up corporate groups and subcontracting *keiretsu* relations as a weapon with which to engage in large-scale global competition, have now found this method to be ineffective. In its place, Japanese corporations are now working to expand their overseas operations by emphasizing co-operative businesses and the creation of consortiums with foreign multinationals. These corporations now feel the need to change fundamentally the previous structures of capital accumulation, including the systems to control subcontracting and labour.

The shift to a multinational corporate strategy

Japan's giant multinationals are seeking to advance their management strategy based on the following conditions:

1 As the Japanese economy enters the 'post-growth era', high profits through expanding domestic markets are hard to guarantee.
2 With the majority of companies unable to keep up with the sharp appreciation of the yen, and acknowledging the need for restructuring and for setting up operations overseas, from now on they have to plan to secure profits in the context of the contraction and stagnancy of domestic market.
3 In order to secure their place as global corporations, companies will increasingly have to plan to carve out international markets based on co-operation with multinational corporations, while handing over part of their right and interests in the domestic market to US and overseas corporations, as can be seen in the case of semiconductors, cars, public works and insurance.

In this way, large Japanese corporations are being forced to pursue a management strategy that can ensure an increase in profits even when growth falls, and the production and sales of domestic companies falls, by separating the growth of their individual companies from the growth pattern of the Japanese economy. In essence, Japanese corporations are adopting one of the most avaricious multinational strategies in the world.

This multinational corporate strategy emerged first as moves towards the setting up of overseas operations, centred especially on East Asia, and the large scale restructuring of production activities. The moves made towards setting up operations overseas include the rapid expansion in the procurement of parts and purchase of manufactured goods from overseas; the increased transfer of production bases and the development of production on commission overseas; the overseas establishment of management centres and technology development facilities; and the development of a system for the international division of labour that covers Japan, the NIEs, ASEAN, the special economic zones of China, NAFTA and APEC. The results of this major move overseas are undermining Japan's industrial base, and producing the 'hollowing out' of the Japanese economy.

Changes in corporate control

During the current process of restructuring, the existing framework of monopolistic control is not just being altered, but is undergoing fundamental transformation. Particularly important are the following three points:

- break-up and reorganization of the employment system;[13]
- reorganization of subcontracting and *Keiretsu*;
- lowered working and living conditions.

The break-up and reorganization of the Japanese-style employment system and industrial relations

In the workplace the ruthless use of human resources is being promoted in various forms (movement of labour, change of job and dismissal). Examples of this trend are the frequent movement of support workers between shops and enterprises within a corporate group; the daily enforcement of dispatch and change of employment within and beyond a corporate group; the working conditions and expulsion of middle-aged and older workers; the large-scale dispatch of permanent employees and replacement with part-time employees. The expulsion of middle-aged and older workers has reached the extent whereby the labour mobilization policies within corporate groups can no longer cope. Even for the permanent employees of large companies mandatory retirement age no longer applies, with the lifetime employment system already becoming a thing of the past (Figure 11.1). In turn, this is giving rise to the introduction of a subdivided, discriminatory and diverse employment system with regard to employment practices, wages, and working conditions. Contractual working and the annual salary system are also leading to the expansion of discriminatory and temporary employment, which often resembles a system more akin to self-employment. This system excludes as much as possible agreement made on a group basis, preferring individual contractual arrangements made directly between the company and individual worker; unstable employment is continually expanding.

Together with flexibility of human resources and the breakdown of the lifetime employment system, other distinctive Japanese employment practices, such as seniority based promotion and pay, workplace hierarchy, collective recruitment of new graduates, and on-the-job training, are also being re-examined. Other innovations include the move towards the simplification but also intensification of work duties due to a shift from seniority-based hierarchical organizations to 'flat' organizations; the introduction of an ability-based promotion system and of a specialist's and technician's post system, premised upon self-education; and the systemization of information in group work (the exclusion of independent and critical agreement). Micro-electronic technology has also been mobilized,

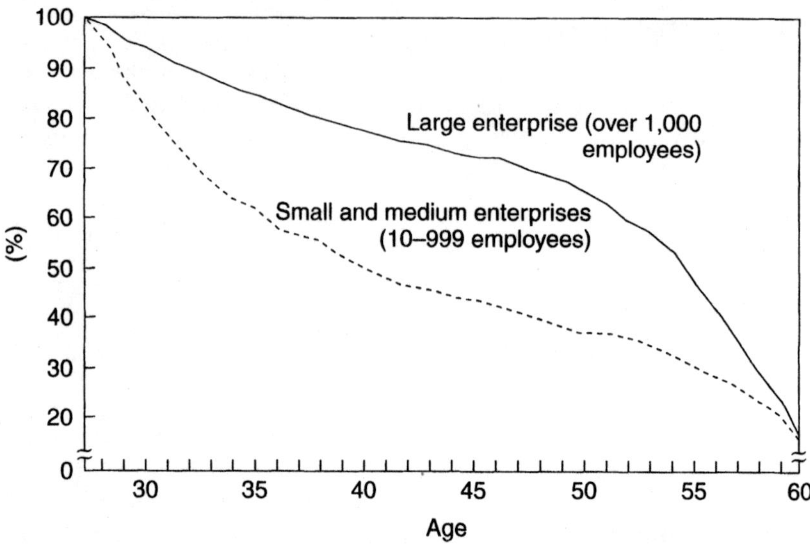

Figure 11.1 Percentage of male employees working in the same enterprise (all educational careers)
Source: Rōdōshō 1994: 188

and the systems of personnel control and management for individual workers have been carefully strengthened.

The progress of these types of conditions has meant that the spread of 'non-unionism' in the workplace has become an important issue. As has been pointed out already, the company unions affiliated with *Rengō* have already begun to lose definitely the characteristics of labour unions. These unions fail to promote the interests of their members, and today are even prepared to push forward with redundancies as if they were the company managers, with the result that the estrangement of members from the union is becoming more and more serious. Even the managerial staff, who in the past supported the company union, have now become the object of personnel downsizing with the result that they are allying with workers critical of the company, ignoring the union, and seeking to protect their own interests. This is undermining the basic conditions for the existence of the company union. On the other hand, top management is adopting policies which ignore and deny the role of labour unions, such as proposals to end the ritual of the spring labour offensive, a reluctance to make any agreement on wages and working conditions through collective bargaining and labour agreements, the shelving of issues related to industrial relations, one-sided decisions on working conditions by the use of shop regulations, and the refusal to allow union activities in new plants and subcontracting companies. The top management of large corporations is encouraged to take these policies by their experience of being able to create industrial relations in overseas business establishments that effectively prevent union activities. Now, as proved by the case of Toyota, which has recently stopped using the slogan 'mutual trust between labour and management', it appears that even the collaborative activities of company unions is becoming an obstacle to the new strategy of Japanese big business.[14]

Reorganization in the control of subcontracting and keiretsu

Presently, one of the greatest changes that affects labour is occurring in the system of control for subcontracting and small to medium-sized companies, and regional economies. The vertical and horizontal *keiretsu* relations which were carefully constructed by every large corporation are now being destroyed. This has resulted from a conversion to 'dry' trading relations with subcontracting and allied companies, the moves to entrust production and subcontracting to overseas plants aided by trading companies, the discovery of the potential of overseas labour, the expansion and construction of overseas production bases, and moves to reorganize in the face of drastic cost competition brought about by 'price collapse'.

In terms of regional relations as well, the concentration of production and technology in particular domestic regions, which have been typically seen in the processing and assembly industries, are now being dissolved, and even in building up new plants these concentrations are consciously being avoided. Domestically and internationally, we can increasingly find a global operation which seeks low costs by allocating production to areas where this can be achieved most effectively. Particularly noticeable in this regard is the organization and development of everyday economic activity that connects Japan and Asia. This trend is demonstrated by the formation of an economic zone around the Yellow Sea, including Kyūshū, the Yamaguchi region, South Korea, Taiwan, and China's special economic zones. This marks the rise of a regional economic grouping that transcends national frontiers.

However, this development is also undermining local domestic economies. As the competition among corporations intensifies both at home and abroad, and as the exploitation of small and medium-sized subcontractors by large corporations increases, this has led to an unprecedented number of closures and failures among small and medium-sized enterprises, and an absolute decrease in the overall number of business establishments. The result has been deteriorating employment opportunities and poverty in the regions.

Lowered working and living conditions

Currently in Japan, with the changes in the framework of control by big corporations and progress in the rationalization and restructuring described above, one of the most important policies that has appeared to improve the profits of leading corporations is the lowering of workers' living and working conditions. According to government statistics, real wages have fallen two years in succession, but these do not show the true extent of the situation.[15] Workers in most industries, including white-collar workers, have experienced a large fall in take-home pay of around a fifth of monthly income. These falls in income are not just due to reductions in allowances for overtime and night shifts, reductions in bonuses, and policies of wage restraint, but also because of the spread of discriminatory wages, based on the strengthening of ability-based wage systems, more rigorous assessment of results, and wider differentials of bonuses and rises in salary according to rank. With the spread of more labour-intensive work and unpaid overtime, the hourly wage rate is decreasing to a significant extent.

As a result, the number of workers who are finding it difficult to repay housing loans and to subsist just on the wages received from the employer is increasing even among the permanent employees of large corporations. Table 11.3 provides evidence that a considerable number of family budgets are in the red, with the family being forced to have many working members. Furthermore, given the structural changes in Japanese capitalism, these problems cannot be considered to be only temporary. Top corporate managers and company union officials now consider the 'restructuring' of the life styles of workers to be necessary over the long term: their call is for a 'simplification' of life styles. In this way, many workers from large corporations, and especially middle-aged and older ones, are now beginning to fall into the ranks of temporary workers (or the unemployed). The decline in working conditions, redundancies by the 'domino effect', and unemployment resulting from closures of small and medium-sized enterprises will continue over the long term after the collapse of the 'bubble economy'; the massive 'collapse', 'subsidence' and 'fluidity' of the structure of the working class is now in progress. A similar situation is also evident in self-employed businesses in cities and agricultural communities.

Table 11.3 Example of reduction in the household income of a Toyota employee

Income item	*Jan. 1992*	*Sept. 1992*	*Increase and decrease*
Basic wage	352,260	362,390	+ 10,130
Overtime allowance	145,400	24,310	− 121,090
Night shift allowance	60,630	63,710	+ 3,080
Deductions (e.g. tax)	− 167,178	− 166,765	+ 413
Wages subtotal	391,112	283,645	− 107,467
Wife's contribution	0	81,000	+ 81,000
Children's part-time work	0	52,000	+ 52,000
Family income subtotal	0	133,000	+ 133,000
Household income total	391,112	416,645	+ 25,533

Source: Aichi Labour Research Institute, 1994: 143

Contradictions in the new structure of control

The creation of a new structure of control by big corporations, as outlined above, has as one of its main tenets the recent political structure where 'all (but the Japan Communist Party) are ruling parties' – a similar set-up to the *Yokusan* (Imperial Rule Assistance) politics of the war years. The implementation by national and local government of massive public works projects worth 630 billion yen has ensured not only markets and profits for large corporations, but has also been seen as a way to resolve the contradictions connected with industrial 'hollowing out' and the difficulties faced by local citizens. Added to this, deregulation not only emphasizes the creation of new domestic markets for multinational monopolies, deprives citizens and workers of their vested interests, and sacrifices small companies and businessmen, but also works as a policy tool to involve citizens and workers in fierce international and domestic competition. If these policies are carried out in accordance with the expectations of large corporations, then, under the constraints of a contemporary system of *Yokusan* politics, labour movements are likely to face great problems. As a result, it will become very difficult to build trade unionism to replace the company unions.

However, in the medium and long term, the system of control now being put into place by giant corporations will face a number of unprecedented and serious destabilizing factors. First, such a system of control will lead to the loss of the multinationals' domestic industrial, technological, and workforce bases. In turn, when they are unable to maintain and secure these domestic bases, the business giants will simultaneously find it difficult to secure the bases for their development as global companies. Second, the new control system will be a production and labour management system that will integrate Japan and East Asia, and opinion critical of such a system will increase both domestically and in Asia. Combined with questions over responsibility for aggression in the Pacific War and colonialism, the democratic morals of Japanese corporations will be further questioned. If multinational corporate activities are not accepted by local workers and citizens in the host countries, and receive no support from local consumers, then the corporation will be unable to establish itself. Third, and as was proved by the 1995 'Hanshin' earthquake, the construction of a sophisticated global division of labour increases the risk of the whole system being thrown into chaos by problems at just one business establishment. Fourth, the new international system of control also carries the risk that the vicious circle of reduced cost and rises in the cost of living will also be reproduced in Asia. In this case, the possibility exists that Japanese corporations and the Japanese economy will be negatively influenced by the increasing problems of underdeveloped infrastructures, labour shortages, and inflation in Asia. Fifth, the management strategy of Japanese multinationals is premised upon a consistent low wage system in all countries – at home, in Asia, and, indeed, all over the world. As a result, international solidarity between workers and labour unions centred upon Asia will inevitably emerge to confront Japanese capital and corporations.

These factors have already begun to have a concrete effect. Within the domestic mass labour movement, *Zenrōren* has begun to seize the initiative, and in every region joint actions between labour unions affiliating *Zenrōren* and Spring Struggle Committee are developing, and organizations of small enterprises and farmers, demanding 'democratic control of big corporations', have sprung up. Recently, *Zenrōren* has been creating ties with labour unions in East Asia, and it is probable that the management strategy of massive Japanese corporations will be increasingly subject to heavy domestic and international criticism.

Today, many Japanese managers accept the inevitable collapse of the Japanese style of employment relations characterized by seniority-based promotions and wages, but they stick tenaciously to enterprise unions as company unions. It is nevertheless doubtful whether or not the enterprise union can survive as a company union in the twenty-first century. Company unions are certainly making efforts to respond to difficult conditions (for example, moves by company unions to organize part-time workers and workers of allied companies; the promotion of the organization of workers from diverse industries, by shifting from unions organized by individual industry to general unions that include workers in various industries; and the creation of large industrial unions by amalgamating unions), but there seems to be no obvious solution to the company unions' fundamental problems. Indeed, the future of Japanese labour unions seems to be reliant upon whether or not those independent and cross-enterprise unions, which were established in opposition to company unions, can create organizations and movements which go beyond the limits of the traditional enterprise unions and can exercise a social influence among the ranks of the working masses in both the workplace and the region, and so overcome the problems of non-unionization in large corporations.

NOTES

1 Those who first identified the characteristic of Japanese labour unions as enterprise unions, different from Anglo-American unions, were Suehiro (1950) and the Institute of Social Sciences at Tokyo University (1950). Since then various studies have been conducted but we may say that they were all based upon these basic works.

2 In the reactionary offensive of capital since the 1950s, many enterprise unions have experienced a split or suffered organizational dissolution. A representative figure who identified the weakness of enterprise unions in connection with their historical experience is Fujita (1982).

3 Ōkochi (1951) argued the inevitable birth of enterprise unions from the

Dekasegi-type of wage labour as a characteristic of the pre-modern nature of the Japanese labour market. This argument has been replaced today by the theories which argue the inevitability of enterprise unions from the unique seniority-oriented industrial relations and internal labour market (Shirai 1968).

4 It was Ōtomo (1981) who criticized Ōkōchi's theories of enterprise unions and others in this perspective.

5 In the latter half of 1950, under the orders of the US occupation forces, communists and their supporters were purged from public offices, public and private enterprises and the mass communication world.

6 The '*Shuntō*' began in 1955. At first it was only a liaison forum for wage increase negotiation among major private industrial federations of enterprise unions. It was in the 1960s, after the Japan–US Security Treaty struggle of 1959–60, when it began to develop as a unified wage increase struggle for all organized workers.

7 See Ōki and Aichi Labour Reasearch Institute (1986). This is the first research which identified how the union officials of company unions are tied to the labour and personnel sections of a company, on the one hand, and how the running of the unions is undemocratic, as in the case of the election of the union officials, on the other.

8 The membership of *Rengō*, according to a Rōdōshō survey in July was 7.72 million, accounting for 61.2 per cent of all organized labour.

9 The union membership of *Zenrōren* is said to be 1.4 million, whereas that of the Rōdōshō survey of July 1995 was 0.86 million, accounting for 6.8 per cent of organized labour. The gap between the two figures, according to *Zenrōren*, is due to the exclusion of various unions in local areas, which are not affiliated to industry-based union organizations.

10 See Bratton (1992) for the influence of Japanese-style production methods in Britain.

11 Labour management at Toyota extends not only to the lives of workers in the workshop, but to living and education in the local communities. Saruta's work (1995) is an example of recent research which sheds light on this issue.

12 Rōdō Mondai (Labour Issue) Research Centre conducted research in 1992 in order to investigate the rapid deunionization of workers and identify the realities of changes occurring in enterprise unions, which can be considered as factors for deunionization. The survey entitled 'Contemporary Theme of Labour Unions and Union Leaders' was carried out with 1,050 enterprise unions (a majority of them were members of *Rengō*). The analysis, based upon the survey, was done by Inagami (1995). He identified the fusion and unification between the union organization and that of the company.

13 Reform of Japanese-style industrial relations was proposed by the Japan Federation of Employers Associations (Nikkeiren 1995) and this is being put into practice in both industrial organizations and local employers associations.

14 A New Employer–Labour Declaration of Toyota (January 1996) upholds 'execution of mutual responsibility and respect of rights'. 'Execution of responsibility' is understood to imply that the union stands in the forefront of corporate policies, and 'respect of rights' is to agree to management prerogatives to pursue global strategies. See Ōki (1996) for how far the unions have shifted from 'company union' to a kind of *Yokusan* organization.

15 According to a monthly statistical survey of Rōdōshō on the wage index of the manufacturing industry (1990: 100), it was 100.1 for 1991, 99.6 for 1992, 98.6 for 1993, 100.1 for 1994. According to a survey by the tax authorities of salaries in private companies, it was a 0.6 point decrease in nominal terms in 1994.

REFERENCES

Aichi Labour Research Institute (1994) *Henbō suru Sekai Kigyo Toyota* (A changing global enterprise, Toyota), Tokyo: Shin Nihon Shuppansha.

Bratton, J. (1992) *Japanization at Work*, London: Macmillan.

Fujita, W (1982) *Sengo Rōdō Kumiai Soshikiron* (Essays on the organizations of post-war Japanese trade unions), Tokyo: Sanichi Shobo.

Inagami, T. (1995) *Seijuku Shakai no naka no Kigyōbetsu Kumiai* (The enterprise union in mature society), Tokyo: Japan Institute of Labour.

Institute of Social Science of Tokyo University (1950) *Sengo Rōdō Kumiai no Jitta* (The actual conditions of post-war Japanese trade unions), Tokyo: Nippon Hyōronsha.

Nikkeiren (1995) *Atarashi Jidai no Nihonteki Keiei* (Japanese-style management in a new era), Tokyo: Nikkeiren.

Ōki, K. and Aichi Labour Research Institute (1986) *Daikigyo Rōdō Kumiai no Yakuin Senkyo* (On the election of union officials in the big enterprise unions), Tokyo: Ōtsuki Shoten.

Ōki, K. (1996) 'How can we see the Japanese unions changed?', *The Quarterly Journal*, Tokyo: The Japan Research Institute of Labour Movement.

Ōkōchi, K. (1951) 'Rōdō kumiai ni okeru Nihon gata ni tsuite' ('On the Japanese-type of trade unions'), *Ōkōchi Kazuo Shū* (Collection of Kazuo Ōkōchi), 1981, Tokyo: Rōdō Junpōsha.

Ōtomo, F. (1981) *Nihon Rōdō Kumiairon* (Essays on Japanese trade unionism), Tokyo: Miraisha.

Rōdōshō (annual) *Rōdō Hakusho* (White Paper on Labour), Tokyo: Rōdōshō.

Saruta, M. (1995) *Toyota Shisutemu to Rōmu Kanri* (Toyota system and labour management), Tokyo: Zeimu Keiri Kyōkai.

Shirai, T. (1968) *Kigyōbetsu Kumiai* (Enterprise unions), Tokyo: Chūō Kōronsha.

Suehiro, G. (1950) *Nihon Rōdō Kumiai Undōshi* (History of the Japanese trade union movement), Tokyo: Kyōdō Tsushinsha.

Index